The
RIGHTS of MAN
in AMERICA

1606-1861

The
RIGHTS of MAN
in AMERICA

1606-1861

Gilman Ostrander

UNIVERSITY OF MISSOURI PRESS

COLUMBIA

PREFACE

MORE than fifty years ago the author of that marvelously capacious *History of the American People,* John Bach McMaster, published three concise lectures on *The Acquisition of the Political, Social, and Industrial Rights of Man in America.* It was a unique study at the time McMaster presented it, and, remarkably enough, it has remained a unique study. Although historians have accepted the rise of democracy as the central theme in the nation's history, no historian since McMaster has written the history of American democracy itself, in the broad meaning of the word suggested by McMaster's title. The purpose of this book is to present such a history of American democracy from its seventeenth-century English origins to the Civil War.

The problem of defining democracy was less difficult in the nineteenth century than one would suppose who knew the word only as it is used today by a variety of conflicting authorities, ranging from Herbert Hoover to Chou En-lai. In the twentieth century the term has been so fought over as to have passed out of the category of words for which there is a broadly acceptable definition. Such was not always the case. In the early eighteenth century "democratic" was a term of abuse, synonymous with "leveling"; that is, descriptive of mob rule. It had no other generally accepted meaning except the inapplicable meaning of direct democracy as practiced in certain bygone Greek city states. By the mid-nineteenth century, this old abusive definition had given way to a new one, and "democracy" had come to mean a political and social system having the characteristics of contemporary American government and society. The French aristocrat Alexis de Tocqueville's *Democracy in America* was accepted as constituting the most authoritative available definition of the word.

The basic requisites of this new democracy were representative political institutions based on manhood suffrage (or at least white manhood suffrage), the ultimate rule of the majority, and equal protection under the law. But democracy was not thought of as a purely political and legal phenomenon. Tocqueville said that the key to American democracy was "equality of condition," and social equality was an essential characteristic of the system. The comparative lack of class distinctions in America rested upon a comparative lack of major economic inequalities, but this approximate economic equality was so taken for granted that it failed to become a positive tenet of democracy. The true system, Abraham Lincoln said, was one which permitted each man to get rich as fast as he could. The assumption was that the system would continue as it was in Lincoln's youth, when it had produced few really rich men, and when the majority of free American men started the race of life on a more or less equal footing as poor boys. The first part of the assumption was soon to prove quite false, but the assumption nevertheless remained basic to American democratic thought.

American democracy contained an inherent inconsistency which has never been resolved, either in theory or practice. The basic democratic tenets of individual liberty on the one hand and majority rule on the other are logically incompatible. The majority, if it is sovereign, has the authority to deprive the minority of its rights, which are inalienable. This problem, which absorbed the attention of the founding fathers, did not much worry the Jacksonian democrats, who put great faith in the wisdom and goodness of the majority and also in the "sacred" system the founding fathers had devised. American democracy, however, had by then become a permanent contest between the libertarian eighteenth-century Constitution and the majoritarian nineteenth-century constituency.

Nor did the democratic ideals of liberty and equality always travel easily together. The condition of liberty gave the strong an opportunity to rise above the weak and to maintain themselves as a superior order in society. This had been no problem to eighteenth-century republicans. They had understood that all men were created equal in the limited sense of being equal under God and being equally entitled to their God-given natural rights to life, liberty, and property. At the same time, it had been taken for granted by the founders that all men were unequal in intellectual and physical endowments, character, social rank, and economic position. It was therefore self-evident that all societies would naturally divide themselves into superior and inferior ranks and stations and that rank and station would determine the role the individual would play in a republican form of government. Participation in political affairs was not a natural right but a privilege, extended only to those whose property holdings gave them some tangible stake in society. Democratic America rejected this aristocratic view of equality. Equality, for the age of Jackson, meant that every man was as good as the next one and had as good a right to share in the affairs of government. This equalitarian theory was partially implemented by the extension of white manhood suffrage and by the spoils system, but it never was in as close accordance with reality as the older aristocratic view had been.

The ideal of fraternity or brotherhood was also an essential quality of American democracy. In the American language, it is true, "fraternity" is the word for exclusive college organizations, and it is comparatively little used in any other context. Americans have coined no word of their own to serve as a synonym for the warmly encompassing *"fraternité"* of the French—brotherliness or brotherhood or fraternalism being not entirely satisfactory translations. It might be supposed that, if the Americans lacked a word for it, they probably lacked the sentiment itself. Nevertheless there welled up in American society in the years after the War of 1812 an engulfing fraternalism compounded of hopeful ambitions, patriotism, humanitarianism, evangelism, and equalitarianism. Democratic America, for all its vaunted individualism, was a nation of boosters, joiners, reformers, flag-wavers, and brothers' keepers. For the want of a better word this spirit may be identified as a sense of brotherhood. It formed an American ideal which remains basic to American democracy and which, in the age of Eisenhower, is captured in the terms "togetherness" and "team spirit."

Sensitive to the dangers of majority tyranny and group conformity, American liberals have tended to underestimate the importance to American democracy of this often intolerant spirit of brotherhood. Indeed the very survival of limited government was made possible only because the boosters, the joiners, and the evangels created business, social, and religious societies which operated outside the framework of politics and pre-empted areas into which government would otherwise have penetrated. After the decline of aristocracy, with its ordered social discipline, American society relied for stability not upon authoritarian government, but upon the social cohesiveness which these autonomous organizations helped to provide and upon the national willingness to conform which these organizations exemplified.

It would have proved incomparably more useful for European democrats if the French Revolution, instead of the American, had led successfully to the first modern democratic state. It would have resulted in a democratic state created out of circumstances similar to those faced by other European countries, instead of one created out of the exotic American wilderness. It would presumably also have been a system of popular rule based upon some political theory of universal application. American democracy, on the other hand, did not come into being as the fulfillment of a political theory, and even after it had arrived it developed no theory in its own defense. The well-tempered theorists—John Adams and James Madison, John Marshall and Chancellor Kent—were all on the other side.

American democracy was an historical development and not a logical system. Even its most cherished principles were themselves historical developments, which were clearly comprehensible only within the American historical context, if at all. The doctrine of the separation of church and state, for instance, while originally a logically defensible aspect of Lockian political theory, became rather mysterious and indefinable in the course of several generations of sectarian struggles. The difficulty was not the result of the need to apply a known principle to a new situation. It was rather that the doctrine was employed as a precedent and not as a principle. American politics was thoroughly legalistic, and what Justice Holmes said of the common law applied equally to the American political system: that experience and not logic was the life of American democracy.

No nation in western Europe uses its history in quite the reverential and authoritative way that Americans use theirs. The English are proverbial for the reliance they place upon precedent and for the strength they derive from the consciousness of a long, continuous, and lucky past. But surely a responsible political figure in England today would strike a false note if he were to concern himself seriously in public with speculation on how William Pitt would have met current fiscal problems or what Palmerston would have done in the present world crisis. Yet American politicians do not hesitate to call upon Washington or Jefferson or Jackson or Lincoln to support them in their arguments.

Rip Van Winkle was put to confusion, after a twenty-year sleep, when a "short but busy little fellow pulled him by the arm and, rising on tiptoe, inquired in his ear, 'Whether he was Federal or Democrat?'" He could not answer the question, and, in spite of the whole literature of Jefferson-Jackson and Lincoln Day dinner addresses to the contrary, it is doubtful that the sages and patriots of America's pre-industrial past could do much better with a similar question today. They will nevertheless continue to be asked the question and it will be in a good cause; for this paradoxical conservatism of American democracy is the main reason it continues to exist. Lord Acton wrote that England owed her free institutions, not to the independent spirit nor the magnanimity of her people, but only to "the consistent, uninventive stupid fidelity to that political system which originally belonged to all the nations that traversed the ordeal of feudalism." Bringing its institutions from England, America held fast to the old ways in a new world until after several centuries it found itself transformed into a democracy.

For giving friendly and considerate critical attention to all or part of the manuscript, I wish to thank Carl Bridenbaugh, Foster Rhea Dulles, James Henle, Theda Henle, Charles Mullett, Katharine Ostrander, and Frank Pegues. Extensive quotations from the following works have been made possible by permission of the following publishers: *Ideas In Motion,* by Dixon Ryan Fox. Copyright, 1935, D. Appleton-Century Co., Inc. By permission of Appleton-Century-Crofts, Inc., *The English People On The Eve Of Colonization,* by Wallace Notestein. Copyright, 1954, Harper & Brothers. *Self-Government At The King's Command,* by Albert B. White. Copyright, 1933, University of Minnesota Press. *Mind Of The South,* by W. J. Cash. Copyright, 1941, Alfred A. Knopf, Inc. *A Little Rebellion* by Marion Starkey. Copyright, 1955, Alfred A. Knopf, Inc. *The American Revolution Considered As A Social Movement* by J. Franklin Jameson. Copyright, 1926, Princeton University Press. *Democracy And The Organization Of Political Parties,* by Mosei Ostragorski. Copyright, 1908, The Macmillan Company. William Peden director of the University of Missouri Press and Judith A. Jenkins of the Press have given the manuscript all the attention that an author would want and none that one wouldn't.

GILMAN OSTRANDER

East Lansing, Michigan
April, 1960

CONTENTS

Chapter 1

ENGLISH
LIBERTIES

THE history of democracy in America began at least as early as 1578, when Queen Elizabeth issued to Sir Humphrey Gilbert letters patent authorizing colonization on the North American mainland. Sir Humphrey's ventures ended in expensive failure resulting in no permanent settlement, but the patent itself proved of enduring importance to the history of the United States. It contained a provision, until then probably unique in the history of European colonization of America, and one which was to remain an enormously important precedent throughout English colonial history. The patent declared that all Englishmen emigrating under the terms of the patent "shall and may have, and enjoy all the privileges of free denizens, and within our allegiance: any law custom or usage to the contrary notwithstanding."

England, unlike France or Spain, intended to extend the laws and liberties of the realm to her colonial possessions. French and Spanish colonists when they departed from their native lands departed also from whatever rights they had previously enjoyed as citizens. And in the seventeenth century all other colonizing nations of Europe except England followed this same principle. Dutch citizens in the early seventeenth century enjoyed at home liberties at least as generous as those possessed by Englishmen, but in America New Netherlands was dictatorially governed under a charter which stripped the colonists of their rights as citizens of the homeland. Two generations later the conquest of New Netherlands was facilitated by the willingness of the settlers to exchange such liberties as they enjoyed under the charter of the Dutch West India Company for the liberties of Englishmen.

In 1584 Sir Walter Raleigh received a colonizing charter similar to that of Sir Humphrey's and containing the same guarantee of English liberties. Sir Walter's colonizing attempts followed a similarly disastrous course, but in the generation that followed two developments occurred which made such ventures practicable for the first time for Englishmen. The defeat of the Spanish armada reduced the Spanish threat in America, while the development of the joint-stock company made possible more heavily financed enterprises than had been feasible with the merely personal resources of even a Gilbert or a Raleigh. In 1606 James I, laying claim to a large expanse of the North American mainland, issued charters to two such joint-stock companies, the Virginia Company of London and the Virginia Company of Plymouth, and with the successful establishment of American plantations by the Virginia Company of London the promised introduction of English liberties to America became a practical consideration.

The charters of 1606 were, in most respects, quite in keeping with the crafty, selfish, antilibertarian character of the first Stuart King. George Bancroft, the great democratic patriot historian, tended to see American colonial history as a titanic struggle between liberty-loving Americans and English tyrants, and those charters of 1606 were well suited to his theme.

> Thus the first written charter of a permanent American colony, which was to be the chosen abode of liberty, gave to the mercantile corporation nothing but desert territory, with the right of peopling it and defending it, and reserved to the monarch absolute legislative authority, the control of all appointments, and a hope of ultimate revenue. To the emigrants themselves it conceded not one elective franchise, not one of the rights of self-government.

All this was true, so far as specific provisions were concerned; yet the charters quite incongruously proceeded to follow precedent by declaring that the settlers "shall have and enjoy all liberties, franchises, and immunities, within any of our other dominions, to all intents and purposes, as if they had been abiding and born, within this our realm of England. . . ." And, however James I may have interpreted this provision, Englishmen in both England and America assumed that it meant something and that it constituted a basic tenet of English colonial policy. The same principle was later extended to all English colonies in America and was vigorously affirmed by English courts of law. It defined the issue for repeated altercations between the crown and the colonies, it permitted the English colonies a degree of self-government unheard of in the possessions of other nations, and finally it was the text for the argument which culminated in the American Revolution.

Like Bancroft, the patriotic frontier historian Frederick Jackson Turner was loath to dwell upon the debt which American democracy owed to English institutions and English colonial policy. In his most famous statement on the subject, Turner declared that American democracy was not brought to Virginia on the *Susan Constant* or to Plymouth aboard the *Mayflower*. "It came out of the American forest, and it gained new strength each time it touched a new frontier." Still, although they chose not to emphasize it, Bancroft and Turner would hardly have denied that these ships brought *something* to America which was denied the emigrants to Montreal and Mexico City and New Amsterdam. It was from the liberties of Englishmen that Democracy was fashioned in the American forests.

The attempt to transplant English liberties to the American forest was made difficult by the difference in environment and by the lack of any clear definition, even in England, of what constituted an Englishman's liberties. Some strange sea change was bound to result. Nevertheless, from the perspective of the mid-twentieth century one of the most evident characteristics of American democracy is the continuing strength of its English inheritance. With that deep conservatism which won such rich praise from Edmund Burke, Americans have preserved the old English forms of law and of municipal, county and state government through revolution, civil war, transcontinental expansion, and three world wars. When one considers the immense gulf of time and space separating seventeenth-century Devon from twentieth-century Nebraska, the similarities in the field of government and law become more striking than the differences.

I

Seventeenth-century Englishmen, both in England and America, used the term liberty, or liberties, in two quite different, if not downright contradictory, ways. There was the familiar idea of liberty as a general condition of men deriving from natural law, or a condition of Englishmen, deriving from the legal and constitutional past. At the same time there was the medieval idea of a hierarchy of liberties which varied according to the station and purpose in society of the individual or group. Parliament possessed certain liberties which were the specific properties of that body. The freemen of particular municipalities possessed defined liberties, which they were obliged to forfeit if they moved elsewhere. Liberties, in this sense, were often exemptions from the normal obligations or punishments to which the unprivileged were subject. Most commonly the distribution of liberties bore some relation to the distribution of property. This remained true in the thought of John Locke and probably even of Thomas Jefferson, but for them liberty had become one thing which all property holders possessed in common.

It was not generally supposed that a man was deprived of his liberty because he was denied the privilege of self-government. Charles I, in his last words before his execution, made this point. "For the people . . . their liberty and freedom consists in having government. . . . It is not in having a share in government; that is nothing appertaining to them." And though the Roundheads had condemned Charles I to death, this was not the point at issue. Nor would the leaders of the Massachusetts Bay Colony have seen reason to contest this statement. For them, as for Charles, liberty was a state of submission to duly—which was to say divinely—constituted authority, as opposed to suffering the tyranny of unauthorized control or of suffering the natural liberty of wild animals.

This definition of liberty as submission to duly constituted authority was interpreted in the context of the medieval cosmography of Englishmen in the early seventeenth century. The world of James I remained at the center of that same universe which St. Thomas Aquinas and Dante had described centuries before. In this universe the sun, moon, and myriads of stars, each tended by officers of the celestial hierarchy, were moved in their courses around the fixed and unmovable earth, where new souls were born and where the main purposes of the Creator were working themselves out. Living harsh, barren lives, the masses of the people might gain some consolation from gazing upon the firmament and reflecting that they were at the center of what they saw. It was perhaps true, as Arthur Lovejoy noted, that this geocentric cosmography served for man's humiliation rather than for his exaltation, since the Earth, as the farthest removed from the Empyrean, was the vilest place in the universe, and since the innermost center of the earth, Hell, was the vilest place possible. Still, men could hardly have avoided a sense of pride at having been singled out for so central and uniquely humiliating a position.

Within this universe there extended a great chain of being, ranging from the foot of God's throne to the meanest form of life on earth. As a fifteenth-century English writer described this chain of being,

> In this order angel is set over angel, rank upon rank in the kingdom of heaven; man is set over man, beast over beast, bird over bird, and fish over fish, on the earth, in the air and in the sea; so that there is no worm that crawls upon the ground,

no bird that flies on high, no fish that swims in the depths, which the chain of this order does not bind in most harmonious concord. Hell alone, inhabited by none but sinners, asserts its claim to escape the embraces of this order. . . .

On earth there was established by divine plan an ordered society, ranging down harmoniously from the anointed king through barons, knights and yeomen, to the husbandmen, cottagers and farm laborers, who, although technically free, possessed little more practical freedom than the serfs of earlier centuries. In the realm of religion the hierarchy descended from the Unmoved Mover through archangels and angels to the King, the bishops and the lesser prelates to rector, vicar, and curate. Each office held its duties and its privileges; each officer might say of himself that he served by divine right, that is to say, in accordance with the divine plan, and each might speak of his liberties, not as something to be shared with other men, but as special privileges associated with his special position in that great chain of being.

This was the theoretical rather than the actual English world of the early seventeenth century. There was another more dynamic England of sea dogs and explorers, of enterprising farmers, merchant venturers, wool and cloth merchants, Puritan reformers, Baptist sectarians, lawyers, politicians, pirates, wreckers, footpads, thieves, and roving beggars. Against these busy people the old order might appear to be maintaining itself on all levels, from the courts of Star Chamber and High Commission down to the local parish. In fact dissatisfied, ambitious and restless people in English society were sweeping away much of the medieval web of privilege and duty, and those Stuarts who stood on principle were swept along into the discard. And those who fought the established system justified themselves, as likely as not, on the grounds of their liberties as Englishmen.

One may avoid having to fit early seventeenth-century England into a period by quoting F. M. Powicke, who has written that "Properly speaking, there is no mediaeval and no

modern history of England; there is just English history,"
a history characterized to an extraordinary degree by the
omnipresent sense of continuity even in times of revolutionary
change. Serfdom had been a thing of the past for more than
a century when James I came to the throne; yet certain of
the old manorial restraints remained to plague tenants until
Parliament legislated against them in 1922. No break—not
even the Great Rebellion—ever brought a repudiation of the
English past. As Sir Edward Coke demonstrated in the early
seventeenth century, and as American revolutionists demonstrated a century and a half later, a most effective weapon
for the English radical was constitutional precedent. In the
case of England, and of the English colonies in America, the
more it was the same, the more it changed.

Cutting across the antilibertarian medieval connotations
of the word liberty was the conception of liberties common to
all Englishmen. The right to hold property was a liberty
common to all, and if one held property the government could
not arbitrarily take it from him. If laws were to be passed
which affected his property interests, notably laws taxing
property away from him, then he must share in the passing
of those laws, by direct vote or through his elected representative. Even those who did not hold property had the right to
life, liberty, and equal justice under the law. Those without
property would probably be in a poor position to defend their
liberties, but they were at least at leave to think that they
possessed them.

The idea of English liberties as rights commonly held by
all gained strength from England's peculiar situation as a
centrally governed island kingdom. Freed from the constant
fear of invasion, the king and his people were freed also from
the burden of a large standing army or the maintenance of
personal armies by the great noblemen of the realm. The
Tudors used this advantage to create a truly civil government.
Henry VII, while liquidating the liveried armies of the great

lords at the turn of the sixteenth century, maintained but a small palace guard for his own defense. He rested his authority upon the will of the people, backed by the centuries-long tradition of centralized monarchy, and instructed by the bitter memory of the Wars of the Roses. The citizen soldier was the ultimate basis for national security, and the rule long since had been accepted which three centuries later was incorporated into the American Constitution, "A well regulated militia being necessary to the security of a free State, the right of the people to keep and bear Arms shall not be infringed."

The lack of a military caste had much to do with the fact that, in comparison with most continental societies, there was a marked fluidity in the English class structure. If the English nobleman's daughter married the son of a yeoman in the county, she was scorned for marrying beneath her station, but such things were not unheard of, and no law prohibited them. Nor was it absolutely necessary for her brothers to uphold the family honor by slaughtering the scoundrel. Continental aristocracies maintained themselves in rigid hierarchies based upon the stable economy of landed wealth and ordered for military purposes into a clear-cut chain of command. England, by contrast, was a civilian kingdom, and its aristocracy was based upon a more complex and changing economy. Land remained the basis for aristocratic privilege in England, but land could always be purchased by the well-to-do merchant or lawyer, and the privileges went with the property.

There was constant movement up and down the English social scale by marriage or by change in economic fortune. There was a close interrelationship between the landed classes and the townspeople, with the younger sons of the nobility going into trade along with the sons of lesser people; the son of a cottager acquiring a university education, making his fortune as a lawyer, and perhaps even gaining a seat in

Parliament. Of course if one were born into one of the lower classes, the likelihood was that one would die at that same station, and very likely at an early age under unspeakable circumstances. England was not the land of opportunity; certainly it was lacking in the spirit of equalitarianism which characterized a later American society. Nevertheless, the class distinctions it made were not quite so fine nor so rigid as those generally made on the continent. This slight blurring of class lines contributed to the idea of an Englishman's liberties.

A circumstance of immeasurable importance to the development of English liberties was the Black Death, which destroyed from a third to a half of the English population in the mid-fourteenth century and then periodically continued its devastations, especially in the towns, during the next centuries. There has been much controversy concerning the economic and social consequences of the Black Death, but that it altered the character of English society can hardly be questioned. It created in England the same condition which Frederick Jackson Turner saw as the main formative influence upon the development of democracy in America. It created an abundance of free land, and in its wake the areas of untilled English farm land continued to increase for a century and a half.

An immediate advantage of the plague to the common man was the labor shortage, which enabled him, if a free man, to wring higher wages from his employer or, if still bound to the manor, to flee the condition of villainage and work elsewhere as a free laborer. At a time of great labor scarcity a man was apt to be hired without being closely questioned as to his legal status elsewhere. But more important than this to the history of English liberty is the fact that this was the age which saw the main rise of the English yeoman. Enterprising farm laborers and former serfs were placed in a position not only to bargain for higher wages, but to acquire substantial land holdings of their own under a bewildering variety of legal conditions, and then to pass these holdings on to their children. By the close of the fifteenth century, the areas of vacant land finally began to diminish in the face of increasing population and the increasing use of formerly vacant areas as pasture for sheep. By the time of the early Stuarts the great age of the English yeoman was declining, under the onslaughts of enclosing landlords and their lawyers. At a time when the yeomanry was on the decline in England, the class was to revive itself in America; and there it was destined to play a role in society such as had never been conceivable in the old country.

II

It remained true in the England of 1606 that the large majority of the population was without land by freehold tenure and, being so placed, was apt to be substantially without rights. Lowest on the scale were the landless farm laborers, who, though free, were hardly in a position to assert their rights as Englishmen at all, unless it were by committing a crime sufficiently serious to warrant a jury trial. Under any circumstances, the story of their plight has little direct bearing on the development of English society in America. The English colonists worked out their own degraded systems of labor in the form of slavery and indentured servitude, but the availability of free land everywhere frustrated attempts to transplant the English class of free farm laborers.

Above the farm laborers existed a class of husbandmen clinging to plots of land by virtue of a wide variety of legal claims, against the ceaseless encroachments of ambitious landlords. In the exceedingly complicated struggle for possession of land, the advantage went against these cottagers to those who could command the services of the best lawyers. Living at the perilous margin of subsistence, the cottager held a position in society which was both humble and insecure. He took little or no active part in the direction of affairs, even at the local level. It was to this class that the large majority of Englishmen belonged in the seventeenth century, a class which, like the class of farm laborers, did not transplant itself well to land-rich post-feudal America.

It was the English yeoman, standing above the subsistence level of the cottager, who of all English classes was most easily transplanted to America. Sometimes defined as a forty-shilling freeholder, the yeoman belonged to a broad and not very clearly defined class of relatively substantial farmers, who supported himself largely as a farmer rather than as a landlord. Such a man possessed a modest amount of economic and social independence, and he might play a modest role in political affairs as well. He might possess the right to vote in Parliamentary elections. His service in the militia was the basis of the English system of national defense. In the civil wars his military service was instrumental in the defeat of the royal armies. The petty constable was likely to be selected from the yeomanry, and the more substantial of his number might serve as high constable, helping to enforce laws, collect taxes, and set wages, assisting the churchwardens in administering the Poor Law, and assisting the justice of the peace, while at the same time acting as the spokesman for village opinion.

It was as churchwardens that the more affluent of the English yeomanry assumed the most active role in civic affairs. The churchwardens were the trustees of the parish church, acting in the interests of the parishioners. They held legal control of the church, they supervised its upkeep, and they were responsible for levying rates for its support. Beyond that, their duties had been expanded during Tudor times to supplement the efforts of the justice of the peace at the village level. With overseers of the poor they could levy a poor rate on the parish, and they were expected to organize what aid they could muster for the indigent and the needy, and to look out for the general interests of the village.

In spite of this broad political participation, there was not much democracy in the English parish system. It was "regarded by no one as an organ of autonomous self-government," wrote Sidney and Beatrice Webb. "It was, if we may coin a new phrase, an organ of local obligation . . . the allocation of unpaid offices and burdensome duties among the ordinary citizens serving more or less in turn," under the strict subordination of the justice of the peace. The English yeoman furthermore paid for his privileged position by a constant struggle to wring returns from the land, defend property tenure, provide for a numerous family, and—living in chilly houses, farming by ancient methods, and reasoning in an age of superstition—to fight the unremitting fight against sickness, evil spells, and death.

"The sorrows of our ancestors we fail to realize," wrote Wallace Notestein,

> because they recorded their losses with little comment. Some solace they received, no doubt, from what the parson promised, but it was a kind of stolid endurance that carried them through. They did not pity themselves. They were not philosophic and they did not rationalize their experiences; they went on doing the next things as well as they knew how. People of that kind could even face perilous seas and settle on a stern and rockbound coast. Their daily lives had given them a hardness that was not soon bred out of the English stock in Devon or Massachusetts.

The American colonies, especially in New England, drew heavily from this yeoman class, and the yeomanry made up the most numerous part of the free population even in Maryland and Virginia. The parish system of local government also was transported to the American colonies, where it underwent a variety of mutations. In the southern mainland colonies, where the Anglican Church was established, the vesterymen were drawn from the gentry rather than the smaller landholders, and the system to that extent partook even less of democracy than was the case in England. In New

England, however, the township system developed to some degree upon the model of the English parish and village government, and there, joined to the Congregational Church organization and dominated by the yeoman class of "pumpkin gentry," it developed into a thoroughly democratic center of local self-government.

Ranked above the yeomanry, the gentry ruled the English countryside, maintaining a station in society and government which was readily emulated by the American gentry of the eighteenth century. A country gentleman, strictly speaking, was a man who possessed in his own right or through his ancestors a heraldic title to gentility, founded upon the possession of land. But such acquisitions could be purchased by those who had the money, and in any case they were not essential. The class of squires became almost as indefinite as that of yeomen. Its ranks were constantly replenished by enterprising yeomen, by decayed nobility, and by prosperous lawyers and merchants from the towns or from London, seeking the social status and political power which accompanied ownership of land. The country gentleman was well-to-do and perhaps wealthy. The minimum income required for membership in the class is indicated by the law which required that a justice of the peace hold lands and tenements to the value of £20 per year, but most justices of the peace were probably a very great many times wealthier than that. The gentry drew their income from rents rather than from tilling the soil, although they might farm their lands as well.

The gentry supplied Parliament with most of its members, and it administered local government. The lord lieutenant, it is true, generally was selected from the leading noble family of the county, but his position as head of the militia, though theoretically of great importance, tended in times of peace to be largely honorary. The sheriff, the chief law enforcement officer of the county, was also chosen from the nobility, or at least from among the wealthiest few in the county, if for no other reason than that the office was an expensive one, involving heavy fees and a responsibility for large debts owed the King. The office was highly influential in its direction of law enforcement and in its control of elections. It was an annual post, however, and despite its political power it probably was avoided wherever possible because of the expense it entailed.

The heavy burden of local government was borne by the justices of the peace. There were forty to seventy in a county, appointed by a royal commission from gentlemen of consequence locally, ranging from the small gentry to the nobility. Tudor power had based itself upon the local authority of its justices of the peace, against the pretensions of the great nobles. Pains had therefore been taken to select gentlemen who could command authority in their own right. The list of justices became a roster of provincial eminence.

Clothed with broad general powers, the justices sat in judgment on criminal cases which were not subject to jury trial. They supervised poor relief, game laws, road repairs, the fixing of wages, the control of prices, the licensing of taverns, and the suppression of religous heterodoxy. The office was transplanted to America in various forms. It was in Virginia, probably, that it followed most closely the lines of the English model.

Above the gentry ranged the great nobles, commanding wealth and high honors. From the class of nobles came the presidents of the Council of the North and the Court of the Marches of Wales, exerting all but royal authority in those territories, until the offices were abolished in 1641. The nobles served as lords lieutenants of the counties, exerting great military authority in time of war. Nobles advised the King from the House of Lords, and some of them took an active part in the administration of the nation, whether as members of the Privy Council or as court favorites of the King. Still the power of the nobles as a class had declined since the Wars

of the Roses, and it reached a low ebb during the reigns of
the early Stuarts. The Tudors systematically undermined the
authority of the nobles, and it was further diminished during
the reigns of James I and Charles I by the expense of court
life, which bankrupted the ambitious and placed them in the
King's power. The House of Lords had long since ceased to
rival the Commons in power. The Great Rebellion stirred the
energies of the nobility, and they played a more important role
during the Restoration than earlier they had.

In America during the seventeenth century, Maryland,
the Carolinas, and New York were placed in the possession of
titled nobility, while certain individual nobles, such as the Earl
of Southampton, assumed a leading role in the founding of
other American colonies. Ambitious plans were devised at
various times to establish in certain colonies classes of nobles
enjoying vastly greater authority than the English nobility
itself had commanded for centuries. Ultimately all such
attempts failed; nevertheless, in certain areas—New York
and South Carolina, for example—the efforts were at least
influential in forming aristocratic societies.

III

Although many thought that James I made too much of
the point, the vast majority of his subjects were willing to agree
that he ruled, in a manner of speaking, by divine authority,
and that his rule was virtually supreme, so long as he used
only his own revenues and took some care to stay within the
laws. Even the law courts and the Parliaments which battled
the Kings to defeat in the seventeenth century could be viewed
as hardly more than extensions of the royal power. The
King was the fountainhead of justice. The common law was
enforced in the King's courts by judges whom the King had
appointed. To many it seemed a contradiction in terms to
say that the King could commit an illegal act. As to Parliament, F. W. Maitland wrote:

Consider how very much that assembly depends for its constitution, for its very existence, on the king's will. It comes when he calls it, it disappears when he bids it go; he makes temporal lords as he pleases, he makes what bishops he pleases, he charters new boroughs to send representatives. After all, is not this body but an emanation of the kingly power? The king does well to consult a parliament—but is this more than a moral obligation, a dictate of sound policy?

Both the Tudors and the Stuarts found it possible to rule England for years at a time without summoning Parliaments, and when Parliament was not in session there was no effective check upon the authority of the King. In practice the King managed the affairs of the nation through his chosen advisors, Henry Hallam wrote, "as if it had been the household and estate of a nobleman under a strict and prying steward." Acting in the capacity of the Privy Council, the advisors formulated state policy, including American colonial policy, and then executed these decisions, sometimes down to minute details. Acting in a separate capacity as the Court of Star Chamber, the King's advisors interfered directly with purely local legal and political matters, reversing the judgment of a justice of the peace concerning a conviction for poaching, perhaps, or intervening to suppress a village riot. The Star Chamber acted informally, quickly, and with authority limited only by the facts that it did not inflict the death penalty and that it was open to public scrutiny. Justified as an emergency body, the court was attacked under the Stuarts and destroyed by Parliamentary statute in 1641.

Justices of the peace were overseen in their labors by the royally appointed judges at the quarter sessions. Three or four times a year the King's judges appeared at the quarter sessions, traveling on their assize circuit, to decide on matters which had arisen since their last visit. They summoned a grand jury, from which they elicited a report and to which they addressed remarks concerning the King's view of the conduct of the district. They presided over jury trials, they examined local conditions, and they paid close attention to the way taxes were being collected. They held wide administrative as well as judicial authority. Indeed, the two functions were inextricably combined at all levels of English government. The maintenance of the highways by the inhabitants, for instance, was part of the common law, which the justices enforced.

The Stuarts inherited a system of civil government which had enabled their predecessors to wield despotic authority without military force. Upon examining this system, the Stuart Kings concluded that those "liberties" to which their subjects laid claim were not the inalienable heritage of Englishmen, as was widely and incessantly alleged. They were rather privileges which the Crown had seen fit to bestow upon the people, and they existed upon royal sufferance. Against this view Sir Edward Coke and others asserted that these liberties were ancient rights, held by the people independently of royal authority. But, although Coke studded his argument with precedents from ancient documents, the Stuart position probably accorded better with the facts of English constitutional history. Where the Stuarts chiefly erred was in supposing that these privileges, once given, could, as a practical matter, be revoked by subsequent monarchs.

Over the centuries, the English Kings had developed an administrative system which Albert B. White has described as "self-government at the king's command." It was the power of the crown which had forced so many of the King's subjects to perform a multitude of onerous duties without compensation and without military coercion. "The English kings," wrote White,

> working in what they believed to be their own personal interest, so used the English people in government, laid upon them for centuries such burdens and responsibilities, that they went far toward creating the Englishman's governmental sense and competence . . . . [Charles I] did not know that all divine right authorities had received a mortal blow. He did not realize that

a long line of his own predecessors had been forcing "a share in government" upon very many generations of Englishmen. Now came the harvest of this long premeditated planting: the English people *could* do the thing that they now had come to wish to do. That one fact makes much of seventeenth-century history whether in England or on American shores, and conditions much of governmental growth in the centuries following.

So long as the Tudor system of government was functioning successfully, its practitioners had not concerned themselves with arguments as to where sovereignty ultimately rested. Certainly they did not act upon the assumption that it rested exclusively with the Crown, and even the Stuarts did not take so extreme position. Although Parliament and the law courts were called into being at the King's command, it was never supposed that they were in existence merely to do the King's bidding. The law was glorified as the collective wisdom of the English people, and it was a normal occurrence for the King's judges to decide in favor of private citizens against the interests of the King.

To administer the law, the lay legal profession had emerged in the late middle ages, governing its own conduct through its craft guilds, the Inns of Court, and working into its system the rival legal procedures of the Church and Crown. By the end of the fifteenth century the Inns had gained exclusive authority to train the lawyers who practiced in the King's courts. Under the rule of law equal protection was in theory extended to all Englishmen, and with it freedom from arrest and imprisonment except by explicit charge and according to due process of law. The true ruler of the kingdom, Coke declared, was not the King but the common law, which ruled the King himself. Unquestionably it was to the authority, independence, and attentiveness of the English bar that the English colonies owed those guarantees of English privileges and immunities upon which they based their forms of self-government.

In practice, the common law might be flouted by lords, lay as well as clerical. It might be avoided, as well, by some members of the lower orders who enjoyed a lord's protection, and it was repeatedly set aside by Stuart Kings, as it had been by their predecessors. Coke's view, nevertheless, was the one which prevailed by the eighteenth century, and one which influenced American thought from the beginning. In America the common law itself played no important direct role until the eighteenth century, when American society had developed a sufficient complexity to warrant adoption of the complex English legal structure. The principle of equality under the law, however, spread easily through America, in the relative absence of feudal obstructions, and in the eighteenth century an American legal profession arose to shape the common law to American needs. On the eve of the Revolution, American lawyers studied the *Commentaries* of Blackstone, the Tory advocate of Parliamentary supremacy, and from Blackstone they constructed the case for American liberties, solidly based on English legal precedents.

The law which the American colonies inherited contained a vengefully bloody penal code which America adopted as well. Mild misdemeanors brought whipping and the stocks. The sentence for minor crimes was mutilation, such as cutting out the tongue or branding through the gristle of the ear. The penalty for almost all else was death. America preserved this form of justice in most states until the democratic age of Jackson, although in practice the death penalty was much less frequently inflicted in America.

Parliament plainly shared some measure of sovereignty with the courts and the Crown. James I agreed that legislation required the assent of Parliament, although he argued that in an emergency the King could issue proclamations on his own authority. Without question, Parliament's assent was necessary for the taxation which in the seventeenth century was increasingly vital to governments no longer able to live on royal revenues alone. The statesmen of Elizabeth's reign probably had held the abstraction, King-in-Parliament, to be supreme, above the King and above the law. Certainly that was the theory which Henry VIII had come to act upon. The "practical despotism of the Tudors," Maitland wrote, "had laid a terrible emphasis upon the enormous powers of parliament." The authority by which Henry VIII broke with the Roman church was King-in-Parliament, and when Queen Mary returned England to Roman Catholicism, she called upon Parliament for the authority to do so. The question which remained to be answered by civil war and revolution in the seventeenth century was how great a share Parliament possessed in the sovereignty of the nation.

As a feudal institution, Parliament represented not the people or the nation, but the three separate estates of nobles, clergy, and commoners. It came into being as a realization of the medieval view that the King should act in council with his vassals like any other lord, and that his vassals should be especially consulted before the King exercised his authority in any unusual way. In particular, the royal need for money necessitated the calling of such assemblies in England as on the continent.

The English Parliament early developed along distinctive lines as compared with similar feudal institutions on the continent. The fourteenth-century organization of a house of commoners and a separate house containing the lords and upper clergy gave the English Parliament a special character. The relatively large influence enjoyed by the commoners was especially striking. The town burgesses had risen to a position of strength in England earlier than on most areas of the continent, and those sharp class distinctions were lacking, which divided nobles and commoners elsewhere. The rural gentry, which on the continent were classed as lesser nobles, in England consented to be represented in the House of Commons, and they gave that body an authority which the towns-people alone could not have won for it.

According to the medieval view, the House of Commons represented all commoners, and it could authorize taxes in their name, regardless of whether individual taxpayers had taken part in the selection of the representatives. This was to be the official English justification for taxing Americans, who were not directly represented in Parliament. It was argued that, as members of the third estate, Americans were "virtually" represented in the House of Commons. But a different view had arisen much earlier in the House of Commons itself. "When a representative voted a tax," Louise F. Brown wrote of the Elizabethan House of Commons, "he thereby bound his constituents."

> They expected something in return, and the member was supposed to get it for them. Out of this situation grew two political ideas. One was: "Redress of grievances must precede supply." The other was that if the queen did not release imprisoned members, "some countries [counties] might complain of the tax of these many subsidies, their knights and burgesses never consenting unto them nor being present at the grant."

This idea that members of the House of Commons represented, not simply the whole third estate, but rather their own constituents, was put forward with especial force by the Puritan element in Parliament. It was the view of Sir Simonds D'Ewes among others that furthermore "the poorest man ought to have a voice, that it was the birthright of the subjects of England." Three centuries passed before all of these principles triumphed in England, but already they had gained currency among some Parliamentarians at the time of America's settlement. Elizabeth's last Parliament acted such a forward part as to persuade the Queen's chief minister that "those persons would be glad that all sovereignty were converted into popularity." The complaint was one which colonial governors and proprietors were to find endless occasion to echo with reference to the colonial assemblies.

IV

It is a charming historical fact that modern England rose most conspicuously in national power under the rule of Queens, while the great struggles for liberty were waged mainly against Kings. During the periods which intervened between the glorious reigns of Queens Elizabeth, Anne, and Victoria, England was ruled by Kings who were successively pedantic, conscienceless, traitorous, stupid, slothful, insane, un-English, and, as often as not, grossly immoral. In one way or another all of them served to bring the royal authority into disrepute. Under any circumstances, barring violent countermeasures on the part of the King, royal authority was destined to diminish during the seventeenth and eighteenth centuries with the rise of the middle classes, the spread of Puritanism, and the increasing economic dependence of the Crown upon Parliament. The extent of the Parliamentary victory of 1689, however, was made possible by the signal incompetence and contrariety of James I, Charles I, and James II.

A spendthrift Scotsman and a personally unprepossessing exponent of the divine right of kings, James I inherited a government which was becoming increasingly dependent upon Parliament for financial support, and he inherited a church which was increasingly under attack from the dominating Puritan element in Parliament. Two decades of threats and arguments failed to alter the demands of Parliament for reforms, and in his last years the need for money forced James to capitulate. His son Charles I took up the father's old cause with a vengeance. He redoubled persecution of dissenters, he squandered money with a prodigal hand, and he insisted upon the complete subservience of Parliament to his wishes. Failing to win pliant Parliaments, he ruled England for eleven years without the assistance of Parliament, but in the end the need for money brought him also to terms.

Parliament thereupon forced Charles I to accept a series of conditions. It outlawed unauthorized taxes. It abolished the courts of Star Chamber and High Commission, the Council of the North, and the Court of the Marches of Wales. It passed a triennial act calling for the summoning of Parliament at intervals of not more than three years. Then it divided over the efforts of the Puritan majority to abolish the office of bishop, to eliminate the prayer book, and to place Parliament in command of the army. Taking advantage of this division, Charles I raised the royal standard at Nottingham and launched the Civil War.

From the point of view of official English constitutional history, the events of the subsequent eighteen years became, in retrospect, as if they had not taken place: the defeat of the King, the failure of the attempt to establish a national Presbyterian church, the subsequent victory for the idea of toleration, the execution of the King, and the series of unsuccessful republican experiments. But the memory remained of the regicide and a decade of republicanism. The failure of the republican experiments may have strengthened the appeal of monarchy in England, but the American colonies were an ocean apart from the English crown, and, after the Restoration of 1660, libertarian ideas, born of the civil conflict, were permitted trial there while they were vigorously obliterated at home. Novel political ideas of the Rebellion influenced the constitutions of the Carolinas, Pennsylvania, and Delaware, while Rebellion-born religious sects, particularly Quakerism, found refuge in America from Restoration England.

Memory of the unhappy period of the Great Rebellion joined with the violently impolitic conduct of James II to make the Glorious Revolution of 1688 the momentary, moderate, and successful event that it was. James II alienated the gentry by his support of Roman Catholics and by his arbitrary conduct toward Parliament, the Anglican Church, and the office of justice of the peace. Sturdy royalists, who might once again have paid the purple testament of bleeding war to a less subversive monarch, embarrassingly enough found their own positions attacked by the King. James II left them no course but dignified desertion, and William of Orange moved without opposition to London and the English throne.

A convention was called to regularize the proceedings, and the convention, transformed into a Parliament by the King it had appointed, in 1689 passed the Bill of Rights, a detailed assertion of the power of Parliament to limit the King's authority. It prohibited Roman Catholics from holding the royal office. It prohibited the King from suspending or dispensing with the laws, from interfering with elections and debates in Parliament, from maintaining a standing army without the permission of Parliament, and from levying taxes except by Parliamentary grant. The Toleration Act, though it excluded non-Anglicans from office, extended religious freedom to virtually all but Roman Catholics, who, in practice, were not denied the freedom. The annual meeting of Parliament was permanently secured, and Parliament gained ultimate, although indirect, control of the army.

Various English colonies in America simultaneously held their own glorious revolutions and drew up their own bills of rights, all of which were vetoed by the Privy Council. In England during the eighteenth century the Glorious Revolution came to be interpreted as a victory for the idea of parliamentary supremacy. In America it came to be viewed rather as a victory for the idea of legislative supremacy, and Americans came to view their own provincial assemblies in this light. In time it turned out that this difference of opinion could be settled only by revolution.

The Revolution of 1688 influenced political thinking throughout western Europe in the next century. It had occurred during the age of Louis XIV, when the idea of the divine right of kings was in vogue, and it broke the prestige of royal divine right absolutism. It was not simply that England moved decisively against the reigning doctrine of the age; it was, also, that afterwards the Revolution proved remarkably successful in terms of national power. The practical effect of the Revolution, in shifting power from the King to Parliament, was to shift power into the hands of those who controlled the nation economically. In the ensuing age of confidence England rose rapidly as the commercial and financial center of the world, and, under the Duke of Marlborough, as a military power of the first rank. Liberalism, which became the path of virtue for reformers in the eighteenth century, became the road to power for enlightened despots.

The Glorious Revolution was a victory for Parliament, for property rights, and for the rule of law. It opened the way for three-quarters of a century of quiet, unheroic development of Parliamentary government, the creation of the office of Prime Minister, and of the cabinet responsible both to the King and to Parliament. "The consequences ripened slowly," Lord Acton wrote, "and a time came under George III, when it seemed that they were exhausted. It was then that another and more glorious Revolution, infinitely more definite and clear-cut, with a stronger grasp of principle, and depending less on conciliation and compromise, began to influence England and Europe."

Chapter 2

TRANSPLANTATION

I

IN ACCORDANCE with company instructions, after more than a decade of military rule, the chief company officer in Virginia summoned a representative assembly in 1619. It consisted of the governor, his council, and twenty-two burgesses. The burgesses were elected by universal manhood suffrage, including, apparently, all males in the colony over sixteen years of age. With the calling of the assembly on July 30, representative government began in America, as a business policy of the Virginia Company. The summoning of this legislature was the company's effort, in the absence of any clear precedent, to fulfill the charter clause guaranteeing the settlers their rights as Englishmen. If there was any serious opposition within the company to this momentous decision, no evidence of it has been made available.

The assembly wrote into law previous instructions from the company to governors and added a number of laws based on the legislators' own experience in the colony. It requested of the company that its laws henceforth be considered immediately operative, even though the company might eventually disallow them. It requested permission to express disapproval of company laws. Then it adjourned to meet again the following March. In 1621 the burgesses received assurance from the company that "no orders shall bind the colony unless they be ratified in the general assembly."

Three years later Virginia became a royal colony. On the eve of this transfer of ownership to the King, the infant Virginia assembly, a curious novelty among English forms of local government, proceeded to legislate itself rights which exceeded those claimed by Parliament:

> The governor shall not lay any taxes or impositions upon the colony, their lands or commodities other way than by the authority of the General Assembly, to be levied and employed as the said Assembly shall appoint.

It further requested that the Privy Council limit the authority of Virginia governors and that it permit the Virginia general assembly to continue in its advisory capacity. "In these two utterances," Charles M. Andrews wrote, "are contained all the law and the gospel as far as self-government in a colony is concerned."

James I ignored these claims, and Charles I after him withheld approval for many years. From 1624 to 1629 the Crown summoned various conventions in Virginia to discuss specific problems, but they did not meet annually, and they did not have the character of a continuing elective body. Despite lack of authorization from the Privy Council, however, general assemblies met annually on their own authority from 1630 to 1638. In England, meanwhile, the autocratic Charles I appeared to be succeeding in his attempt to rule the nation without the aid of Parliament. Finally, in 1639, the Virginia assembly received official sanction from Charles' Privy Council. By their steadfast exertions the Virginians had won recognition for a precedent which henceforth would apply to all royal colonies in America. It was under divine right monarchs in the seventeenth century that the English colonies formed their representative institutions; it was against divine right Parliaments in the eighteenth that the colonies, defending these institutions, won their national independence.

Stuart tolerance of free American institutions was mainly Stuart indifference toward the subject. James I personally hated libertarianism just as he hated the tobacco habit. Both, as it turned out, were encouraged by the Virginia experiment. James, however, was interested in the colony as a possible source of revenue, and both tobacco culture and the general assembly were incidentally tolerated in the hope of financial returns. How a small, distant colonial venture arranged its internal affairs did not concern the English Crown greatly.

A generation before the settlement of Jamestown, Queen Elizabeth had illustrated this same attitude when she had advanced a scheme to found a colony for Roman Catholics in America, where Catholicism might flourish beyond the reach of English persecution. Within England, Elizabethan religious policy was implemented by the hanging, drawing, quartering, and disemboweling of Roman Catholics before shrieking English mobs. At home Roman Catholics were viewed as potential royal assassins and members of a subversive organization. Three thousand miles away in the American forest they might be as subversive as they liked without danger to the national security or the royal person.

James I viewed the English Puritans as enemies to royal power. If they would not conform to his views of religion he would harry them from the land. Still, having harried the Separatists from England, James gave his consent, if grudgingly, to the establishment of a Separatist colony in New England. Under Charles I persecution of Puritans was increased; yet no critical objections were raised when leading Puritans, removing to Massachusetts, established virtually an independent commonwealth. Cromwell, during the period of the English Commonwealth, attempted to suppress the appearance of royalism in Virginia, but only the appearance, and in Maryland he upheld the proprietary rights of the Roman Catholic Lord Baltimore. Charles II violated colonial charter rights irresponsibly and recklessly, but not as part of any comprehensive scheme to gain greater control over colonial affairs. James II, an experienced colonial administrator, did attempt to unify the colonies under systematic royal control, but the scheme was supported by no adequate method of enforcement.

During a century of civil and religious struggle in England, the colonies were left much to themselves.

The English governments viewed the American colonies as a sewage system, draining England of some of her religious malcontents, convicts, and beggars. Seventeenth-century England believed overpopulation to be among the great evils of the time. The colonial system happily served to remove some of the less desirable elements of the population at little expense to the nation. It was a system which also gave employment as administrators to needy members of the upper classes. Under such circumstances it was to be expected that colonial America would fall below English standards; that was the defect of its virtue.

While Virginians in the 1630's, guided by no democratic theories, were asserting, on the basis of no clear legal right, a system of self-government based on universal manhood suffrage, Maryland was being founded on the basis of a system of feudal authority such as had existed nowhere in England for more than a century. Maryland was an attempt by the Roman Catholic George Calvert Lord Baltimore to establish a haven in the New World for English Catholics. Baltimore brought to his task a life of experience in English public affairs and a long connection with American colonizing efforts. In his efforts to devise a charter suited to his purposes, Baltimore was freed, as the Virginia Company had been, by the lack of any clear precedents, and he chose as his pattern the fourteenth-century charter of the bishop of the palatinate of Durham. The charter, styling Baltimore absolute lord and proprietor, gave him complete ownership of the land and the right to make any laws he wished, subject to the laws of England and the "advice, assent, and approbation of the freemen of the province." All the settlers in Maryland were to be his tenants, obligated to perform such feudal services as he required. He in turn was required to pay the English King two Indian arrows annually. This arrangement, which gave the Calverts greater legal power in Maryland than Charles I enjoyed in England, was looked upon as a reasonable application to America of a feudal authority which had been wielded in the medieval English marches, at a time when England had endowed the feudal lords on its own frontier areas with vast powers in exchange for their performance of important military duties.

In America the system faltered at once. Protestants from the first greatly outnumbered the Catholics, and religious disputes commenced during the voyage to America. Perhaps from conviction, but certainly from necessity, Lord Baltimore's son Cecil Calvert advocated a broad policy of toleration which found expression in the toleration act of 1649, extending protection to all sects of Trinitarian Christianity. The support of a strongly established Catholic Church was denied him. Indeed, the struggles with a Protestant majority were complicated by an equally bitter struggle against the pretensions of the Jesuits. It was in part to frustrate the Jesuits that Baltimore pressed for the toleration act.

A more basic threat to Calvert's authority was the almost unlimited availability of land and the short supply of settlers. The Calverts bestowed upon their friends manorial estates complete with the trappings of medieval privileges. But, to meet the competition of neighboring colonies, they also leased land to yeoman farmers on terms which amounted practically to free private ownership. Such holdings became the basis for voting privileges.

Undercutting Calvert's feudal authority was the charter stipulation requiring the "advice, assent, and approbation" of the freemen. The charter reserved to the proprietor the right to call whatever form of freeman's assembly he chose, whenever he wished, and its duties were to be limited to assenting to such laws as the proprietor proposed. Still, the assembling of such a body apparently was a legal necessity, and, once assembled, thousands of miles from the seat of established authority in England, it presented a formidable front. In 1638, one year before the Virginia assembly was confirmed in its legislative rights by the King, the Maryland proprietor assented to the demand of the assembly that it share the right to initiate legislation. Within a dozen years the settled custom had developed of annual sessions, triennial elections and a two-house legislature, the lower house being composed of freemen whose consent was required for all laws. Maryland and Virginia, created for different purposes under sharply contrasting charters, rapidly developed systems of society and government which were in major respects very nearly identical, the result of a common culture adjusting to a common geographical setting. Tobacco could be raised profitably in the Chesapeake region by single-family farming units, but it was better suited to production by large agricultural factories, where simple, uniform tasks were performed by many hands operating under the supervision of overseers. Until the Restoration Period, this manual labor was performed mainly by indentured servants who were earning their freedom. With the rise of the Royal African Company in the 1670's, however, slavery rapidly supplanted indentured white labor, and by the close of the century the Chesapeake aristocracy was securely established, modeled self-consciously upon the English landed gentry.

Beneath this landed gentry there ranged independent yeomanry, holding its own land, supplying the greater part of its own needs, and possessing the franchise. This counterpart to the English yeomanry made up the majority of the white population of the Chesapeake area, and, since it was a voting part of the population, it was able to exert influence upon the colonial governments. With the actual operation of government, local as well as colonial, however, it played little part. County government in the Chesapeake region was modeled on county government in England. The justices of the peace, appointed from the leading local families, possessed the same wide judicial and executive authority. The Anglican Church came to be established in Maryland as well as in Virginia, and the vestrymen in both colonies were self-perpetuating. "These," wrote Jefferson, "are usually the most discreet farmers, so distributed through their parish, that every part of it may be under the immediate eye of some one of them . . . . They find sufficient inducements to execute their charge well, in their philanthropy, in the approbation of their neighbors, and in the distinction which that gives them." The parish became a unit of local government on the Chesapeake as in England. The sheriff of the county, the coroner, and the county lieutenant were all appointed. Local self-government was virtually nonexistent.

Though the lower houses of the legislature of Virginia and Maryland continued to be elected by a broad suffrage, the legislators were selected mainly from the same class of slaveowning gentry which controlled local government, while in Virginia the governor and his council and in Maryland the proprietary interest assumed some of the characteristics of a local nobility. In political and in social behavior, Chesapeake society modeled itself as best it could upon mother England. It succeeded as well as it did in the new lands of America by force of slavery, which created its own subordinate class while dividing the freemen into classes of slaveowners and non-slaveowners. The result was two quasi-independent societies representing, not alienation from England, but rather the inevitably imperfect attempt, supported by the novel expedient of slavery, to reproduce rural aristocratic England in a new environment.

II

The bitter geography of New England repelled all efforts to erect a medieval palatinate such as had been contemplated for Maryland, and it prohibited the rise of a country gentry on the English model, such as did develop in Maryland and Virginia. The original effort of the Virginia Company of

Plymouth to establish a plantation at Sagadahoc in 1606 was much like that of the Virginia Company of London at Jamestown. Where last minute exertions of the London Company and the production of tobacco sustained the Jamestown venture, however, Sagadahoc developed no source for quick profits. It struggled briefly on an unfriendly terrain and failed. Members of the Council for New England, notably Ferdinando Gorges in upper New England, strove to create just such a feudal barony as Lord Baltimore contemplated for Maryland. Gorges capped a long career of failure in New England enterprises in 1639 when he obtained from Charles I a proprietary charter to the "Province of Maine," covering one-half of New Hampshire, one-eighth of Vermont, and three-eighths of Maine. The terms of the patent were almost identical to those of the Maryland patent.

Moved by dreams of feudal splendor in a land of vast baronial estates, Gorges drew lavish plans, which he did his best to carry out; yet at the time of his death, seven years later, his barony consisted, in addition to the scattered fishing villages which had previously established themselves, of two small plantations. Upon the news of Gorges' death, these two communities drew up a social compact by which, for the next few years, they ruled themselves without authorization from England, until they were summarily annexed by the vigorous, expanding Massachusetts Bay Colony to the south. The Massachusetts Puritans, meanwhile, finding the environment suited to their needs, were immigrating by the thousands and multiplying townships in all directions.

New England's rocky shores and stony hills preserved it for settlers whose primary motive for settlement was not concerned with the goods of this world. Material incentives no doubt played a part in the Great Emigration. Depression conditions in the 1620's helped to persuade Puritan merchants in England that little would be lost by removing to New England. Despite the assertions of numerous authorities to the contrary, the religious motive was evidently dominant, however. Unlike Virginia, which originally was settled chiefly by single young men, Massachusetts was settled by groups of families, drawn heavily from the yeoman class. It is not to be supposed that these men would have uprooted their families to resettle them in a distant mysterious wilderness on the off-chance that the change might improve their material fortunes. Furthermore, the immigration figures, as Edward P. Cheyney pointed out, give honest measure of the role played by religious zeal in the founding of New England. During the first twenty years of the settlement of Virginia, where religious incentive was least strong, less than six thousand settlers came over; during the first twenty years of the settlement of New England, where religious incentive was most strong, more than twenty thousand came. By that time Puritanism had temporarily triumphed in England, and the immigration stopped almost completely.

The great purpose of the New England Puritans was not that of the Chesapeake planters, to recreate England in America; it was to found a New Zion, purged of the evils of English church, society, and government. From the first, therefore, New England exhibited a more thoroughgoing spirit of independence than did the colonies to the south. The Puritans of Massachusetts Bay Colony did not consider themselves separated from the Church of England, as did the Pilgrims who settled Plymouth in 1620. In theory the Puritans were members of the Anglican Church, wishing only to reform it from within. Still their leaders acted vigorously upon the assumption that the "service of raising and upholding a particular Church is to be preferred before the bettering some part of a Church already established." Upon arriving in America they set at once to establishing congregations which repudiated the authority of the English bishops and much of the doctrine of the Anglican Church.

In the political field the Puritans followed a much more flagrantly independent policy than did the small Pilgrim band. The Pilgrims of Plymouth Colony considered themselves subject to the English King. Not so the Puritans in Massachusetts. They were determined to organize a holy state, openly independent of England. They recognized the King as the temporal leader of the country from which they had come, but they made no acknowledgment of his authority over the New Zion. They availed themselves of English law and of their own charter rights wherever such a course suited their interests; where their charter violated their intentions they ignored it.

The leaders of the Massachusetts Bay Colony included intelligent and influential men, who used their advantages to obtain exactly what they wanted. In their original patent of 1628 they acquired from earlier patentees a large grant of land and a wide grant of power. Then, to avoid the consequences of possible flaws in their patent, they reorganized a year later into the Massachusetts Bay Company under a new charter received directly from Charles I. It was a conventional trading company charter. The colony would be ruled by the governor and the board of assistants, elected by members of the company. The board, or General Court, was given "ample power to govern and rule all his Majesty's subjects that reside within the limits of our plantation."

It was assumed by the crown, of course, that the colony would be governed from England like any other chartered trading company. But such an arrangement would have threatened the security of the New Zion. Company stock might have been bought on the open market, and leaders of the company feared that stock might fall into unsympathetic hands. The danger was avoided in 1630, when radical Puritans gained control of the company and sailed for New England, taking the company charter with them. By this highly original and legally questionable act the company practically severed its legal connection with England, and for the next half century it expanded its business charter, by additions and violations, into the Commonwealth of Massachusetts.

John Winthrop, the dominating figure of the company, favored a highly centralized government controlled by the governor and the board of assistants, or magistrates as they were called. The company imposed a suffrage qualification of membership in one of the recognized churches of the commonwealth, a qualification which probably eliminated a sizable majority of the settlers. Even so, Winthrop was as little willing to share power with the house selected by this electorate as Charles I was to share power with Parliament. But Winthrop's centralized, autocratic system of government commenced to crack almost at once. The freemen won the right to elect deputies from each town to represent them in three of the four annual meetings of the General Court. The company magistrates asserted their right to veto the decisions of these deputies, who were in the majority. In 1644 the struggle over this assertion resulted in the dividing of the General Court into two separate houses.

Meanwhile, a kindred struggle for political rights was being waged by non-churchmembers, who, in the townships, were on the same economic footing as their sanctified neighbors. The struggle was supported by freemen, who wished to share the many onerous duties of citizenship with their fellows. In 1647 the General Court admitted non-freemen to active, although non-voting, participation in local affairs, and in 1648 non-freemen were permitted to take part in any town meeting, council or court proceeding in the Commonwealth. In the same year, again in response to popular pressure, as well as in response to pressure from England, the Commonwealth published its *General Laws and Liberties,* a conglomeration of General Court legislation, Mosaic law, and altered English common law. Henceforth freemen and non-freemen alike were at least in a position to inform themselves of their legal rights. In 1662 the Half-Way Covenant broadened the franchise by admitting to church membership persons who had not given evidence of their divine election. The Massachusetts Bay Company within a generation had altered itself into a commonwealth based on a working compromise between the authoritarian theocratic principles of the leaders and the demands of the majority.

In the meanwhile the Massachusetts leadership was at least successful in heading off the immigration of high born Puritans whose coming would have threatened to place mere squires like Winthrop, Dudley, and Saltonstall themselves in the second rank of Massachusetts society. In 1635 Lord Say and Sele and other lordly gentlemen suggested that they might themselves remove to Massachusetts, if the government were reformed to accommodate two classes of citizens, gentlemen and freeholders, the former to share in the rule of the province through membership in an hereditary house of lords; the latter to elect representatives to a house of commons. To this offer John Cotton replied, as instructed, that such men in Massachusetts were recognized simply as part of the gentry, in common with worthy persons of lesser means; and also that the hereditary principle might result in the selection of political leaders who were not suited to the task.

Although essentially Calvinistic, New England Puritanism was not based directly upon Calvin's *Institutes* and does not appear to have followed Calvin in his aristocratic theory of predestination. According to Samuel Eliot Morison, the Puritan clergy assumed that salvation lay within the reach of every person who made the effort; that "Christ helped those who helped themselves." Support for this view is to be found in Michael Wigglesworth's *Day of Doom,* the lengthy rhyme about the day of judgment read by generations of New England children. *Day of Doom* is especially illuminating on the subject, because it is an attempt to explain the Puritan theory of salvation in a clear, simple, complete, and noncontroversial fashion, to children who do not as yet know what the theory is.

At one point the rhyme quite inconsistently refers to the elect as having been chosen by God before the creation of the world, but it goes on to assert repeatedly that salvation is open to all. The damned who venture boldly to Hell, it declares, had been offered salvation and had refused it. Those who had died young and were about to go to Hell are reminded that they had been given at least a brief period to save their souls and that they should have made better use of their time. And, finally, the theory of predestination is specifically denied.

'Twas no vain task to knock and ask,
   whilst life continuéd.
Who ever sought Heav'n as he ought,
   and seeking perishéd?
The lowly, meek, who truly seek
   for Christ and for Salvation
There's no decree whereby such be
   ordain'd to condemnation.

Living in an aristocratic age, the political and religious leaders of New England were naturally aristocratic in their views, but their theology, itself, was not necessarily aristocratic in its implications.

Central to the doctrine of New England Puritanism was the idea of the Covenant of Grace. Originally God had made a Covenant of Works with man, but man, following Adam's fall, had become incapable of carrying it out. By the terms of the subsequent Covenant of Grace, man would be redeemed from the natural consequences of his depravity on the simple condition that he put his faith in God. This covenant was a permanent contract, like a business contract, directly binding on both God and the individual. Under the terms of this contract, the individual was free to choose between damnation and salvation through faith.

To this extent New England Puritanism was thoroughly individualistic. In practice, however, this individualism was tempered by the Puritan's awareness of man's totally depraved condition. The Bible was the rock on which man's faith rested, and theoretically the individual might achieve salvation by his own unaided reading of Scripture. That was by no means thought to be the normal way to Grace, however. The Devil, certainly more ingenious than ignorant men, might guide them easily into error in their uninformed reading of the Bible. The chief instrument of salvation was the sermon, where the Bible was expounded by a learned clergyman, but even the learned clergyman was open to error. Against so resourceful an opponent as Satan, the best guarantee was the congregating together of those who had reason to believe that they were on the way to Grace. These placed themselves under a trusted minister and then watched the minister to be sure that he himself did not fall into error. This, the New England Puritans believed, had been the form of church organization of the primitive Christians in the purest age of Christianity.

The result of this reasoning in New England was the Congregational system. At the center of each town was the church, its membership including those of the community who could offer satisfactory proof of their sanctification. Non-churchmembers were required to attend church and to support it by taxes, but they were permitted no active part in church affairs. The minister was selected by the congregation and, on occasion, discharged by it. In the town meetings, held in the same meeting house, the elect originally exerted the same control over secular affairs.

American conditions also favored Congregationalism. In Old England, Puritans were divided on the question of church organization between the adherents of Presbyterianism, on the model of the Scotch Calvinists, and the advocates of absolute Independency. In America, the wilderness conditions favored the latter course. The First Church of Christ in Salem, the original Congregational church in America and the model for later churches in Massachusetts and Connecticut, was independent geographically as well as doctrinally. There was no unity of opinion, even among the early Puritan leaders, on so important a matter as church organization, but the Congregational system was the one best suited to the environment.

Local government in England functioned through the Anglican Church, and in the Chesapeake colonies the parish similarly became the basis unit for local government. Congregationalism became the established religion in Massachusetts and Connecticut, and there it formed the basis for that distinctive institution of local government, the town meeting. The system developed almost by itself. The early Puritan leaders of New England, intent on controlling the central government, originally allowed the local communities wide latitude in forming their own local governments. The result was an institution formed out of English village tradition, out of the fact of general equality of land ownership, and out of the political consequences of Congregational church organization. The county officials, including the justices of the peace, were appointed by the governor. The towns governed themselves, however, each one rotating dozens of unpaid jobs among its citizens.

The town meeting system tended strongly toward democracy, "the meanest and worst of all forms of government," according to Governor John Winthrop. The tendency was one more testament to man's natural depravity. One of many. Zealous as the Puritans were, they were not zealous enough to satisfy their leaders. Although the power and persistence of New England Puritanism was to demonstrate itself through the centuries and across the continent, the American Zion had hardly been founded before the leaders began to lament the decline in religious devotion and public morality. Even the leaders themselves, secure at last from English persecution, were found to be "not so lively in their profession as they were wont to be many years ago." The dangerous democratic tendencies of the town meeting system, as compared with the parish system on the Chesapeake, were meanwhile early in evidence.

III

The founders of Massachusetts sought to combine complete freedom from English Kings and bishops with complete authority over their inferiors. The result, in their minds, was perfect liberty. "There is a twofold liberty, natural (I mean as our nature is now corrupt) and civil, or federal," declared John Winthrop in his most famous statement on the subject. Natural liberty, he said, reduces man to the level of beasts; civil liberty

> is maintained and exercised in a way of subjection to authority; it is of the same kind of liberty wherewith Christ hath made us free . . . if you will be satisfied to enjoy such civil and lawful liberties, such as Christ allows you, then will you quietly and cheerfully submit unto that authority which is set over you, in all the administrations of it, for your own good.

Liberty was the state enjoyed by the citizen who submitted freely to the divinely sanctioned authority of his secular master as the bride submitted gladly to the authority of her lord, to be "refreshed, supported, and instructed by every such dispensation of his authority over her." Submission to the authority of Charles I and Bishop Laud was slavery, for they were falsely guided; submission to Governor Winthrop and John Cotton was liberty, for they had perceived the true word of God and ruled according to His plan.

Opposition to the official view of liberty in Massachusetts came in the main from two sources: from the belief that Winthrop was right in his definition of liberty but wrong in believing himself its divinely appointed instrument; and from the belief that Winthrop was wrong in his definition of liberty. The settlement of Connecticut was stimulated by the first kind of opposition, the settlement of Rhode Island by the

second. Both colonies were established within the first decade
of the Massachusetts experiment.

Connecticut was settled mainly by Puritan leaders who,
agreeing with the underlying principles of the Massachusetts
experiment, were antagonized by its ruling group or were
simply attracted by the richer Connecticut farm land. In
1639 these new settlements, except for New Haven, united
under the Fundamental Orders of Connecticut. At first
Connecticut accepted the direction of the Massachusetts General Court, and it never placed itself in direct opposition to
the mother colony. Nevertheless, it did constitute a dissenting
from dissent. It demonstrated a fundamental weakness in the
Massachusetts experiment, the difficulty of establishing a
precise decentralized Protestantism which would admit of no
further protesting. Connecticut was settled by men who considered themselves orthodox Puritans, but the apparent effect
of their continuation of the Protestant process was the infusion
of a mild libertarianism, most evident in the omission of a
religious test for citizenship.

New Haven was settled by men who remained in harmony with the Massachusetts leadership and avoided the cor-
rupted colony of Connecticut, until forced into its company
by the threat of annexation to New York. In establishing
their first government, the voters unanimously passed a resolution that "the scriptures do hold forth a perfect rule for the
direction and government of all men," and they declared their
intention of following it. New Haven remained pre-eminently
the center of Puritan orthodoxy in New England, but the
future of America lay less with New Haven orthodoxy than
with that rampant heterodoxy which characterized the colony
of Rhode Island.

Rhode Island was the reduction of Protestantism to an
absurdity; its settlements, banished from Massachusetts for
disagreeing with the official dissenting doctrine, fell into vigorous dissension among themselves. From the first, Rhode Island

was marked by an extreme of libertarianism which, during the seventeenth-century religious struggles, manifested itself in the free exercise of Brownism, Antinomianism, Arminianism, Anabaptism, Seekerism, and Quakerism, and which in the more worldly eighteenth century manifested itself in smuggling, piracy, privateering, revolution against English rule, and, finally, dogged opposition to the authority of the federal government of the United States.

Rhode Island was one of the first societies in the history of the world to be based on principles of religious freedom and political individualism, bringing to a sudden fruition ideas which were, in the course of the ensuing century, to develop gradually in other of the colonies and in England. The colony was founded by Roger Williams, upon his banishment from Salem in 1636 for preaching unacceptable doctrines. To escape deportation from America, Williams fled to unoccupied country, where he purchased land from the Indians and founded the town of Providence. Banishment of Anne Hutchinson shortly thereafter resulted in the settlement of nearby Portsmouth, and friction within the Portsmouth settlement resulted a year later in the founding of Newport. In 1643 friction within the Providence community resulted in the settlement of Warwick. In 1647 a disharmonious union of the four settlements was achieved, lasting four years. A reunion was affected by Williams in 1654 and was sanctioned by a royal charter in 1663.

Roger Williams demonstrated in his career, as did William Penn after him, that under American wilderness conditions the visionary idealist could become the creative statesman. Williams had fallen out with the Massachusetts clergy chiefly over his belief in freedom of conscience and the separation of church and state. Whatever other disagreements developed in Rhode Island, the four settlements agreed upon these principles. Quakers, for whom Williams conceived a fierce hatred, were freely permitted to settle in his community although they came in such numbers as for a time to gain control of the government. In Massachusetts, by contrast, Quakers were whipped, put to hard labor, and, at the height of the anti-Quaker fury, hanged.

It was Williams' argument that, "All civil states with their officers of justice in their respective constitutions and administrations are proved essentially civil, and therefore not judges, governors or defenders of the spiritual or Christian state and worship," and that

> It is the will and command of God, that (since the coming of His son the Lord Jesus) a permission of the most paganish, Jewish, Turkish, or anti-Christian consciences and worships, be granted to all men in all nations and countries: and they are only to be fought against with that sword which is only (in soul matters) able to conquer, to wit, the sword of God's spirit, the word of God.

Against the unrelenting opposition of Massachusetts and the divisive tendencies of his own principles, Williams successfully defied the "bloody tenet of persecution for cause of conscience," to erect a permanent state on the principles of freedom of conscience and, incidentally, political democracy.

Connecticut and Rhode Island both enjoyed the advantage over Massachusetts or Virginia of having been founded independently of any aid from England. There were no corporate connections to make difficulties. When these colonies eventually received their permanent charters from Charles II—Connecticut in 1662 and Rhode Island a year later—they received just what they asked for. No control whatever was reserved expressly by the King, either over legislation or over the administration of justice. Except for tokens of fealty, no express demands were placed upon the colonies. These charters, the most liberal granted to any of the colonies, so far as the majority of settlers were concerned, remained in force into the nineteenth century.

IV

In their remarkable liberality the Connecticut and Rhode Island charters were typical demonstrations of the lighthearted colonial policy followed by the government of Charles II. Although steps were taken during his reign to control colonial commerce, Charles continued to grant lands, liberties, and privileges with a prodigal hand. An extreme example of this careless indulgence was the granting of Virginia to several court favorites, an act of generosity which put the colony itself to a burdensome expense. More permanent fruits of this prodigality were the granting of the Dutch-owned New Netherlands to his brother the Duke of York, the granting of the Carolinas to eight aristocratic proprietors, and of Pennsylvania to William Penn, the son of a court favorite and royal creditor.

The intent of the Carolina proprietors was indicated in their Fundamental Constitutions, which prescribed an aristocratic hierarchy, based on the size of the landholdings, ranging from the lords proprietors down through landgraves, caciques, gentlemen, and commoners, to the yeomanry. The Fundamental Constitutions never obtained the necessary approval of the freemen of the colony, however, and so never passed into law. Nevertheless, the document guided the proprietors for a generation, and the aristocratic pattern of South Carolina society developed early.

The rich South Carolina lowlands were early pre-empted by those who could afford to purchase them and to purchase Negro slaves as well. Others were obliged to take possession of the poorer land in the upcountry. The lowlands were richer than the farming land around the Chesapeake, and the contrast between the profitable lowlands and unprofitable hinterland more clear-cut. South Carolina rice plantations proved to be most efficiently operated in relatively small units, and the high profits made absentee ownership and the hiring of overseers practicable. The malarial conditions of

the low country during the summer made it advisable for all
who could absent themselves to do so, and for half of the
year the planters habitually resided in Charles Town, the
only city to develop south of Philadelphia in the course of
the colonial period.

In Charles Town there emerged an ingrown, aristocratic
society markedly different in its political and its social orientation from the aristocracy of the Chesapeake. Where the
rural gentry of Virginia, living the year around on their
plantations, took as their pattern for politics and behavior
the English squirearchy, the Charles Town aristocracy took
its cues from the royal court in England and from those English landed aristocrats sufficiently opulent to afford town
houses in London, just as the South Carolinians were able to
afford town houses in Charles Town.

Again in contrast to the Chesapeake society, where a
vigorous small-farmer class developed, society in the Carolina
low country was divided "into opulent and lordly planters,
poor and spiritless whites and vile slaves," while the hill
country, with its Scotch-Irish and German population, was
beyond the pale, denied substantial representation down to
the Civil War and through much of the colonial period given
no form of government whatever. The tight group of aristocrats controlled the government through very high property
qualifications, disfranchisement of the back-country, absentee
political representation, establishment of the Anglican Church,
and the social and political pressures created by a preponder-
ance of slaves. In 1719, restive under the abuses of the current
proprietors, the South Carolina aristocracy performed a mild
revolution, declaring the colony independent of the proprietors and placing themselves directly under royal authority.
Under this more dignified arrangement the aristocrats continued to govern their colony throughout the rest of the
colonial period.

New York alone, among the American colonies, was governed for the first generation of its English existence without the calling of a legislative assembly. Its ultra-aristocratic proprietor, the Duke of York, accomplished this feat through the skilfull efforts of his deputy in New York, Richard Nicolls, who ruled the colony under the "Duke's Laws," a legal code made up of existent Dutch law, New England law, and English common law. The chief basis for this aristocratic rule was the consent of the Dutch colonists, who had not previously possessed representative institutions, and who had not enjoyed any government so efficiently and honestly operated. The chief objection to the lack of a legislature came from the English colonists on Long Island, who complained to the Duke of York of the "slavery" of taxation without representation. Their complaints met with the authorization to draw up a constitution creating such a legislature, but before the constitution received approval the Duke of York became James II, the proprietary colony became a royal one, and the creation of a legislature was delayed until after the Revolution of 1688.

The Duke of York acquired with New Netherland a highly aristocratic land system which bestowed vast tracts and the title of patroon upon Dutch settlers who brought fifty additional settlers with them. The system had not worked well. Only two patroons remained in possession of their land at the time the English assumed control. Those were confirmed in their possessions, and a similar and more workable English modification was introduced, creating huge English estates and a Dutch-English landed aristocracy along the Hudson. These manorial lords received feudal rights which they successfully asserted, controlling local trade, holding leet courts, and in some cases being privileged to send their own personal representatives to the Assembly. Still the English were faced with the same condition which had hindered the patroon system: the existence of much free land and the need for settlers. The Roman Catholic duke, who in England later pressed for a policy of toleration which would benefit the English Catholics, followed in New York a policy of wide toleration to encourage settlement. In competition with neighboring colonies, particularly Pennsylvania, a favorable land policy also was instituted. The owners of the great manors themselves competed with each other for settlers to work the manorial lands, offering land in freehold tenure to those who would settle it. The result was a thriving, independent—although politically passive—yeomanry developing beside a wealthy landed aristocracy.

A similar situation developed in the city of New York, where a mercantile aristocracy owed its prosperity to privileges accorded it by the English King, and where commercial prosperity permitted the development of a strong, independent, voting artisan class. In the early years the landed aristocracy and the mercantile aristocracy were indistinguishably mingled. In time they came to separate and to oppose each other on economic grounds, providing an opening for democratic pressures from the strong middle and lower-middle classes of New York. In New York, more than in any other English colony in America, aristocratic origins were at loggerheads with democratic environment. One result was an aristocracy comparatively dependent on and loyal to the English Crown; an aristocracy which, during the Revolutionary War, proved more heartily loyalist than that of any other colony. Another result was that division within the colony which produced evenly fought class struggles resulting, during the early nineteenth century, in some of the most fruitful early experiments in American democracy.

In Pennsylvania the similarly democratic potentialities of the environment were harnessed from the first to a Frame of Government which was by far the most liberal of any of the royal or proprietary colonies in America. Its author William Penn was to his contemporaries a wildly radical, democratical idealist. He devised a visionary scheme of government and administered it with soft headed ineptitude to create a society which was, from the first, one of the most richly successful of the English plantations in America. Pennsylvania was the Rhode Island of the middle colonies, dangerous to its neighbors for the obviously fruitful consequences of its libertarian principles. Like Rhode Island, it demonstrated that in America political liberty was the practical formula for material success.

Penn was a member of the Quaker sect, which George Fox had founded amid the religious ferment of the English civil wars. The Quakers brought the individualism of Protestantism to its logical conclusion with the announcement of the priesthood of all men and women. No particular form of worship or indoctrination was prescribed by the Quakers. The source of a man's religious experience was an inner light, private to each soul. While not original with the Quakers, the doctrine of the inner light was given a central position in their religion as in no other. In England they remained a minor though influential sect; in America they shaped the commonwealths of Pennsylvania and Delaware, and to some extent of New Jersey, North Carolina, and Rhode Island. For a time it appeared that they might establish Quakerism as the dominant religion of America. They lacked organization, however, and lacked also an intolerance of rival sects, and they were soon overtaken by the more evangelical religions. In America their importance to the history of liberty has proved greater than their importance to the history of religion. They have remained to the present day, as a group, the most thorough-going defenders of conscientious individualism in the whole national society.

Under the Frame of Government, revised in 1701, the proprietor ruled with the assistance of an elected council of eighteen men and an elected assembly. In the eighteenth century the assembly, rather than the governor and council,

became the ruling body in the colony. Outside Philadelphia
the assembly was elected on the basis of a broad franchise.
In Philadelphia, on the other hand, political participation
was rather narrowly restricted. Local government in Pennsylvania, unlike all other royal and proprietary colonies, was
democratic. The local officers—sheriff, coroner, assessors,
commissioners, and burgesses—were locally elected. The
justices of the peace, in common with other judicial officers,
were appointed by the governor.

In later years Penn, impoverished by the expenses of the
colony and legislated against by the assembly he had created,
wished to curtail some of the liberties he had originally extended. He was then to find what other proprietors had
found: that in America, except for the spread of slavery,
the currents flowed in the direction of liberty. It might be
possible to anchor the ship against the currents, but movement
was all in one direction. The settlers in America, Penn complained, "think nothing taller than themselves but the trees."
The government of Pennsylvania was a constant struggle of
the assembly for independence from the proprietor, and a
constant struggle within the assembly against aristocratic control. By the eve of the Revolutionary War, the Pennsylvania assembly had won a large measure of independence both from
the proprietor and from the Quaker aristocracy, an advanced
position which gave Pennsylvania as little cause, perhaps, as
any mainland colony to see its interest in outright independence from England.

Chapter 3

SELF-RELIANCE

FROM the reign of James II to the eve of the American Revolution the apparent tendency of the mainland colonies was toward increasing submission to royal authority. In 1684 there were two royal colonies among those which eventually won their independence; in 1763 there were eight. In 1684 the Church of England was established in one colony; in 1763 it was established in six. The Glorious Revolution had been echoed in America by little Glorious Revolutions. But when various colonies passed their own bills of rights after 1689 these were all disallowed by the English government on one pretext or another.

The navigation laws controlling colonial trade were administered haphazardly in 1684 by a committee of the overworked Privy Council; following the Glorious Revolution an independent advisory agency, the Board of Trade, was established to help bring the colonies under more effective economic control. The Board of Trade exerted wide and detailed supervision. The Treasury officials, Admiralty officers, the War Office, and the Secretary of State for the Southern Department all played overlapping roles in eighteenth-century colonial affairs. During the first half of the eighteenth century, imperial control extended itself over additional important articles of trade, and additional laws were passed prohibiting or curtailing the manufacture of certain articles of trade in the colonies. This extension of royal authority created resentments, and it often brought little more than lip service to the crown. Still the colonies mustered no really formidable opposition to these continual encroachments.

The French and Indian War revealed glaring weaknesses in the imperial system while at the same time suggesting effective new administrative methods. In the 1760's the time seemed to the English government propitious for a broad colonial reorganization, and for a decade the English government acted accordingly. It was only then, even in America, that men began to realize the extent to which American society had developed, since the Glorious Revolution, along independent lines. Silent changes had been producing a new society which was not entirely English and which no longer was reducible to the subordinate colonial status, where English government men relegated it as a matter of course. Furthermore, where American society departed from the English model the tendency was generally leveling, democratic, and, from the point of view of the American as well as the English upper classes, rather uncivilized.

I

Above all else the colonial tendency toward bigness altered the imperial relationship. Between 1700 and 1750 the population of the colonies increased by roughly five times. Between 1750 and 1800 it increased once again by about five times. The population of England, meanwhile, increased by less than twenty per cent during the first half of the century and less than thirty per cent during the second. On the eve of the American Revolution, Englishmen in the homeland still outnumbered the mainland colonists three to one, and it was sixty years more before the American population outstripped the English. Nevertheless, the tendency was clear as day to leading Americans. Within the empire the center of gravity was shifting inexorably toward the New World. England should take that into account.

In at least one respect the English government certainly was beginning to take America's rapid growth into account. It had been well enough in the seventeenth century for the sparse English settlements in America to call for English aid and protection. It had seemed less justifiable during the French and Indian War for a colonial population of two million, more or less, to rely so heavily on redcoats. If the horde of colonists could not defend themselves, at least the time had come for them to help pay their own way.

The imperial crisis of the sixties also opened English eyes to a situation, harmless enough in the seventeenth century, which was becoming a matter for concern in the eighteenth, due mainly to the increase in American population. It was one thing to permit a thousand settlers in Virginia to elect their own little assembly in 1619; it had become something else altogether when the Virginia House of Burgesses, in the mid-eighteenth century, backed by a century and a half of tradition, spoke for a society of three or four hundred thousand persons. Such systems of government as the Virginia House of Burgesses had been devised in the seventeenth century, entirely by royal sufferance, to regulate the affairs of small communities. In the eighteenth century these governments were developing lives of their own, independent of royal or Parliamentary authority, and with the rapid growth of American society they were assuming an importance which originally had never been intended.

Though the eighteenth-century expansion of the colonies was predominantly a rural expansion, it manifested itself most obviously and impressively in the rise of the provincial cities. The largest of them, Philadelphia, was one of the largest cities in the British Empire. Its "natural advantages, trade, riches," Peter Kalm declared, were "by no means inferior to those of any, even of the most ancient towns in Europe." New York and Boston also were major cities by eighteenth-century standards, while Charles Town and Newport led an impressive number of thriving towns. These cities gave abundant evidence of the growth and complexity of colonial life in the eighteenth century. In the imperial struggle they assumed an importance far out of proportion to the numbers of their citizens, in relation to the total colonial population. They became both the focal points for revolutionary agitation and the communication centers which made possible the uniting of the revolutionary forces.

Geographically also, America was becoming unmanageably big from the imperial point of view. Amercan colonists were moving westward beyond English control, and these frontiersmen, unlike the majority of seaboard settlers, were not mainly of English descent. Rather they were the Germans and Swiss, driven from Europe by the ravages of war and by religious persecution after the Treaty of Utrecht in 1713, or they were the Scotch-Irish, driven from Ireland by English economic repression. In the one case they were simply un-English; in the other they were likely to be downright anti-English. More than 300,000 of these immigrants were in America on the eve of the revolution.

The energies of these immigrants extended the settled area west from the coastal regions and river fall lines inland for from one to two hundred miles into the Appalachians. Two removes from the English seat of aristocratic power, these frontier settlers resisted all efforts of the colonial governments to control, and most particularly, to tax them. "There," wrote the French observer, Hector St. John de Crevecoeur, "remote from the power of example and check of shame, many families exhibit the most hideous parts of our society." On the frontier he found that men appeared to be no better "than carnivorous animals of a superior rank." Then, as settlement increased and the sharp edge of the frontier moved beyond, a wonderful transformation occurred. Industrious folk moved in and "a pleasing uniformity of decent competence appears throughout our habitations." In contrast to the predominance of English on the seaboard, the western settlers were "a mixture of English, Scotch, Irish, French, Dutch, Germans, and

Swedes. From this promiscuous breed, that race now called Americans have arisen."

This new race of Americans shared qualities which their critics called anti-social, brutal, and leveling, and which their friends called individualistic, self-sufficient, and democratic. "From the beginning of the settlement of America," Frederick Jackson Turner wrote, "the frontier regions have exercised a steady influence toward democracy." Equalitarian ideals came naturally to a society of equals. Living on the fringes of organized government, the frontier farmers became unused to governmental control and therefore sensitive to it. Beyond the reach of schools and manor houses, these westerners came to view with suspicion the educated gentlemen, putting their trust rather in common virtues, useful to everyday life on the western farms.

In an age when almost all Americans were farmers, the mere existence of the unsettled West exerted an equalizing influence throughout the colonies, depressing land values in the East and giving bargaining power to the eastern worker. "The inhabitants of our frontiers," Governor Spotswood of Virginia wrote, "are composed generally of such as have been transported hither as servants, and, being out of their time, settle themselves where land is to be taken up that will produce the necessaries of life with little labour." Governor Spotswood saw the open West work to his own disadvantage when German settlers, to whom he had refused to sell land, in turn refused to work his iron furnaces, moving west to settle lands of their own instead. With the acquisition of a small amount of land in Virginia came the right to vote, resulting, Governor Spotwood said, in the election of "persons of narrow fortunes and mean understandings," some of whom had "so little shame, as publicly to declare that if, in Assembly, anything should be proposed which they judged might be disagreeable to their constituents, they would oppose it, though they know in their conscience, it would be for the good of the country."

England's West Indian island colonies, while they were still in frontier stages during the seventeenth century, had followed much the same independent courses as had the mainland colonies. They had developed independent representative institutions, while their churches had succumbed to Puritanism. Once the sugar islands were well settled, however, the tendency had reversed itself. Sugar plantations were consolidated into fewer hands, and the aristocratic planters tended to view their fields of operations as sources of wealth rather than as the homeland. The center of the universe for the Jamaican or Barbadan aristocrat was aristocratic England, to which West India planters aspired to return, to purchase that landed estate which would provide entree into English society and politics. The center of interest for the colonial landed aristocrat on the mainland, by contrast, tended to be the unlimited West, where vast opportunities for land speculation remained to be exploited.

II

A striking manifestation of the increasing size and complexity of colonial society was the swift rise of American lawyers from despised obscurity to prominence and honor in the generation before the Revolution. Nothing in the early legal history of the colonists, wrote Charles Warren, "is more striking than the uniformly low position, and the slight part they played in the development of the country until nearly the middle of the Eighteenth Century." Yet at the third quarter of the eighteenth century, twenty-five of the fifty-six signers of the Declaration of Independence were lawyers. Of the fifty-five men who attended the constitutional convention, thirty-one were lawyers. Rising suddenly, the American legal profession grasped power with the American Revolution. From that day to the present the American bar has dominated

American politics to an extent perhaps unparalleled elsewhere in the world.

During the eighteenth century the westward expansion, with its endless opportunities for litigation in land law, provided incentive for a rising legal profession. The rise of the colonial cities and the expansion of merchant capitalism opened many additional fields of opportunity. The colonies in the seventeenth century had functioned on too simple a level to justify the introduction of the complex common law. Amid the complexities of eighteenth-century society it became increasingly necessary.

No systematic standards of legal training were established in the colonies, and the preparation of American lawyers ranged from Patrick Henry's few weeks of study to John Adams' extended, scholarly research. One might train for the law by understudying a successful lawyer or by attending the Inns of Court in England, as was the case particularly with lawyers in Virginia and South Carolina. Wherever one studied, the standard text, until a decade before the Revolution, had been *Coke on Lyttleton,* the all but incomprehensible classic by the great seventeenth-century defender of English liberties. By the eve of the Revolution, however, most of the younger lawyers were turning to the more lucid prose of Blackstone's *Commentaries,* first published in 1765-9. Blackstone, Warren writes, "taught them for the first time the continuity, the unity, and the reason of Common Law—and just at a time when the need of a unified system both in law and politics was beginning to be felt in the colonies."

The shift from Coke to Blackstone was a shift from a redoubtable Whig to a thorough Tory, and to an expounder of the absolute power of Parliament over the colonies. Colonial lawyers succeeded in refashioning Blackstone to suit patriotic American needs, but Thomas Jefferson in later years found that the Tory influence had prevailed at last. He wrote:

Coke on Lyttleton was the universal elementary book of law students and a sounder Whig never wrote . . . profounder learning in the orthodox doctrines of British liberties. Our lawyers were then all Whigs. But when his black letter text and uncouth but cunning learning got out of fashion, and the honeyed Mansfieldism of *Blackstone* became the student's hornbook, from that moment, that profession (the nursery of our Congress) began to slide into Toryism and nearly all the young brood of lawyers are now of that time. They suppose themselves indeed to be Whigs because they no longer know what whiggism or republicanism means.

At the time of the Revolution the list of lawyers in the colonies, still by no means an extensive one, read like a roster of the revolutionary leadership: in Virginia, Peyton and John Randolph, Edmund Pendleton, Thomas Jefferson, George Mason, Richard Henry Lee, and Patrick Henry; in Massachusetts, James Otis, father and son, Oxenbridge Thacher, Sam Adams, and John Adams; in Pennsylvania, Francis Hopkinson and James Wilson; in South Carolina, Edward Rutledge, John Laurens, C. C. Pinckney, and Timothy Pinckney; in Connecticut, Roger Sherman and Oliver Ellsworth. Most of these were young men. Some of them were from the ranks of the colonial aristocracy; others, though these were probably in the minority, were ambitious men from the lower classes.

Most illustrious among the common people who chose the law as an avenue of advancement was John Adams, who made the decision after some hesitation. "The study of law," he wrote William Cushing, "is indeed an avenue to the more important offices of State and the happiness of human society is an object worth the pursuit of any man. But the acquisition of these important offices depends upon many circumstances of birth and of fortune, not to mention capacity, which I have not and I can have no hopes of being useful in that way." The event which did much to prove John Adams wrong was the American Revolution, freeing America from aristocratic

English control and placing American lawyers firmly in the seats of power. Ambitious American lawyers brought the law to the side of liberty and the American Revolution; once in power they took the side of property and position just as effectively against the threatening advance of democracy. The history of the American bar helps to explain why the Revolution came in the first place and why it then took the moderate course that it did.

III

Colonial political history in the eighteenth century was one long struggle by the colonial ruling classes for greater autonomy, a struggle waged mainly between the assemblies and the governors. By the eve of the Revolution the clear advantage in each of the colonies had gone to the assembly. Despite the authority and social prestige of the crown, the governor's use of the patronage, and the threat of royal veto, the viceroys found that their powers were repeatedly nullified in practice. The great distance from England vitiated royal authority, and the governors, living in the colonies, were subjected to strong social pressures not to violate the feelings of the best people. In most of the royal colonies the governors were subjected to economic pressures as well. Except in Georgia and Virginia the governor was, practically speaking, dependent for his salary upon grants of money by the assembly, and the assemblies followed the practice of paying the governors in annual grants in order to limit their independence.

In Maryland, where the proprietors ruled through appointed governors after 1733, the assembly maintained full control of public money, and went so far as to deny the right of the governor to veto legislation. In Pennsylvania the bitter struggle against the proprietor culminated in resolutions of condemnation passed without a dissenting vote. Thereafter the assembly was somewhat quieted by the change to a new and more obliging proprietor. In all the colonies, by the time Lord Grenville was preparing to overhaul the American system, the assemblies had long had the upper hand of the viceroys.

Within the assemblies no clear permanent party lines developed during the colonial period. In New England the assemblies tended to divide on the issue of paper money, between the merchant interests on the one hand and the farmers and lesser merchants on the other. The issue reached a major crisis in 1740 with the land bank scheme for the issuance of paper money, finally disallowed by the Privy Council. In New York, politics remained chiefly a struggle for power among the leading families. In Pennsylvania the Quakers with German support controlled the assembly until the middle of the century, against the proprietors, who by then had joined the Anglican Church. In the tobacco colonies the division was chiefly between the large and small planters, while in South Carolina the chief contests were between the merchants and the major planters, the "plain people" being largely unrepresented.

Most of the colonial assemblies, in their turn, experienced growing western opposition to seaboard control in the decades before the Revolution. In three colonies, Pennsylvania, New York, and North Carolina, the opposition broke into active, if ineffective, insurrection, while the latent western opposition in Massachusetts later erupted into Shays's Rebellion during the period of the Articles of Confederation. Western resentment fed on complaints of overtaxation, support of an established church which most westerners did not attend, underrepresentation, unreasonable legal expenses, graft, government influence in land speculation, and inadequate Indian defense. In New York the tenant farmers rose in arms against their landlords, to be suppressed swiftly by British redcoats. In Pennsylvania the unwillingness of the assembly to defend the frontiers inspired the abortive march of Paxton's Boys on Philadelphia. In North Carolina the Regulators were aroused by a variety of grievances, chiefly maladministration of western counties and wholesale government corruption, which bore particularly hard on the West. The Regulators were defeated at the Battle of Alamance, but they were not without their effect on North Carolina politics. One result was the manifestation of strong loyalist sentiment in western North Carolina during the Revolution. Another was the development of militant democratic sentiment among the westerners, a sentiment which the eastern Whigs felt obliged to appease in drawing up the first state constitution.

Western South Carolina enjoyed no regular government at all, to the very eve of the Revolution. In 1769, in response to desperate western appeals, the South Carolina assembly finally created four grossly underrepresented western counties. Largely as a consequence of this cavalier treatment, a bitter internecine struggle was waged in the state throughout the Revolution, and the political struggle within the state continued into the nineteenth century down through the Civil War. The aristocratic patriots of South Carolina, while fighting England in defense of their liberties, refused to make any substantial concessions to western demands. Elsewhere, with the coming of the Revolution, however, eastern patriots seeking unity against England were willing to satisfy some of those grievances of westerners, which were so embarrassingly similar to their own.

IV

Just how democratic the colonial governments actually were is a matter which has recently received increasing historical attention, the most thoroughgoing investigation being Robert E. Brown's examination of colonial Massachusetts. It is Brown's conclusion that "not many adult men in colonial Massachusetts were excluded from voting because of property requirements," and briefer studies of other areas have resulted in similar conclusions. According to Brown, representation was apportioned in such a way that the farmers, rather than any merchant aristocracy, had complete control of the legislature. In fact they had greater representation than they wanted. According to the election law of 1692 it was compulsory for towns of forty voters to return a delegate. Small communities, feeling that this worked a hardship on them, successfully petitioned to be permitted not to send a representative if they preferred not to.

Older studies of colonial voting, notably the work of A. E. McKinley, place emphasis upon the narrowness of the franchise; yet this emphasis is not altogether justified by their statistics. McKinley estimated that about 16 per cent of the population of Massachusetts and Connecticut was entitled to vote, which would have included a substantial majority of the total adult male population. The middle colonies were subject to a much heavier eighteenth-century immigration, and partly for that reason the electorate seems to have been smaller than in New England, about 8 per cent of the population in rural Pennsylvania. In Virginia, according to Charles Sydnor, nearly all the free white landowners would have met the requirement of twenty-five acres of improved land, but only a third to a half of the total adult white male population was entitled to vote. In this estimate Sydnor sides with Thomas Jefferson against Governor Dinwiddie and St. George Tucker, who both thought that a majority of the white men in Virginia could vote.

Virginia had moved from universal manhood suffrage in the early seventeenth century to the property qualification in the eighteenth of twenty-five acres of land with a house twelve feet by twelve in size. But the purpose of the property qualification, as Sydnor points out, was less to disfranchise the poor than it was to restrict the political power of the rich, who otherwise would have been able to command the votes of their landless "tenants & retainers." The smallness of the qualification in Virginia, as in most other colonies, demonstrates the lack of any intent to restrict voting to members of the upper classes. The property qualification satisfied the convention, which died hard in the age of Jackson, that a voter ought to have some tangible stake in society.

Generally such qualifications were American equivalents of the British forty shilling freehold, the property required in England to vote in county elections. In land-rich America most farmers who owned a freehold at all were probably able to meet this requirement, which ranged from twenty-five acres to three hundred. It was in the cities that the property qualification was most restrictive, especially in the six colonies which specifically required real property. Only an estimated 2 per cent of the population of Philadelphia was enfranchised as compared to about 8 per cent in New York City and a considerably higher proportion in Boston. Still, a city mechanic might well have been able to vote whether he had the legal right to do so or not. Governor Hutchinson of Massachusetts complained that "there is scarce ever any inquiry" into the property qualifications of the voters.

The electorate in the late colonial period was winnowed by other restrictions as well, but the extent to which these restrictions were systematically implemented is open to question. Belief in one god was a general requirement for voting, but it does not appear that voters were ordinarily questioned on the matter. Catholics and Jews were widely denied the vote by law, but the colonies contained few of either, the laws were not rigidly enforced, and in some cases specific laws were passed admitting certain Catholics or Jews to political life. A strict interpretation of the Virginia election laws would have excluded from the vote all who were not members of the established church. At the same time, the law, late in the colonial period, contained a provision permitting Quakers to meet the voting requirements by affirmation rather than by oath, and dissenters seem generally to have been admitted as voters. Women, Negroes, indentured servants, and men who had not reached "full age" were excluded from the

polls, and there were additional residence requirements ranging from three months to two years.

The legality of plural voting gave added power to large
landholders in some colonies, and unequal apportionment of
representation generally favored the old settlements at the
expense of the new. Apportionment of representation thus
tended to favor the seaboard over the western areas, and this
advantage was increased, in a day of horse-drawn transportation, by the eastern location of the provincial capitals.
Jefferson believed that, theoretically, the eastern counties
did not have sufficient representation to control the assembly at Williamsburg, but that the eastern location of the
capital enabled them generally to command a majority. And
yet colonial apportionment certainly was no more unrepresentative than the apportionment of the vote for most state
legislatures in the twentieth century, when the expanding
cities, instead of the expanding West, have come to be
underrepresented.

The methods of elections themselves left much to be
desired from the democratic point of view. Polling places
were often as much as a day's journey away from the voter's
residence, sometimes as much as three days away. The sheriff
commonly held the same wide control over elections that he
had in the English counties. He could set the time and place
for the election. He could often call the election to an early
halt, delay it interminably, or arbitrarily move the polling
area. R. P. McCormick's study of voting in colonial New
Jersey reveals that apparently all freeholders could vote, and
in some cases those who were not freeholders could vote also.
Furthermore, the study does not find that such limitations as
existed were systematically enforced. Nevertheless, the influence of the sheriff, the distance from the polls, the normal
apathy of the electorate, and the large number of uncontested
elections indicated that the system was less than democratic

in its operation, even though in theory it was based upon virtual manhood suffrage.

Oral voting was the rule, so that pressure was on the voter to comply with the wishes of the influential men in the community. The secret ballot, however, was already in use in Massachusetts, Connecticut, and Pennsylvania. Elections were often accompanied by intimidation, violence, bribery, and liberal treating with food and liquor, and any hotly contested election was likely to be won only by a man of consequence and substance. To some extent, that was already ordained by the property qualifications for office holding, generally much higher than those for voting. But this circumstance does not appear to have been popularly resented, even in western communities, where large landholdings were comparatively rare among the settlers and where grievances against the seaboard were often strong. Illiteracy accompanied poverty, particularly outside New England, and the lack of suitable training would have disqualified the vast majority who were specifically disqualified by the higher property qualifications.

The colonial voting restrictions, serious as they were, fail altogether to explain the aristocratic character of colonial politics. The really significant fact was that the overwhelming majority of the people apparently did not vote, even though many of them were qualified to do so. Virginia, where voting was compulsory, probably had the best voting record of any of the colonies, an average of about 9 per cent of the population participating in elections in the generation before the Revolution. New England, with a larger electorate, had a much sorrier voting record. Consistently in Massachusetts and Connecticut, before and during the Revolution, the major issues were decided by about 2 per cent of the population, or one out of eight legal voters. Apparently most men in colonial America, unlike their descendants in the nine-

teenth century, were willing to leave political matters to
their betters.

V

Colonial Americans were accustomed to thinking of society in terms of proper ranks and orders, even though American society lacked the sharply defined distinctions of society
in England and Europe. Rank was ultimately based on wealth,
but colonial America did not look upon wealth itself as the
measure of a man's value. "To men of that age," Carl Bridenbaugh has written, "status seems to have bulked larger than
economics and, in large measure, to have governed the course
of political events."

In every well settled community, particularly on the
seaboard, there was a self-conscious group of the "better
sort" of people, the planters, the merchants, and their close
associates, who were recognized by the community as the
natural custodians of political power. Ranked beneath these
"gentle folk" were the "middling sort" of substantial yeomen
and lesser merchants and successful craftsmen; beneath them
the "plain people," the subsistence farmers and artisans;
beneath them the "meaner sort," indentured servants, sailors,
tenant farmers, drifters, and indigents; and finally, at the
bottom of the scale, the Negroes, virtually all of whom were
enslaved in the northern as well as the southern colonies.

The fight to maintain class distinctions on the American
mainland was a losing one, even in the colonial period. Laws
were passed prohibiting members of the lower classes from
riding in carriages or from otherwise aping their betters.
The most famous such law, passed by the Massachusetts General Court in 1651, prohibited "excess in Apparel . . . especially
amongst people of mean condition." The General Court expressed its "utter detestation and dislike that men or women
of mean condition, should take upon them the garb of Gentlemen," and it therefore prohibited this garb to all of those who
could not claim an estate worth £200, or some other title to

gentle condition, such as superior education or the holding of public office. In various colonies laws were passed exempting gentlemen from humiliating punishments such as whipping.

The difficulty always remained of deciding what the nature of the class system was, and who fit where. In the royal colonies the royal governor was the center of society, presiding over an aristocracy of royally appointed councillors, except in Massachusetts, where the council was elected. In Virginia an early statute prohibited all but the members of the governor's council from wearing gold braid. These councillors, chosen from the most substantial families in the province, held a more secure tenure of office than did the governor himself. They gained control over the best positions available in the colonial government, they voted themselves special privileges and exemptions, and they took on some of the airs of a local nobility. Their political—and indirectly their social—position depended upon royal support. Royal favor tended, in turn, to coincide with colonial affluence, but many well-situated planters and merchants nevertheless struggled without success to wring favors from the distant and graft-ridden court of England. Not a few of the revolutionary leaders had tried in vain to obtain the royal preferments which they considered due their economic and social position.

The difficulty of maintaining distinctions increased as one descended from the first rank of society. Titles were of great importance to people of the time, but it was found impossible to use them in any meaningful or consistent way. "Esquire" was about as honorable a title as one could well aspire to in the colonies. It was reserved for councillors and magistrates and other holders of high political office, and it was not always bestowed upon them. "Squire," on the other hand, was used in speech when addressing a broader group, which would include justices of the peace. And "Gent." followed the name of an even broader classification of members of the wellborn ruling social group. The title was often given to ministers. Except for "Esquire," however, these marks of distinction were not very systematically applied, and as further descent was made in the social scale, the confusion increased still further.

Goodman or Goodwife were the customary forms of address for the substantial yeoman or artisan. Goodman received a definition from The Right Worshipful John Winthrop Esquire, when he opposed the efforts of several ministers to deny the title to non-churchmembers. "Goodman," Winthrop argued, did not imply moral worth, but worth as a citizen capable of serving his community in civic matters. "Mr." was a decided cut above Goodman as a mode of address. One citizen of Boston, Josias Plastowe, achieved a trifling immortality as the one known instance of a man who was officially deprived of his title of "Mr." as part punishment for a criminal offense.

The established churches were staunch supporters of class distinctions. This was most obviously the case with the established Anglican churches, but even the Congregational churches of Massachusetts and Connecticut were often meticulous about maintaining nice distinctions. Though the elect were perhaps all equal before God, they were not equal before their fellow churchmembers. Seating arrangements were carefully made to maintain proper precedence, such rules being laid down as "the fore seat in the front gallery shall be equal in dignity with the second seat in the body." The church people in one town were separated into seven classes, for seating purposes, by vote of the town.

Where the Anglican Church was established it lent sanction to social hierarchies, but the church lacked its own hierarchy in America, no American bishop being appointed during the colonial period. And wherever the church was established, it faced the hostility or indifference of the non-Anglican majority. The Great Awakening of the 1720's, and

1730's brought widespread conversions in all of the colonies to nonestablished churches, while it challenged the entrenched, aristocratic leadership of some of the older nonestablished churches. The Dutch Reformed churches in New Jersey were captured from the older controlling group by Theodore J. Frelinghuysen, who arrived in America in 1719, organized private prayer meetings, and spread the gospel with the assistance of lay helpers. Conservative elements in the church broke away temporarily, but by the eve of the Revolution they returned to a church more evangelical and more democratical than they would have liked.

At the same time, the Presbyterian Church produced an evangelical, and in some ways democratical, leadership, strongly influenced by Frelinghuysen. By the eve of the Revolution the Presbyterian Church had been formed into a distinctly American church, primarily under the direction of William Tennent and his sons, and formed out of an alliance of Scotch-Irish Pennsylvanians and Yankee New Yorkers. In doctrine it differed little from Massachusetts Congregationalism, and even in matters of church organization it did not greatly differ from Connecticut Congregationalism, which early in the eighteenth century adopted a rather Presbyterian form of church government. But unlike these churches it was not a state church, and its ministry, so far as leaders of the Awakenings were concerned, was not an aristocratic calling. Its most effective ministers were trained by William Tennent in his Log College, and these were often drawn from the humble classes. An affront to the genteel Presbyterian leadership, they split the church for a time, but by the eve of the Revolution the church had reunited and they provided it with its leadership.

In the same period, Baptist revivalism spread through Virginia under the leadership of former Congregational ministers who had been converted away from infant baptism by the persuasive English evangelist, George Whitefield. Persecuted in Virginia for not obeying the licensing laws, the Baptists rapidly gained adherents in the years preceding the American Revolution, winning numerous conversions even in the stronghold of New England Congregationalism itself. Enemies to established religion, immune from religious hierarchy, and distrustful of an educated ministry, the Baptists were a militantly equalitarian force wherever they rooted themselves.

Colonial Americans thought naturally in terms of an ordered society of classes, but American circumstances made it impossible to classify people as was done in older, more settled societies. As one observer noted, "the levelling principle here, everywhere operates strongly, and takes the lead, and everybody has property, and everybody knows it." The democratical consequences were an endless source of grievance, especially to colonial governors. "The Elections are just ended," Governor Gooch of Virginia wrote, "and a great many of the old Members dropt, Gentlemen here having no influence over the meaner People, who are vastly the Majority of the Electors." And opposition to aristocratic control always threatened to become opposition to imperial control. Joseph Galloway saw this clearly in 1765 when he warned that "Democratic notions in America may lead to the independence of the Colonies from England."

Chapter 4

THE TRIUMPH OF
THE RADICALS

EARLY in the course of the prerevolutionary struggles with England, colonial gentlemen began to learn that aristocratic opposition to the royal authority in England encouraged leveling tendencies at home, and not only among the common people. Gentlemen themselves in many cases adopted a democratic tone which for them would have been almost unthinkable in the old days of Walpole. Driven by circumstances to curry favor with the inferior orders, the patriotic aristocrats were driven also from sensible bread-and-butter arguments to the assertion of their rights as Englishmen and thence to the assertion of the rights of man. Afterwards the philosophy of the Declaration of Independence could not easily be repudiated by those who had supported it in 1776, and the principles of the Declaration had obvious applications which some of the most ardent revolutionists could not stomach. The Revolution was directed by men who professed to abhor democracy just as they loved liberty, but when they appealed to the people against the King they worked in harmony with the leveling tendencies of the time, and when they broke with England they consigned themselves to an America free of feudal restraints.

I

The Proclamation of 1763 closing off western lands to settlement afterwards proved to have been the first important step by the British government in an ambitious attempt to reorganize the colonial system and consolidate royal authority in America. At the time, however, it was accepted in America, even by men whose interests were injured, as a purely temporary emergency measure to check western expansion pending the postwar settlement of the Indian problem. Passage of the Sugar Act a year later was therefore the first occasion for widespread organized colonial opposition to the postwar program of the Grenville Administration in England. News of the Sugar Act, according to Governor Bernard of Massachusetts, "caused a greater alarm in this country than the taking of Fort William Henry did in 1757." The act placed a three penny per gallon duty on foreign molasses imported into the colonies. This in itself was no cause for alarm, for previously the duty had been sixpence per gallon. However the British government had never seriously attempted to enforce the old Molasses Act; it did, apparently, intend to enforce the new one, encouraged and instructed by the degree of success it had enjoyed during the French and Indian War in enforcing the navigation laws. Parliament served notice with the Sugar Act that the old policy of "salutary neglect" was at an end.

The merchants' opposition to the Sugar Act was characterized by no dangerous political radicalism. Mention was made now and then of the rights of Englishmen, but the emphasis was rather on trade statistics, proving that England herself would suffer from the act. It was mainly a businesslike appeal to British business interests. But, while the merchants were waiting amid depression conditions for the argument to sink home, the Sugar Act, according to James Otis, "set people to thinking, in six months, more than they had done in their whole lives before."

A year later the Stamp Act was passed, requiring the purchasing of tax stamps for all newspapers, business documents, and legal papers, as well as for miscellaneous articles of general purchase. The act was unprecedented, and the colonists did not doubt that it was illegal. And unlike the Sugar Act, it directly touched the interests of all the ruling classes in all the colonies. When that happened, those classes, which had always been the chief reliance of the crown, rose up in defense of their liberties, and they called upon the lower classes to assist them in the struggle. The violence and unanimity of their reaction took the English government completely by surprise; the radical consequences of their disorderly conduct surprised many of the colonial gentlemen themselves.

Upon news of passage of the Stamp Act, months before the law was to go into effect, organized opposition began in "Mobbish Boston." A group of shopkeepers and artisans organized the Loyal Nine, later expanded into the Sons of Liberty. They greatly augmented their strength by recruiting Ebenezer McIntosh, a shoemaker and leader of the South End mob. McIntosh demonstrated his effectiveness with a violent mass outburst which the authorities were hopelessly unable to control. A second anti-Stamp Act riot was directed against Lieutenant Governor Hutchinson's house. A day later, in Rhode Island, a mob drove the King's officers from their houses. In one colony after another royal officers and stamp collectors were brought to heel.

In October, nine colonies sent gentlemen to the Stamp Act Congress in New York. There they resolved that the American colonists possessed all the rights of Englishmen, that Americans were not represented in Parliament, that by the nature of things they could not be, and that therefore the stamp tax, levied upon them by Parliament, had "a manifest Tendency to subvert the Rights and Liberties of the Colonists." Then they went home, and it appears that some of them put on old clothes and helped the mob to burn stamp collectors in effigy.

Sons of Liberty organizations arose in all of the thirteen colonies that later revolted, and everywhere they received strong aristocratic support. "The episodes of violence which defeated the Stamp Act in America," write Edmund and Helen Morgan, "were planned and prepared by men who were recognized at the time as belonging to the 'better and wiser part'." In North Carolina and Virginia, gentlemen openly took part in the riots. In South Carolina Henry Laurens, mobbed by rioters in the middle of the night, identified nine of his acquaintances beneath the "soot, sailors habits, slouch hats &c." In New York De Lanceys and Livingstons sponsored the Sons, while in Rhode Island, the organization, according to Ezra Stiles, contained "some gentlemen of the first figure." The Boston Sons were led by lesser merchants and craftsmen, but they appear to have enjoyed strong support from more substantial elements in the community, notably John Hancock, the great merchant.

Governor Bernard of Massachusetts saw the potential danger of such organizations to the men of fortune who were encouraging them. He did not appreciate the extent to which the American aristocrats could channel class hatred away from themselves and against the British. In Boston, McIntosh was able at a moment's notice to overawe the city; yet he permitted himself to remain an instrument in the hands of others. Nevertheless a new political force had been created, and in subsequent crises the Sons were to grow increasingly radical and self-assertive. Meanwhile the colonial aristocracy, though united in its opposition to the Stamp Act, began to split on the issue of support for the Sons. The division was roughly along the line that later divided patriots and loyalists in the Revolution.

Radical aristocrats in America were not the only aristocrats in the world to hit upon the scheme of arousing a certain amount of mob violence, judiciously directed, in order to win their point. The same thought was to occur to aristocratic English Whigs in the 1770's and to enlightened members of the French upper classes in the early stages of the French Revolution. The result in France was the conquest of the Revolution by the Paris mob and the rise to power of Robespierre. The result in England was the Lord George Gordon riots, the sacking of London, and a reaction among Whig leaders against such tactics.

The result in America was the rise of a new organized political force of artisans and craftsmen, more substantial and less lawless than the mobs of Paris and London. With the organization of the Sons of Liberty this new political element, lower-middle-class rather than proletarian, entered American politics permanently. It continued through the revolutionary era in mechanic's associations and Tammany Societies to exert a leveling influence upon the politics of the states.

To the Stamp Act fight the Sons brought terrorism and violence abundantly sufficient to defeat enforcement. Shocked by the ubiquitous show of violence, Parliament repealed the act four months after it was declared in effect. The Stamp Act had by then perceptibly weakened conservative political control in the colonies. In Virginia Patrick Henry and a group of radical aristocrats used the crisis to win control of the assembly from Speaker Robinson and the old guard. In Massachusetts James Otis and his radical followers succeeded in defeating for re-election members of the General Court who had stopped short of wholehearted resistance. In Pennsylvania Joseph Galloway survived his part in the proceedings and went on to lead the conservatives in the First Continental Congress, but his collaborator John Hughes was permanently discredited for having accepted the office of stamp collector.

When the passage of the Townshend Acts reopened the crisis in 1767, aristocratic opposition was notably less unanimous and emphatic against the crown than it had been two years earlier, while the Sons of Liberty were showing an ominous tendency to act independently of their aristocratic patrons. The Townshend duties, as John C. Miller points out, "struck at the roots of colonial liberty; but unlike the Stamp Act they did not greatly injure business." Sam Adams and the Boston Sons of Liberty called for immediate and militant opposition to the duties, but it was only the creation of the

American Board of Commissioners of the Customs which convinced the Boston merchants of the need for economic sanctions against Britain. Other colonies were slow to follow. When the merchants in the various colonies finally worked out a nonimportation agreement, the Sons of Liberty, suspecting merchants of the tendency to smuggle, moved to take the responsibility for enforcement upon themselves. In Boston the mob addressed itself additionally to harrassing the British troops, creating those inflammatory incidents which culminated in the Boston Massacre in 1770.

II

The New York Sons, particularly, showed tendencies subversive of the established aristocratic order. Although the colonial assembly of New York was narrowly aristocratic, the government of New York City rested on a comparatively broad franchise. The middle and lower classes of New York showed a corresponding independence of spirit, and control of the New York Sons early began to slip from the hands of the great aristocrats. While the Stamp Act crisis was at its height, a fight developed within the Sons between the aristocratic William Livingston and one of the less prominent merchants, Isaac Sears. Livingston favored reliance upon petitions, while Sears advocated direct action. Worse than that, Sears argued for a program of reform which would secure the interests of the rank and file of the people. So unmanageable did the Sons become that the aristocratic element withdrew and organized a separate Sons of Liberty club, one which the gentlemen of standing thereafter patronized exclusively.

The mechanics and shopkeepers, who were the dominant elements in the New York Sons, were in general agreement upon a set of reforms which were unacceptable to the New York aristocracy. They wanted laws passed to protect them from debtors prison, except where intent to defraud could be established, and they wanted the development of a system of public schools. They were not opposed to aristocratic leadership, but they favored frequent rotation in office to prevent the control of government by cliques, and they advocated universal white manhood suffrage. This, it became apparent, was the price the leaders of New York would be asked to pay for plebeian assistance in their altercation with England. As this vision of a new democratic society gained clarity, aristocratic enthusiasm in New York for the struggle against England waned.

Although politically radical, the Sons of New York remained staunchly middle-class in their outlook. When perhaps two thousand New York tenant farmers waged the "Great Rebellion of 1766" against grasping landlords, they called themselves Sons of Liberty and appealed to the Liberty Boys of the city for support. But the city Sons were shocked by this transgression of the sacred right of private property, and they joined the landlords in appealing to British troops to suppress the rent rioters. The city Whigs, it was said, "are of the opinion that no one is entitled to riot but themselves." Thus the economic conservatism of the urban radicals prevented the cementing of a potentially effective nonaristocratic alliance in that politically exclusive colony.

The contest between the New York Sons and the ruling group of the colony broke into the open in 1770 with the publication of a pamphlet by the radical merchant Alexander McDougall, addressed "To the Betrayed Inhabitants of the City and Colony of New York." The New York assembly had defied Parliament by refusing to supply British troops stationed in New York as directed by Parliamentary law. At the same time, the assembly in effect complied by making a gift of money for the purpose. This challenge of Parliament's authority was an advanced stand, and one which most other colonies declined to take at the time. The assembly was therefore offended that McDougall should accuse it of betrayal for having voted the gift of money. McDougall was arrested and jailed, and he immediately became the hero of New York radicals. Elaborate demonstrations were held in his honor, and McDougall himself played the martyr's role to such effect that charges against him were dropped, and he was persuaded to leave jail.

The merchants of New York, in the meantime, were suffering more severely from the nonimportation agreement than any other group of men in the colonies. Belabored as well by the Sons, they withdrew from the nonimportation agreement and reopened trade with England. New York's defection, in the opinion of the Sons, would be "a stench in the nostrils of every true-born American, till time is no more." It collapsed the entire nonimportation movement and put colonial radicalism in abeyance for several years to come. Colonial assemblies returned to their usual struggles with royal governors, and political radicals were driven to such make-work projects as passing resolutions of support for John Wilkes in his efforts to achieve his rightful seat in Parliament. The profligate Wilkes was at best an embarrassing hero for the pure-minded middle-class radicals of America.

In 1772 the burning of the British naval vessel *Gaspee* by the Rhode Island mob gave cheer to the radicals, and in 1773 Lord North gave them their opportunity with an act which permitted the British East India Company to undersell even American tea smugglers on the American market. Boston Radicals (among them, it is said, Sam Adams and John Hancock) boarded East India ships disguised as Mohawk Indians and dumped a fortune in tea into Boston Bay. Amidst widespread disapproval of this destruction of private property, similar tea parties were conducted by other "Mohawks" in other American ports, and the American radicals were within reach of revolution.

The Boston Tea Party lost America the support of its staunchest friends in Parliament and made possible the retaliatory Coercive Acts; and the Coercive Acts broke the power of the conservatives in America by driving American moderates into radical opposition to the Crown. The first of these acts closed the port of Boston until East India Company claims were satisfied. In reply, the Boston town meeting convened, and committees of correspondence were organized to unite the colonists in a Solemn League and Covenant not to trade with England until the Boston Port Bill was withdrawn. In New York the Sons reorganized and campaigned for acceptance of the Solemn League under the leadership of the radicals McDougall and Sears, while Philadelphia radicals pressed for the same conclusion.

Faced with this new challenge, the New York oligarchy bypassed the New York Committee of Correspondence and organized its own group, the Committee of Fifty-One, defeating the radicals partly by holding meetings in the early afternoon when workingmen found it hard to attend. Having outmaneuvered the radicals, the committee moved to head off Sam Adams' Solemn League and Covenant by calling for the meeting of a continental congress. Such a congress, according to conservative calculations, would be controlled by prudent men who could act in unison to curb radical elements in individual colonies. These calculations left out of account the incendiary radicalism of the southern aristocrats, particularly the new order in Virginia. They left out of account, also, the increasingly bellicose program of the British government. By the time the First Continental Congress met in September, the Boston Port Bill had been followed by the Massachusetts Government Act, the Administration of Justice Act, the Quartering Act, and the Quebec Act, acts which drove moderates into the radical camp.

In the face of mounting radical pressure, the conservatives united behind Joseph Galloway in a program which was doomed from the start, since it would have been unacceptable to Parliament, had it been accepted by the Congress. With the defeat of the Galloway Plan, Congress moved in the direction of independence. Urged along by the Philadelphia mob, it organized the Continental Association to bring England to its knees through economic sanctions. Enforcement of the Association was placed in the hands of local committees, where the Liberty Boy element could take control out of the hands of the suspect merchant gentry. All that was required for revolution was the inevitable outbreak of fighting. When the Second Continental Congress met in 1775, the first shots had been fired at Lexington and Concord, and Congress found itself at the head of a nation at war. After more than fourteen months of war and 170 years of colonial history, the colonies declared their independence on July 2, 1776.

III

The Stamp Act brought wholeheartedly to the radical cause the services of the deceptively small and homely colonial press. The radical cause in turn brought to colonial newspapers their first real taste of political power. "It was fortunate for the liberties of America," wrote the South Carolina historian David Ramsay, "that newspapers were the subject of a heavy stamp duty. Printers, when uninfluenced by the government, had generally ranged themselves on the side of liberty, nor are they less remarkable for attention to the profits of their profession." A stamp duty, which openly invaded the first, and threatened a great diminution of the last, struck more directly and heavily at the colonial printer-newspaper editors than at perhaps any other group in colonial society. The newspapers responded with vigor. During the rest of the Revolutionary era the patriots controlled the press to a remarkable extent, and the news sheets became the most effective propaganda medium open to them.

The first successful regular newspaper published in America had been the *Boston News Letter,* started by the local postmaster John Campbell in 1704. Other newspapers appeared but slowly over the next three generations. At the time of the Stamp Act crisis, there was at least one newspaper in every colony except New Jersey and Delaware. In 1775 there were six newspapers in Philadelphia, five in Boston, four in New York, and three in Charleston. They were typically four-page sheets crammed with news, generally two to six months old, which they copied from English papers and from one another. In normal times more local news could be garnered from the advertising section than from the news columns. Where there was but one newspaper in the colony, it had generally served, when its use was thought convenient, as the official organ of the government. Under any circumstances, the first newspapers existed "by authority," and their editors, if they wished to remain at freedom, were well advised not to bring themselves unfavorably to official notice.

The first colonial newspaper to operate without official license and to oppose official policy was James Franklin's *New-England Courant*. Established in 1721 in Boston, the *Courant,* impertinent from the first, received censure after a year and a half of sufferance. Franklin was jailed on grounds "that the tendency of the said paper is to mock religion, and to bring it into contempt." Franklin was ordered to discontinue publication of his paper, and he was released after a month in prison. Despite this official sign of displeasure, Franklin continued to publish the paper for several more years, in the same disrespectful vein, under the nominal editorship of his brother Ben. Nor did he return to jail as a consequence. Despite the undoubted power of the government to control the press, Franklin's paper was finally driven from the field, not by official pressure, but by public apathy. The most significant feature of this first victory for an independent press was the ease with which it was won.

In the next decade, John Peter Zenger fought a harder fight in New York, upon more clear-cut principles. Supported by an influential faction in New York City, Zenger began publication of the New York *Weekly Journal* in 1733, in opposition to the policy of the royal governor, William Cosby.

Cosby, directly attacked in the first issue of the *Journal,* charged Zenger with "Scandalous, Virulent and Seditious Reflections upon the Government," and called for his arrest. Failing to receive the cooperation of the grand jury or the assembly, Cosby persuaded members of his council to bring charges against the editor for "raising sedition."

Brought to trial after months in jail, Zenger, who had undoubtedly printed the attacks upon the government, appeared destined for certain conviction. Under common law his only defense was to deny responsibility, since the truth of a statement was not recognized as evidence to be used against charges of libel. Zenger's case was taken up by the aged and distinguished lawyer, Andrew Hamilton, who risked contempt of court to persuade the jury to ignore legal precedents and to violate the instructions of the judges. The jury, he argued, was qualified to determine the law; not merely to decide upon the facts of the case. And, despite precedents cited by the judges, the truth of a statement was the best defense against the charge of libel. The jury returned a verdict of "not guilty."

The Zenger case had no direct effect upon the law of the land, and not until the nineteenth century was truth officially admitted in a court of law as favorable evidence in certain libel cases. Nor need the judges in the Zenger case have allowed the decision of the jury to go unchallenged, had they chosen to overrule it. But in a dramatic trial, the principle had been asserted successfully that a newspaper ought to be free to criticize the government by presenting statements of fact. Newspaper editors, on the eve of the Revolution, were able to feel reasonably secure in this right, however vulnerable they might technically be in point of law.

Upon the news of the Stamp Act the colonial press launched as gaudy a display of spectacular journalism as the severely limited technical facilities would permit. Perhaps the most successful effort was that of William Bradford, who set the first page of his *Pennsylvania Journal* within the out-lines of a tombstone, decorated with urns and deaths heads. The slogan "LIBERTY PROPERTY and *no* STAMPS" was initiated by the New York *Gazette or Weekly Post-Boy,* and copied by newspapers elswhere. Other newspapers were bordered in black. They sold out to enthusiastic customers who read them and passed them on to a wider and equally partisan audience.

Such fierce popular support for a cause which was so particularly the printers' own served naturally to secure many printers to the radical side. The printers' prominent role in the crisis raised the fourth estate permanently to a new level of power and independence. "Little wonder," as Arthur M. Schlesinger has written, "that the printers emerged from the contest over the stamp act with an exhilarated sense of their importance to the community. They had become acutely conscious of a new political and social force that they con-trolled: the power of the press."

The newspaper editors, like the merchants, were never again as thoroughly united in the radical cause after the Stamp Act crisis. Nevertheless, the large majority of them went on to oppose the Townshend Acts and to support the nonimportation agreements. And virtually all of the Revolu-tionary pamphlets which received lasting recognition were published originally in the colonial newspapers. The printers of the newspapers, in the meantime, were waxing prosperous, so long as conditions permitted their continued operation, with the increased business in the sale of political pamphlets.

With the imperial crisis, the colonial newspapers for the first time gave extended attention to domestic events. The riots which accompanied the Stamp Act were extensively re-ported, and each subsequent development received similarly detailed attention. With the Revolutionary War the whole character of the American press altered sharply. In the early national period, all political factions recognized this new power of the press and made it their concern to cultivate newspaper support. Jefferson worked repeatedly to help establish Anti-Federalist newspapers in areas where the Federalist press held sway. Alexander Hamilton throughout his political life remained a busy writer of newspaper editorials and a patron of the Federalist press. During Andrew Jackson's administration newspapermen rose to a position of prominence and power within the government to a greater extent than ever before, and the age of Jackson may be taken as the culmination of the rising political influence of the press, which received its impetus in the Stamp Act crisis.

Newspapers in the late colonial period were published for the literate and well-to-do minority. The average number of copies of a typical colonial newspaper was probably one hundred, although the reading audience was much wider. It was not until the 1830's that mass production techniques made possible the penny newspaper which the common man could afford to purchase. By the time that had happened, publishing costs of a major metropolitan newspaper had increased to the point where it was no longer possible for a journeyman printer, with moderate local backing, to enter the metropolitan newspaper field and enjoy a decent prospect of success. The development which made possible newspapers for the millions served also to place the newspaper in the category of big business. Despite conspicuous exceptions, it tended to place the interest of the newspaper upon the side of the cautious men of large property interests and against the forces of democracy. During the early national period, however, this tendency was hardly far enough advanced to be a matter for serious concern. The American press continued to be a forceful, not to say murderous, weapon in the hands of all political factions.

IV

The American patriots moved more reluctantly toward the theory of revolution than toward the fact of it. The war had been in progress for a year before the first reasoned defense of revolution was widely circulated, and then it was left to an alien, Tom Paine, to present the argument. Paine was widely acclaimed at the time for bearding the "Royal Brute," but his popularity in America was fleeting. A generation later, his aging revolutionary colleagues were reviling him for his doctrinaire middle-class radicalism and for his deistical religious ideas, by then going out of fashion in upper-class America. Though Paine's *Common Sense* fired revolutionary enthusiasm, his writings have remained alien to the American tradition. His brief vogue in America corresponds to the brief vogue for radical political theory, or, indeed, for any political theory at all. Americans have always been interested in politics, but American concern for pure political theory may almost be said to have commenced with the passage of the Stamp Act, and—aside from the southern defense of the slave society—to have ended with the ratification of the Constitution.

When the American patriots rose up against their king they found little political theory from their own literary past to use in their defense. Despite the seventeenth-century struggles of Massachusetts to protect the autonomy of a Puritan commonwealth, despite the ceaseless contests between colonial assemblies and royal governors, and despite the impact of the Glorious Revolution, no distinctly American argument had been fashioned to defend the right of resistance or to uphold American liberties. Two New England ministers, Jonathan Mayhew and John Wise, produced writings which in time earned them places in the history of American political theory, but each was concerned primarily with religious issues. The writings of Roger Williams, also primarily concerned with religious questions, were unknown to the revolutionists of 1776. And the revolutionary era itself produced no original contribution to political thought, such as accompanied the political struggles of England in the seventeenth century,

France in the eighteenth, and Germany in the nineteenth.

Until the Revolution was actually upon them, the patriots did not feel the need to base their argument mainly upon theoretical points. They were the spokesmen for a system which had been in good working order until the English government had tinkered with it. The leading colonists were all but unanimous in believing that historical precedent was on their side, and that Grenville and Townshend were the revolutionists, or at least the innovators. Although natural rights were mentioned early in colonial resolves, newspaper editorials, and pamphlets, the main appeal was to the historic and legal rights of Englishmen. Until the Coercive Acts moved the discussion into a new realm, the most popular colonial pamphleteer probably was John Dickinson. Dickinson's *Letters of a Farmer in Pennsylvania* were lawyer's briefs. Their purpose was to prove that the colonists were on the right side of the law. When the Declaration of Independence was submitted to Congress, Dickinson refused to sign. He thought it was premature and that there was still room for argument on points of law. By then events had passed Dickinson by. After more than a year of war, the need was at last felt quite generally among patriots for a justification of revolution.

One main line of loyalist argument offered little to challenge the patriot pamphleteers. George III, according to this theory, was the Lord's anointed, the lawful custodian of England's imperial possessions, and the first gentleman in an empire ruled by gentlemen. Therefore, no matter how stupidly he behaved, nothing was to be done. One of the leading exponents of this point of view was Archibald Kennedy of New York, who said:

> Thus you see our Dependence and the Reason of it, is altogether upon his Majesty's Grace and Favour. If we don't approve of our present System of Government, let us pray for a better: In the mean Time, let us not contemptuously treat those Favours the Crown has been pleased already to confer upon us.

Other loyalist pamphleteers, wasting no time sentimentalizing about the divine right of kings, presented arguments which the patriots were not altogether successful in meeting. It is the opinion of Charles Mullett that "as legalists and political theorists if not as practical politicians, the Tories were frequently more shrewd than their opponents." The burden for the Tory defense in America was mainly assumed by Anglican ministers, and of these probably the most skillful was Samuel Seabury of Connecticut. He began his argument with the contention that the King, Lords, and Commons made up "the supreme, sovereign authority of the whole British Empire," and that it was "an impropriety of speech to talk of an independent colony." Since the authority of the colonial assemblies could not extend beyond the colonial borders, the argument that the assemblies could act independently of Parliament was one which led directly to anarchy. Parliament dealt with external affairs and with those affecting the colonies as a whole. It could not properly perform this function without supreme authority over the colonies and their assemblies. Nor did Seabury find merit in the argument that the colonies were united with England only through the King. George III was King of America because he was King of England, and he was King of England by act of Parliament. Seabury's argument was difficult to meet, so long as the colonies remained within the Empire. The patriots met this problem by getting out of the Empire, and in so doing, finding room for more spacious arguments based upon the natural rights of man.

In the year 1776 Anglo-American revolutionists, once they had decided upon outright independence, were hardly likely to be embarrassed for the lack of political theory appropriate to their needs. They were the political legatees of the Glorious Revolution, and they lived in the noontime of the Age of Enlightenment. They were familiar with the history of England and with the major political writers of

Western Europe, and they drew freely upon English and European authorities to prove what all of them—once they had been driven to first principles—assumed to be true. "These are what are called Revolution principles," John Adams wrote. "They are the principles of Aristotle and Plato; of Livy and Cicero, and Sydney, Harrington and Locke; the principles of nature and eternal reason; the principles on which the whole government over us now stands."

Of all political writers, John Locke was most directly to the point, for his treatises on civil government were the all-but-officially accepted version of the justification of an English revolution. It is impossible to separate the influence of Locke from the influence of other natural rights philosophers who had a wide audience in revolutionary America. Nevertheless Locke's essay was considered then, as now, a classic expression of this philosophy. "Locke's little book on government," Jefferson wrote, "is perfect as far as it goes."

Locke based his theory of government upon a view of nature supported both by Christian traditions and by seventeenth-century science. Natural law, he argued with St. Thomas Aquinas, was a reflection of divine reason in created things. Nature endowed all beings with the faculty for preserving themselves, seeking good, and avoiding evil. Men were naturally endowed with certain capabilities and with certain responsibilities to one another, as well as to God, whose property they were. "The state of nature has a law of nature to govern it, which obliges every one: and reason, which is that law, teaches all mankind, who will but consult it, that being all equal and independent, no one ought to harm another in his life, health, liberty or possessions." Such a relationship was possible even outside civil government. "Men living together according to reason, without a common superior on earth, with authority to judge between them, is properly the state of nature."

In the state of nature, according to Locke, all men were

born equal, not in the sense of being born with equal capabilities, but in the sense of being born with "that equal right that every man hath to his natural freedom, without being subjected to the will or authority of any other man." Although man under natural law had a right to his life, to his freedom, and to the fruits of his labor, there remained the difficulty that every man was a judge of his own rights, and that some men refused to live up to their obligations. It therefore became necessary, in order to defend his natural rights, for man to give up his natural condition and to form a political society which would protect his rights.

Such was the purpose, and the justification, of all civil governments. A government which ceased to perform the function for which it was instituted might therefore be dissolved by the people, to be replaced by a new government which better served its true purpose. Locke fortified his argument with references to historical examples, but he was not urgently concerned to show that any actual social compact ever had existed between a government and its people. Rather he was concerned to demonstrate that man by his very nature logically stood in that relation to government. "And thus that which begins and actually constitutes any political society is nothing but the consent of any number of freemen capable of a majority to unite and incorporate into such a society." English colonists in America, operating politically under written charters, developed a more literal belief in the contract theory than was the case in England.

The monarch who refused to abide by the civil law was "as much in the state of nature, with all under his dominion, as he is with the rest of mankind. For wherever any two men are, who have no standing rule and common judge to appeal to on earth for the determination of controversies of right betwixt them, there they are still in the state of nature." His subjects are then justified in resorting to revolution in order to recover the equal protection of a just civil government. The *Declaration of Independence,* which Jefferson wrote without consulting Locke's or anyone else's treatise on government, can to a remarkable extent be pieced together out of passages from the *Second Treatise:*

> . . . being all equal and independent, no one ought to harm another in his life, health, liberty, or possessions . . . . The reason why men enter into society is the preservation of their property . . . . Whensoever, therefore, the legislative shall transgress this fundamental rule of society . . . it devolves to the people, who have a right to resume their original liberty, and by the establishment of the new legislative (such as they shall think fit) provide for their own safety and security, which is the end for which they are in society . . . . People are not so easily got out of their old forms as some are apt to suggest. They are hardly to be prevailed with to amend the acknowledged faults in the frame they have been accustomed to . . . . But if a long train of abuses, prevarications and artifices, all tending the same way, make the design visible to the people . . . it is not to be wondered that they should then rouse themselves and endeavor to put the rule into such hands which may secure to them the ends for which government was at first erected.

Jefferson's adaptation of this natural rights philosophy, as Benjamin Wright has said, "deserves quotation, for it is so concise that it cannot be condensed, and so eloquent as to defy paraphrase."

> We hold these truths to be self-evident, that all men are created equal, that they are endowed by their Creator with certain unalienable Rights, that among these are Life, Liberty and the pursuit of Happiness.—That to secure these rights, Governments are instituted among Men, deriving their just powers from the consent of the governed.—That whenever any Form of Government becomes destructive of these ends, it is the Right of the People to alter or to abolish it, and to institute new Government, laying its foundation on such principles and organizing its powers in such form, as to them shall seem most likely to effect their Safety and Happiness. Prudence, indeed, will dictate that Governments long established should not be changed for light and transient causes; and accordingly all experience hath shewn,

that mankind are more disposed to suffer, while evils are sufferable, than to right themselves by abolishing the forms to which they are accustomed. But when a long train of abuses and usurptions, pursuing invariably the same Object, evinces a design to reduce them under absolute Despotism, it is their right, it is their duty, to throw off such Government, and to provide new Guards for their future security.

The signers, in declaring that all men are created equal, meant, with Locke, that men were born equal, not in their natural abilities or in their equal share of the world's goods or in their right to vote, but in their equal possession of that natural right to life, liberty, and property. By "consent of the governed," the signers meant consent of the property-holding taxpayers. By "the pursuit of Happiness," the signers meant the right to do with their private property as they liked, subject to such necessary limitations as they placed upon themselves through their governments. That the signers viewed the words of the *Declaration* in this rather conservative light is demonstrated by the conservative state constitutions which they proceeded to draw up. The phrase "pursuit of Happiness" was a Jeffersonian touch which gave warmth to the document while in no way binding the signers or the new nation (though the phrase afterwards crept into various state constitutions, where it remained as a perplexing problem for the state courts). But the *Declaration,* whatever the sober intentions of its signers, was inescapably a revolutionary document, and although it bound no one to anything but independence, it remained as a consecrated statement of revolutionary purpose to which American radicalism thereafter could always appeal, reminding Americans that the American Way has a revolutionary tradition.

Part II

EQUALITY

Chapter 5

REVOLUTIONARY
AMERICA

D EMOCRACY spread through the West in the generation following the Revolution. In the second generation
it overwhelmed the established aristocracies of the northern
seaboard and jostled the slave aristocracies to the south. Most
articulate leaders of the cause were professed enemies of democratical government, but their actions spoke louder than their
words. The true nature of the Revolution appeared in its
consequences, not in the declared purposes of its articulate
leaders.

The American Revolution is sometimes said to have been
a "conservative revolution," because its purpose was to con-
serve an established system, not to create a new one. The
revolutionary leaders themselves held to this opinion. John
Adams accused the English government of having "formed
and organized and drilled and disciplined a party favorable
to Great Britain," and of having "seduced and deluded nearly
one third of the people of the colonies" into loyalty to England.
The argument had plausibility. It was true that the patriots
had resisted change in colonial laws, while the loyalists had
acquiesced in them. But a "conservative revolution," as opposed to a *coup d'etat,* is a contradiction in terms. The Revolution was the work of a militant minority, united in the crisis
by a common revolutionary ideology. This minority placed
itself in opposition to the dominant ruling group in most of the
colonies. The aim of the revolutionists was the violent overthrow of the existing colonial governments and the suppression
of the non-revolutionary majority within them, by methods
of war and terrorism. Most leaders wished it to be a severely

limited revolution, but revolutions, once started, assume lives
of their own. "The Declaration of Independence," wrote
Henry Adams, "proclaimed that America was no longer to
be English but American; that is to say democratic and popular in all its parts."

I

The historian John Franklin Jameson, on the occasion of
the one hundred and fiftieth anniversary of independence,
delivered four brilliant lectures on the American Revolution
viewed as a social movement, lectures which gave new meaning to the subject. The colonial world, he argued, had "come
to be characterized in its economic life by democratic arrangements and practices." The Revolution was a defense of these
arrangements; it enhanced them by bringing the most democratic elements and qualities of colonial society to the fore.
"All things considered it seems clear that in most states the
strength of the revolutionary party lay most largely in the
plain people, as distinguished from the aristocracy . . . in
the peasantry, substantial and energetic though poor, in the
small farmers and frontiersmen." These were not the articulate
spokesmen of the Revolution, but they manned the armies,
and they used independence according to their own understanding of its purposes.

The Revolution destroyed feudalism in America. "There
was no violent outbreak against the land-system," Jameson
declared,

> for there had been no grinding oppressions or exactions con-
> nected with it. No maddened and bloodstained peasants rushed
> furiously from chateau to chateau burning court-rolls and
> shedding the blood of siegneurs and chatelains. But in a quiet,
> sober, Anglo-Saxon way a great change was effected in the
> land system of America between the years 1775 and 1795.

The West was reopened, after the royal prohibitions of the
Proclamation of 1763 and the Quebec Act of 1774. The vast
crown lands were placed at the disposal of state legislatures,

which distributed them as popular demand dictated. Royal and proprietary quit rents were no longer collected, and feudal requirements were abolished, such as the right of the royal surveyor to reserve selected white pine trees on private land for the King's use. It had been true that colonists often refused to pay quit rents, that the rents had been small, and that the King's surveyor had been unsuccessful in enforcing the royal right. Even legal limitations which are widely violated still exert restricting influences. In land law after the Revolution, Jameson noted, "fee simple was fee simple."

The great loyalist estates were confiscated by the state legislatures and redistributed at public sales for very low prices. The largest of these holdings were the proprietary estates of the Penn family, but many other enormous holdings were seized, such as the De Lancey estate, and the three hundred square mile Phillipse estate in New York, and in Virginia the Fairfax estate. New York passed a law discouraging the sale of these estates in lots of more than five hundred acres, and the tendency of the sales certainly was to equalize American landholdings. The De Lancey estate was sold to 275 persons. After the war land was given to soldiers in payment for services, and the Confederation period witnessed unprecedented land speculation and land settlement.

During the ten years after independence, all but two states had abolished laws entailing land to a single owner. Within fifteen years all states had abolished primogeniture, and almost all states had substituted a law dividing property not disposed of by will equally among the inheritors. It has been objected that Jameson made too much of this revolutionary change in land law; that the Revolution was merely the occasion for the termination of laws which had already lost much of their force. The ease with which these laws were swept away plainly makes the point that they were not immovably rooted in colonial American society. They nevertheless were the laws of the land, and in Virginia the

law of primogeniture was more restrictive than the like law
in England. It was the circumstances of the Revolution which
swiftly destroyed this legal basis for feudalism.

Religious toleration had long been an accepted principle
of life in most of the colonies, but religious liberty, with the
separation of church and state, was a product of the Revolution. The Anglican Church was established in six colonies
on the eve of the Revolution, and in none of them were the
majority of the colonists Anglican. Disestablishment took
place during the next decade, as a natural consequence of
the Revolution and independence, and by the time of the
Constitutional Convention the process was completed. Only
in Massachusetts, New Hampshire, and Connecticut was the
connection between church and state retained in the early
nineteenth century. At the same time, the Revolution was accompanied by a lessening of the religious restrictions in politics,
notably the restrictions against Roman Catholics.

The revolutionists argued from the theory that all men
were born equally free; yet in America hundreds of thousands
were enslaved, a discrepancy which patriotic slaveholders did
not ignore. The first anti-slavery society in the world was
organized in Philadelphia five days before the battle of Lexington and Concord, "at a time," the society noted, "when
justice, liberty, and the laws of the land are general topics
among most ranks and stations of men." During the 1780's
slavery was abolished in one after another of the states north
of Maryland, freeing about fifty thousand. In the meantime,
twice as many slaves were freed in Virginia through manumission as were freed in Massachusetts through abolition.

The age saw a proliferation of humanitarian reform societies, library societies, humane societies, charitable societies,
temperance societies, societies for distressed prisoners, for
distressed debtors, for decayed mariners, and for prison and
legal reform. The Pennsylvania constitution of 1776 declared
that the "penal laws as heretofore used shall be reformed by

the legislature of the state as soon as may be, and punishments made in some cases less sanguinary and in general more proportionate to the crimes." The reform was delayed by the war, but before the end of the century the death penalty had been abolished except for first degree murder, and flogging had been prohibited. New York abolished capital punishment for fourteen crimes, limiting it to murder and treason. Other states moved more slowly, in some cases leaving undisturbed the death penalty for false swearing, horse stealing, and obtaining money under false pretenses, and continuing such punishments as branding the face, cropping the ears, public flogging, and practically indefinite detention in dungeons and old mine shafts and the like for the slightest of misdemeanors. An American in this period might still legally be sentenced to burn at the stake for certain crimes.

The most widely hated feature of the old penal system was the treatment of debtors, who might be jailed for "spite debts" of as little as two cents, and retained in jail for months or years. The common people lived in continual fear of indebtedness. Debtors, men and women together, were thrown into the same cell with criminals of all classifications. They were given even less consideration in some respects than other prisoners, for in some states no provision was made for feeding and clothing them, and they were left to depend entirely on public charity. Despite the efforts of workingmen's groups in the age of the Revolution, these penal codes changed little until the age of Jackson.

By twentieth-century American standards, the humanitarian instincts of the age of the Revolution seem primitive indeed. "There is indeed scarce a scrap of information bearing on the subject extant," wrote that peerless collector of scraps of information, John Bach McMaster, "which does not go to prove beyond question that the generation which witnessed the revolution was less merciful and tender-hearted than the generation which witnessed the civil war." Nevertheless the revolutionary era pioneered many of those reforms which were carried through successfully in the nineteenth century.

The war resulted in the death or exile of more than one hundred thousand loyalists, including, in the states north of Maryland, the principal part of the old ruling order, in addition to recent immigrants from the lower classes. They were replaced by revolutionists, most of them in their thirties and forties, generally libertarian in thought, and certainly somewhat less aristocratic in background. The emigrés of the American Revolution passed out of American domestic history as members of the ruling group, and it is impossible to measure the consequences to America of their departure. But certainly this purge of the aristocracy gave American democracy sudden room to expand. The personnel in control of the states continued to shift, and after the war it was made up of younger members of the old aristocracy, war heroes, war profiteers, land speculators, and politicians who had moved successfully with the times. These could not all palm themselves off upon the people as the gentle folk who held the reins of power in colonial times, however hopefully some of them might try. Nor were the times right for aristocratic behavior in politics. It was said of the members of the Pennsylvania Constitutional Convention that "they would go to the devil for popularity, and in order to acquire it, they have embraced levelling principles, which you know is a fine method of succeeding." Toadying to the people had replaced toadying to the crown as the path to preferment.

"The Revolution," John Adams wrote, "was affected before the war commenced. The Revolution was in the minds and hearts of the people . . . . This radical change in the principles, opinions, sentiments, and affections of the people, was the real American Revolution." In this famous utterance Adams was undoubtedly speaking the truth so far as he, himself, was concerned. In his case the Revolution had been effected before the war had commenced, and during the war he, himself, experienced a very definite private Thermidorian reaction to it. In the minds and hearts of many of the other participants, however, the Revolution itself worked continuing radical changes, far too leveling to be approved of by Adams, or indeed most of the revolutionary leaders. As witness to this leveling influence of the Revolution upon the hearts and minds of the people, Jameson called upon that pioneer of American Methodism, the Reverend Devereaux Jarratt of Virginia. After commenting in his autobiography on the old-fashioned custom among the plain people of looking upon gentle folk as beings of a superior order, Jarratt continued in sorrow:

> But I have lived to see a vast alteration in this respect and the contrary extreme prevail. In our high republican times there is more levelling than ought to be, consistent with good government. I have as little notion of oppression and tyranny as any man, but a due subordination is essentially requisite in every government. At present there is too little regard and reverence paid to magistrates and persons in public office; and whence do this regard and irreverence originate but from the notion and practice of levelling? An idea is held out to us that our present government and state are far superior to the former, when we were under the royal administration; but my age enables me to know that the people are not now by half so peacefully and quietly governed as formerly; nor are the laws perhaps by the tenth part, so well executed. And yet I know the superiority of the present government. In theory it is certainly superior; but in practice it is not so. This can arise from nothing so much as from want of a proper distinction between the various orders of people.

II

Prudence, the Declaration of Independence asserted, "will dictate that Governments long established should not be changed for light and transient causes; and accordingly all experience hath shown, that mankind are more disposed to suffer, while evils are sufferable, than to right themselves by abolishing the forms to which they are accustomed." The patriots remain prudent, even in the midst of revolution, in their organization of state governments. In nearly every state the constitution was based largely on the colonial charter. In most cases the task was speedily accomplished by the revolutionary group in control, and approved without formal appeal to the people. No state but Massachusetts submitted its constitution to popular vote. Connecticut and Rhode Island merely converted their seventeenth-century charters directly into constitutions, while Virginia created its constitution largely out of the first two chapters of its legislative statutes. Ten states completed constitutions in 1776. New York and Georgia followed in 1777, and Massachusetts in 1780. Five of these irregularly constructed adaptations remained unaltered for more than a half century.

A "Declaration of Independence by the Loyalists" charged the patriots with having "abolished the true system of the English constitution and laws, in thirteen of the American Provinces, and established therein a weak and factious democracy." The conduct of the revolutionary governments demonstrated that there was much truth in the charge; yet the revolutionary constitutions themselves showed no very marked democratic tendencies. All states retained property qualifications for voting, though Pennsylvania and New Hampshire required only the payment of taxes as evidence of property. Considerably higher property qualifications were generally required for legislators. Negroes and women were denied the suffrage. Religious restrictions remained general, some states limiting the vote to Protestants, some to Christians, and some to those who acknowledged a God and a future state of rewards and punishments.

One major innovation in most state constitutions was the addition of those bills of rights which the Privy Council formerly had denied them. The first of these, and the model for the first nine amendments to the Federal Constitution, was the Virginia Bill of Rights, chiefly written by the libertarian aristocrat George Mason. Proceeding from the Lockian compact theory of government, the Virginia Bill of Rights listed the liberties necessary to a free people: prohibition of hereditary offices, an independent judiciary, no taxation without representation, trial by jury, the right of the accused to confront opposing witnesses, the right of the accused to refuse to testify against himself, prohibition of general warrants for searches and seizures, prohibition of excessive bail, freedom of the press, the right to bear arms, subordination of military to civil power, and the free exercise of religion according to the dictates of conscience. Mason's eloquent list influenced French revolutionary thought more, perhaps, than any other document created by the American Revolution. It demonstrated a concern for individual liberty among slaveholding aristocrats in the eighteenth century such as was rarely matched by equalitarian democrats in the nineteenth.

In the Chesapeake region and in the Carolinas the established aristocratic element remained sufficiently strong in the patriots' cause to control the constitutional conventions. Pressure was strong from the middling classes and from the western areas generally, and some concessions were made to this pressure in each case, most of all in North Carolina and least of all in South Carolina. South Carolina's first constitution was merely a stop-gap measure, but the revised constitution of 1778 retained the grossly unequal representation of the colonial government, while making an empty gesture to the West by calling for reapportionment every fourteen years. At the same time, aristocratic control was strengthened by the imposition of extremely high property qualifications for officeholders. The constitution continued to leave substantial political control in the hands of a few Charleston families.

In North Carolina the western Regulators were more powerful and more articulate than those in South Carolina. Their influence, in combination with eastern aristocratic radi-

cals, was such at the outset that the drafting committee resolved "to establish a purely democratic form of government."
Following a violent election, however, the eastern Whigs
emerged in control of the balance of power. The constitution
made a number of concessions to the Regulators, such as
election of county judges and a lower house elected by all
taxpayers. At the same time, an upper house was created
with a higher, though still modest, property qualification for
voters, and the constitution retained in modified form the
apportionment which gave the eastern seaboard its control.

In Virginia and Maryland the tidewater aristocracy,
liberal by conviction, remained substantially in control. The
result in Virginia was a bicameral legislature, elected annually
on the basis of a small property qualification. The governor,
with sharply limited powers, was to be elected by both houses.
The recommendations of the leading figure of the convention,
George Mason, for a broader suffrage and for indirect election of the upper house, were both overruled. In Maryland,
alone among the states, indirect election of the upper house
was achieved. The Maryland senate was chosen by an electoral college, which thereby made its first appearance in
American constitutional history. Thus the upper house clearly
became the guardian and spokesman of wealth and aristocracy, while the governor was required by the constitution to
be a wealthy man.

Except for Georgia, which modeled its constitution on
that of Pennsylvania, the southern states, including even
North Carolina, stopped short of democracy in their building
of independent governments. So did New Jersey, Delaware,
New York, and Massachusetts, in the North. New York, despite the mass exodus of Tory aristocrats, was controlled in its
convention by the younger Whig aristocrats such as John Jay,
Gouverneur Morris and Robert Livingston, and the result
was a constitution similar to that of Maryland. The conservatives, however, lost their scheme for indirect election of the

upper house, while the veto power of the governor was dropped in favor of a cumbersome and less effective Council of Revision.

Early in the making of state constitutions the conservative patriots found their most articulate spokesman in John Adams, while the radicals found theirs in Tom Paine. Among the American patriots these two men represented the extremes of radical and conservative whiggism, the one view finding expression in the Pennsylvania constitution of 1776 and the other, in the Massachusetts constitution of 1780. Paine himself took no part in the Pennsylvania convention, but it was dominated by radicals with whom he was closely associated. John Adams wrote the first draft of the Massachusetts constitution almost entirely.

Paine's *Common Sense,* the most widely read political tract of the time, contained directly only a few words of advice on the subject. Paine's main concern in the constitutional field was the need for a stronger continental government, and his advice concerning state governments was limited to a little less than two sentences: "Let the assemblies be annual, with a president only. The representation more equal, their business wholly domestic, and subject to the authority of a Continental Congress." But the book implies a good deal more concerning Paine's views on government, and, from his discussion of the continental government, it appeared that his state governments would consist of an annually elected popular assembly which would choose its own president. It would rule within the confines of a written constitution containing a bill of rights. A three-fifths vote would be required to enact legislation. No other restraint upon the majority will of the assembly is suggested. Paine reflected the radical opinion which opposed placing checks on the will of the people and which hesitated to entrust power to any single executive.

The Pennsylvania radicals, Benjamin Franklin, George Bryan, the astronomer David Rittenhouse, and others, took advantage of serious divisions within the conservative ranks to gain control of the convention. The conservatives were divided between the proprietary interest, the liberal Quakers, for whom John Dickinson spoke, and the younger aristocratic whig element. As war broke out, the Quakers lost influence because of their pacifism. The reluctance of the assembly to declare Pennsylvania's independence gave power to the Philadelphia Committee of Correspondence. When the authority of the assembly collapsed, the committee called a convention which was heavily weighted in western representation. Dominated by western and Philadelphia radicals, it drew up the most radical constitution of any of the states and speedily ratified it.

This "rascally government," as Benjamin Rush called it, vested power in a single popular assembly, elected by the male taxpayers of the state who believed the Scriptures to be divine revelation. The assembly chose its own president, who was merely a presiding officer. A plural executive, the Executive Council of Thirteen, was created, to be popularly elected for three-year terms. The legislature held the power to appoint and to remove judges, and it controlled the salaries of the members of the executive council. Legislation passed in one session had to be passed again in the next before it became law. Local self-government was secured with the election of sheriffs, justices of the peace, and other local officers. The constitution could not be altered for seven years, at which time a Council of Censors, popularly elected, would be empowered to examine the constitution and summon a constitutional convention if changes were deemed necessary.

This constitution, strongly supported by Benjamin Franklin, among others, aroused a furious storm of protest and continued to inspire bitter opposition until its revision more than a decade later. Certainly it was the most radical departure taken by any of the states. And yet, as Elisha P. Douglass has pointed out, it was not an abandonment of the old charter for untried theories, as its enemies charged. It could more accurately be described as the final fulfillment of the old charter drawn up by William Penn. The only real innovations—the Council of Censors and the provision for suspensive legislation—never took effect. Otherwise the unicameral legislature, the administrative council, and the system of local self-government clearly were derived from the Charter of Privileges of 1701. It was mainly the broadening of the franchise and the revolutionary spirit among the people which altered its form.

John Adams concluded from his reading of *Common Sense* that Paine was a better hand at pulling down than building. Adams had already sketched his own plan of government, and it was one which was destined in the coming years to be much more influential than Paine's. The guiding principle of Adams' plan was a system of checks and balances sufficient to curb the overweening desires both of the multitude and of the aristocracy. The rights of the individual being established, Adams was willing to give his government a broadly democratic base. He recommended that "a full and free representation of the people be chosen for a house of commons," to be elected annually. The commons in turn would choose the upper house, and the two houses together would elect the governor. Once the revolutionary crisis was over, Adams thought, the legislature might pass a law permitting the people to elect the upper house and the governor directly. Judges would be appointed by the governor to serve on good behavior, beyond the reach of popular recall. The governor, council, and house would "be each a distinct and independent branch of the legislature, and have a negative on all laws." Adams was convinced that under this plan of government "human nature would appear in its proper glory, asserting its own real dignity."

Four years later, when Adams was given the task of drafting the Massachusetts constitution, his experiences with the

Continental Congress had led him to the conclusion that human nature required a few additional supports in order to appear in its proper glory. The most notable departure from his original plan was in his conception of the upper house, which he made to represent the wealth of the community. Representation for the upper house was made proportionate to total tax receipts, where for the lower house it was made proportionate to the polls. The Massachusetts constitution was not the most aristocratic in the states, but it was the most influential of the conservative constitutions. Where the South Carolina constitution had little meaning apart from local conditions, the Massachusetts constitution became a model for other eastern states including, in 1790, Pennsylvania.

One general trend which exerted a democratizing influence on state governments was the removal of state capitals westward. North Carolina and Georgia, with no regular permanent capitals before the war, established them inland at Raleigh and Augusta. In Virginia, Jefferson in 1776 proposed the transfer of the capital from Williamsburg to Richmond, and the move was approved three years later. The capital of South Carolina was moved from Charleston to Columbia in 1789. The trend was slower in the northern states, New York and Pennsylvania each delaying for two decades.

Most of the constitutions were rather conservative whig patterns of colonial charters; yet the result in many cases certainly was, as the loyalists charged, "a weak and factious democracy." One difficulty, which the conservatives could not overcome, was the temper of the times, which was revolutionary and leveling. Another difficulty, which some of the states soon moved to rectify, was that, in a struggle of colonial assemblies against royal governors, the patriots had come to associate individual liberty with popular assemblies and to distrust any strong executive. The constitutions reflected these sentiments. Only three states followed Adams' advice concerning checks and balances, and few gave the governor sufficient powers to operate the government effectively. In the years before the adoption of the Federal Constitution the states were generally controlled by popular assemblies, little checked by anything except annual elections. The political situation was unprecedented, and it was not known precisely what order of governments had been established in the American States. It was widely suspected, however, that the governments were democratic, despite the sober intentions of their principal architects.

III

At the outset the period of the Confederation appeared to be opening upon an age of triumph. It began brilliantly with the decisive victory at Yorktown, lifting the American States from a long, doubtful contest into a world of astonishing promise. The treaty of peace two years later secured to the nation a vast empire extending to the Mississippi River in the distant West. Republican arms had thrown off royal power, and the world was now to be edified by the spectacle of a new nation of noble Romans, guiding their own self-reliant republican destinies by the pure light of Scripture and by the self-evident truths of the Declaration of Independence.

Freed from the restrictions of the British imperial system, American enterprise saw boundless possibilities for profit in commercial agriculture, commerce, manufacturing, banking, road and canal building, and land speculation. Before the Revolution the royal governments had been the selfish guardians of British interests. The governments were now in the hands of the people and so could be trusted to help the people to enrich themselves. There would be no limits placed upon a nation whose people were their own masters. The old ruling classes were decimated, and the old order was all but demolished. Positions of power and of social prestige were no longer the prerogatives of the wellborn. They

were open to all. And those who could not attain them
could still rest assured that they were as good as the ones
who did.

The patriotic, republican idealism of the new nation is
to be seen in all its bumptiousness in that delightful comedy
by Royall Tyler, *The Contrast,* written in the time of triumph.
"Exult each patriot heart!" it begins.

> Why should our thoughts to distant countries roam,
> When each refinement may be found at home?
> Who travels now to ape the rich or great,
> To deck an equipage and roll in state;
> To court the graces, or to dine with ease,
> Or by hypocrisy to strive to please?
> Our free-born ancestors such arts despised;
> Genuine sincerity alone they prized;
> Their minds with honest emulation fir'd;
> To solid good—not ornament—aspired;
> Or, if ambition rous'd a bolder flame,
> Stern virtue throve, where indolence was shame.

The "contrast" is between Dimple the Englishman and
Colonel Manly, the American, late of the wars for independence. Dimple has fine manners, recites poetry, and de-
spises all the simple pleasures which America offers, except
those which the virtuous American women of the play refuse
to bestow upon him. Colonel Manly is honest, plain-spoken,
and honorable. If Dimple asserts that the fashionable world
of England is superior to the plain world of America, Manly
is too much of a true gentleman to dispute the point with him,
except to remark that he himself has no desire to travel.

The contrast is also between Jessamy, the servant of
Dimple, and Jonathan, waiter perhaps, but no servant, to
Colonel Manly. "Servant!" Jonathan snorts indignantly to
Jessamy. "Sir do you take me for a neger?" But does he not
stoop to grease the colonel's shoes, Jessamy asks. "Yes; I
do grease them a bit sometimes; but I am a true blue son of
liberty for all that. Father said I should come as Colonel

Manly's waiter to see the world, and all that; but no man shall master me; why my father has as good a farm as the colonel." Jonathan goes on to explain that "we don't make any great matter of distinction in our state between quality and other folks." Jessamy finds that "This is indeed a levelling principle." Colonel Manly triumphs and Dimple is disgraced. Jonathan, however, is ludicrously done in by the obsequious but sophistical English manservant. The play is one long celebration of the virtues of plain republicanism. Patriotism, after all, had no other choice, if it was to make a contrast, but to exalt the equalitarian virtues.

Such buoyant hopes as Americans entertained in the flush of victory were bound to be deflated in the course of everyday events. Not everybody shared Tyler's enthusiasm for republican ways. Even at the moment of victory, many had reason to suspect the new system of inconstancy. The army at the close of the war, unrewarded and ill-cared for, was ominously restless. The older aristocracy, momentarily discredited, still held great power in most of the states, and after the war it was daily strengthened by returning loyalists. The older aristocracy gained strength also from the support of men who had enriched themselves during the war and who now wanted to buy in. To these groups the leveling tendencies of the time were not only distasteful; they were subversive of basic good order. Nowhere was this so apparent to the upper classes as in the paper money schemes passed by the politically powerful yeomanry in state after state to evade—so it was charged—lawful obligations to the community. Even while the war was in progress, men worked for a more centralized and aristocratic union, to protect public order, good taste, and private credit.

Peace had hardly been declared when republicanism was threatened by the army. The main force of the army was wintering at Newburg on the Hudson at war's end, idle and exasperated by the lack of supplies and by the failure of

Congress to fulfill pledges. The officers had been promised half-pay for life—after the European custom—but Congress delayed taking official action. As the army grew increasingly restless, right-wing politicians like Alexander Hamilton came to view it as a potentially useful political instrument. The narrowly aristocratic Gouverneur Morris was enthusiastic about such a prospect. He wrote John Jay that he was "glad to see things in their present train. Depend on it, good will arise from the situation to which we are hastening . . . although I think it probable, that much of convulsion will ensue, yet it must terminate in giving government that power, without which government is but a name."

The crisis reached its climax in March with the circulation of the anonymous Newburg Addresses. Were the men in the army to be the only sufferers in the Revolution? It would not be so "if you have sense enough to discover, and spirit enough to oppose tyranny under whatever garb it may assume; whether it be the plain coat of republicanism, or the splendid robe of royalty . . . awake; attend you to your situation and redress yourselves." If there was any real danger of a *coup d'etat*—in an anti-militaristic nation of armed men—it was ended by Washington's famous admonitory address to his officers. The crisis passed, and the officers disbanded peaceably, without waiting for their demands to be met.

Then in April the Order of the Cincinnati was organized, a hereditary secret order, composed exclusively of the officers of the army and the navy and their descendants. The order was immediately and violently denounced. Sam Adams was convinced that it was an attempt to establish—in as short a time as had ever been seen—a military nobility. In all of the states the order was roundly denounced, some states depriving members of citizenship. It was so unpopular that even in aristocratic South Carolina virtually all the leading politicians felt called upon to criticize it in unmeasured terms.

Plainly, so despised an organization was no grave threat to republican institutions. After eight years of war America had not become a militaristic nation, even though officers had developed a fraternal affection for each other and had become united by mutual interest. The officers wanted money; not titles of nobility. They wanted compensation for having been delayed by the war in the general rush for wealth. General Nathanael Greene probably spoke the mind of the officer class as a whole when he advised a friend to "Get as large a fortune as you can. . . . it is high time for you and I to set about in good earnest, doing something for ourselves."

There remained the problem of the common soldiers. In Pennsylvania about eighty soldiers, ill-treated and unpaid, marched on Philadelphia, demonstrated, got drunk, and surrounded the building where Congress was convened. Congress suffered fear and embarrassment for several days, then fled to Princeton, and finally took up quarters in New York. It made known its attitude toward the military by defeating a bill to create a permanent standing army of 896 men. It authorized instead a permanent force of eighty men, twenty-five at Fort Pitt and fifty-five at West Point. Whereas the officers were finally voted five years' pay, nothing of a like nature was seriously contemplated for the enlisted men.

In Massachusetts, Mercy Warren had thought that here was "a formidable body ready to bow to the sceptre of a king, provided they may be the lordlings who in splendid idleness may riot on the hard earnings of the peasant and mechanic." If there had ever been such a possibility, it ended with demobilization in 1783. In the ensuing years the peasant and the mechanic faced the less dramatic threat of a stronger central government, which might well prove beyond their power to control. The impetus for such a movement came from a group of nationalists, representing the creditor interests in the nation, among them the same men who earlier had looked hopefully upon the activities of the army. Chief among them was Alexander Hamilton. Under the conditions of depression which accompanied the peace, the support for a stronger government, to maintain order and particularly to stabilize finances, gained strength along the eastern seaboard.

The end of the war brought vast new economic opportunities for American businessmen. It also ushered in a commercial depression of continental proportions, compounded by the merchants, who continued to import large amounts of goods at continually falling prices. In 1785 there was a sharp decline in prices for American agricultural produce. There was a ceaseless torrent of complaint from the merchant community, accompanied by numerous bankruptcies among smaller merchant enterprises. Then depression passed over into prosperity. By the eve of the Constitutional Convention, the nation had entered upon good times and was launched upon the world-wide commercial enterprise which independence had promised. The period of the Confederation was the occasion for the depression which created sentiment in favor of a strong central government; it was also the time of return to the prosperity which helped to launch the constitutional venture so auspiciously.

Although businessmen roundly denounced the thirteen democratical states and the weak Confederation for practices inimical to a sound economy, the politics of the time was generally favorable to business except in the realm of financial legislation. In the area of interstate trade, the state governments showed admirable restraint. The cases of discriminatory duties between states were exceptional, writes Merrill Jensen; close cooperation and mutual forebearance was the rule. There were acrimonious disputes over the location of state borders, but these were peacefully settled. Most impressively, the problem of western lands was settled with the acquisition of the national domain from the states and with the creation by Congress of an orderly system for land sales, for settlement, for territorial government, and for eventual statehood. The business community had reason to be well satisfied with the handling of commercial policy and land policy by the states.

The mechanics and artisans also received favorable political treatment in the period of the Confederation. It is estimated that wages for unskilled labor had doubled in the course of the war, and laborers remained in a much improved position, although, of course, miserably impoverished by modern standards. The mechanics in the cities, politically active before and during the war, pressed successfully for gains in the period of the Confederation. In 1785 the master cordwainers of Philadelphia held a meeting to protest the bad effects of the heavy importation of goods from Europe. They agreed not to buy, sell, or mend imported shoes. Their move was noticed with approval by craftsmen in other cities, and Massachusetts, in response to pressure from its own manufacturers—which is to say craftsmen—adopted a protective tariff, as well as a navigation law protecting merchants from English competition. Rhode Island, New Hampshire, and Pennsylvania followed the example of Massachusetts, and states with little manufacturing or commercial interests passed similar laws from motives of revenue, protection, and patriotic duty. The laws were designed to protect the interests of the American States as a whole against European competition rather than to work to the disadvantage of neighboring states.

The yeoman farmers had been the main force of the armies during the Revolution, and they were the chief basis of society in the Confederation period. They were the most numerous voters, and they demanded that their grievances be met. Their economic demands were simple. They lived as they had always lived, in a subsistence and barter economy. They had debts and taxes, and they lacked the money to pay them. They were forced to bear a disproportionately heavy share of the tax burden through the payment of poll taxes, and foreclosure—perhaps the debtors prison—awaited those who could not meet their obligations. Their remedy was cheap money, as it had always been, and as it was to be in the nineteenth century.

In colonial times the Privy Council had consistently fought the issuance of paper money. The Revolution had been financed in large part by state and continental paper currency, which quickly became worthless and was no longer in use by the close of the war. Upon the ruins of the paper money system the creditor group established a hard money policy which enhanced the value of the debts owed them by the people, the states, and the Confederation government. In all states the growing opposition of the small-farmer debtor classes was inflamed by the sharp price decline in agricultural goods in the mid-eighties.

Demands for issuance of paper money became the center of controversy in all states, and seven states responded with paper money bills. In New York, New Jersey, South Carolina, Rhode Island, and Pennsylvania the money was based on land and served a need which was not met again until the establishment of the Federal farm loan banks in the twentieth century. In some states the paper currency system was used to fund state and national debts. In those states where the merchants complied with the law willingly, the measures worked well enough. Debtors found the opportunity to pay their creditors, and the paper money held its value. In states where the measures were fought by the merchants, notably in Rhode Island, the consequences were disastrous to creditors and debtors alike.

The western farmers of Massachusetts, struggling to hold their farms and to stay out of debtors prison, received no satisfaction from the legislature. In some western districts there remained no single citizen who could meet the property qualification for representatives, and those districts were obliged to go unrepresented. Slow to revolt in the period before the Revolution, the western farmers had been trained by Boston and Sam Adams to organize and fight. In 1786 the farmers rose again. "For the second time in a decade," writes Marion Starkey,

> the conch shells sounded on the village greens and the minute-men marched; they were not only animated by the same spirit that had impelled them on the road to Lexington, but many of them were the same men. They were supported by much of the old revolutionary paraphernalia: county conventions, commit-tees of correspondence, resolutions solemnly taken. But this time they marched without the blessing of Boston, which in their eyes had replaced Britain as the enemy.

They took possession of the courthouse at Northampton and at Worcester. They demonstrated at Taunton and Concord and elsewhere. They drilled and marched, and at Springfield, under the command of Daniel Shays, they clashed with the state militia and retreated in disorder. Through a dismal winter, bands of insurgents wandered about the countryside. By spring the remnants returned to their homes, and Shays's Rebellion was at an end. The Congress of the Confederation in the meantime cautiously began to raise troops, asserting the need for frontier protection against Indians. Congress, however, moved too slowly and timidly to be of any assistance to the state of Massachusetts, whose militia proved amply sufficient for the purpose. Even so, Congress was able to raise troops only on the basis of the promises of fearful businessmen to take up a half million dollar loan at 6 per cent to finance the mobilization. Shays's Rebellion, ineffectual as it proved to be, was a straight out example of violent class struggle. It struck fear into the hearts of the old whig revolutionists. The rights of property were threatened. No time should be lost in organizing a central government with the power to secure those rights. Every state except Rhode Island prepared to send delegates to a constitutional convention in Philadelphia.

The American Confederation was a paradox of accomplishment and incompetence. Its brilliant representatives abroad did it great honor and won it real advantages, while at home Congress was unable to persuade the Philadelphia constabulary to protect it from rioting enlisted men. At home Congress gained an immense national domain and developed the system by which republican government was successfully extended in time to the Pacific Ocean; yet Congress was beholden to the states for the few dollars necessary to pay for the normal operation of government, and with increasing frequency Congress was obliged to suspend business for the lack of a quorum. Shays's Rebellion dramatized Congressional weakness in the face of violent, irresponsible democratical tendencies. None of the revolutionary leaders countenanced Shays's attack on the government of Massachusetts except Thomas Jefferson, in a private letter from far-off Paris.

Until the eruption of Shays's Rebellion, the aristocratic Rufus King had been an enthusiastic and powerful leader of the opposition to all attempts to give greater authority to Congress. But in 1787 King wrote, "Events are hurrying us to a crisis; prudent and sagacious men should be ready to seize the most favorable circumstances to establish a more perfect and vigorous Government." From the time of the rising of the western farmers of Massachusetts, King was a staunch Federalist. The nation had triumphed over England, and it had triumphed over its own army. The moment was at hand when it must stir itself to triumph over the masses of its people.

Chapter 6

I

THE men of the Constitutional Convention, as John Bach McMaster once wrote, "were brought together in response to the demands of the businessmen of the country, not to form an ideal plan of government but such a practical plan as would meet the business needs of the people." The founding fathers were predominantly the wealthy men of the merchant-planter community, the economic beneficiaries of independence and of the Revolutionary War. They saw their interests threatened by the disunity of the states and by the leveling spirit of the times. Therefore they met in Philadelphia to halt the revolution and create a stable, orderly system of government. The new federal union soon found these men struggling among themselves for control, but at Philadelphia they were united by a common objective. What was wanted was, in Hamilton's phrase, "a solid coercive union," one which could levy taxes, control interstate commerce, maintain a uniform monetary system, protect private property, and secure the nation against the threat of what, for want of a better name, was called democracy.

Both the events immediately preceding the convention and the method by which the delegates were chosen served to produce an august and conservative body. The delegates were appointed by the state legislatures at a time when Shays's Rebellion caused men of substance everywhere to fear for their safety. The legislatures, following the example of Virginia, rose to the occasion by appointing the most prominent and respected citizens of their states. Substitutions had to be found for some who refused the offer, but the substitutes, though men of smaller reputation, proved to be safe appointments. The few radicals among the delegates were right-wing radicals like Alexander Hamilton, holding monarchist or ultra-aristocratic views. The majority were in close agreement concerning the nature of the problem, and, except where the question of representation of the states entered in, the delegates did not disagree widely concerning the nature of the solution.

Except for the surprisingly large number of men who were still in their twenties, the delegates were the same patriots who had fought for American independence. A number of them were the same men who had signed the Declaration of Independence, and it is not to be supposed that they had repudiated their earlier views concerning the natural rights of man. But now they faced a new problem during new times. The problem was one of making instead of breaking. After all, the revolutionary states in 1776 had not relied on self-evident truths in constructing workable instruments of government, and the founding fathers had even less reason to do so. "Experience must be our only guide," John Dickinson warned his fellow delegates. "Reason may mislead us."

The change in the times was no less important than the change in purpose in accounting for the contrast between the spirit of the Declaration and the spirit of the Constitution. Since the outbreak of the Revolution, eight years of war and four years of postwar adjustment had been accompanied by what Albert J. Nock has called "the politics of public plunder" on all levels of free society. The "profiteer, the *nouveau riche,* the *Incroyable,* the flapper," as J. Franklin Jameson said, all made their appearances in this as in all postwar periods of American history. The times invited disillusioned, realistic reorganization of government to hold in check the limitless greed of the people by balancing against it the limitless greed

of the few. The Constitution was written at the anticlimax
of the Revolution. The nation had lost that "attraction of a
country in romance," which is so endearing a characteristic
of revolutions in their beginnings. It would not have become
some of the men at the convention to have taken a high moral
tone, for a few of the leading plunderers of the nation were
delegates; but the time had come to halt the revolution,
especially that popular tendency in plundering politics most
flagrantly exhibited in the area of paper currency.

The delegates wanted a system of government strong
enough to protect property interests, yet not so strong as to
deprive the states of authority or the citizens of liberty. It
was essential that such a government be kept from the control of "faction," whether popular or aristocratic. The aristocratic delegates had seen and read enough to know that unlimited power in the hands of an aristocratic faction would
lead to corruption just as surely as if it were in the hands
of the people. The delegates wanted a government which
could withstand their own overweening passions as well as
those of the people, but the popular threat was uppermost in
their minds.

In meeting the problem, the delegates used the Articles
of Confederation as their chief working model, adopting much
of it bodily. They had at their disposal thirteen working
models of republican government, and the experiences of the
state governments were freely drawn upon. "While several of
the delegates in preparation for their task read quite extensively in history and government," wrote Max Farrand, "when
it came to the concrete problems before them they seldom,
if ever, went outside of their own experience and observation."

The key to the resulting document was its mechanism for
avoiding, as Madison said, "the accumulation of all powers,
legislative, executive, and judiciary, in the same hands,
whether of one, a few, or many, and whether hereditary, self-
appointed, or elective." The Senate and the House of Repre-

sentatives were designed to balance both wealth against popularity and the large states against the small states. The President could veto legislation, and the legislature, by a two-thirds vote, could still pass the bills into law. An independent judiciary was established, headed by a supreme court, which some delegates, at least, assumed would have the right, contrary to practice elsewhere in the world, of declaring Congressional laws unconstitutional. A separate principle of selection was devised for each branch of the government. The House was to be elected by the people, as the states directed. The Senate was to be appointed by the state legislatures. The President was to be chosen by special electors, which the states might designate as they saw fit. All branches of the government would be bound by the Constitution, which imposed specific limitations upon the powers of all branches of the government and declared itself to be the supreme law of the land.

During the fight for ratification additional restrictions were demanded, and these were incorporated into the Constitution during the first Federal administration, in ten amendments. The first nine of these comprised a bill of rights, limiting the power of the government over the private citizen. The tenth specifically reserved to the states all powers not delegated to the Federal government. The Convention had rejected such a bill of rights when George Mason proposed one during the final sessions. The delegates apparently voted the proposition down because they felt that such an addition would merely duplicate existing state bills of rights, and because it was late and they wanted to go home; not because they opposed a bill of rights on its own merits.

At each step of the way, the Constitution was altered to meet specific, practical objections. In the course of meeting these practical objections, as Madison said, it was "forced into some deviations from that artificial structure and regular symmetry which an abstract view of the subject might lead an ingenious theorist to bestow on a Constitution planned in his closet or in his imagination." Nevertheless, the deviations were not permitted to do violence to the basic political principles of the eighteenth-century, republican, libertarian, antidemocratic American whiggery. The final draft might well have been more aristocratic than it was, except for purely accidental reasons. There were a number of delegates who wanted the president to be elected to serve during his lifetime. At one time four states voted for such a provision, and alternative terms of twelve and fifteen years received serious consideration. Property qualifications for legislators were abandoned only because the problem appeared so difficult to arrange nationally. The majority of delegates favored apportionment of representation in the House according to wealth as well as population. This arrangement was discarded largely because of the difficulties involved in measuring wealth. It was generally agreed that new states should be admitted to the Union, but it was by no means agreed that they should be admitted on a basis of equality with the older states. The Constitution remained ambiguous on this point, and some delegates hoped that it would be interpreted in such a way as to leave political control permanently with the Atlantic states.

The Constitution was not designed to secure power for the mercantile aristocracy at the expense of the agrarian aristocracy. Members of the merchant aristocracy requested specific benefits such as Federal assumption of state debts and establishment of a national bank, and they were denied them on the grounds that these tended to benefit one class at the expense of the whole. Elbridge Gerry of Massachusetts, who proposed assumption of state debts, refused to sign the Constitution and fought its ratification on the grounds that the state of Massachusetts would be a more effective safeguard for commercial interests than the proposed government of the Constitution. Alexander Hamilton was altogether unable to make his influence felt at the convention, and he did not even bother to attend many of the sessions, since he was consistently outvoted by his two fellow delegates from New York. Although he later supported ratification, it had been true, as he said, that the ideas of none of the delegates "were more remote from the plan," than his had been.

The political divisions which later developed into the Federalist and Jeffersonian Republican parties—the struggles between the capitalist and the agrarian aristocracies—did not have their origins in the convention, as Charles Beard argued they did. The statement, by which Beard clinched his argument in his *Economic Origins of Jeffersonian Democracy,* that the opponents of the Constitution within the convention all later became consistent Anti-Federalists and Jeffersonian Republicans is simply wrong. The six delegates who opposed the Constitution and fought ratification represented conflicting interests, opposed the Constitution for conflicting reasons, and afterwards followed conflicting political careers. Three were from the North, and represented mainly the commercial interests; three were from the South and represented mainly, though by no means exclusively, the planter interests. Afterwards one of them withdrew from active politics, one became an Anti-Federalist, one became a Federalist, and the other three shifted their allegiances between the two parties. Their collective reasons for opposing the Constitution included the lack of a bill of rights, excessive power lodged in a single executive, the possible dangers to the debtor classes, and the lack of authorization by state governments to undertake such sweeping governmental changes.

Neither did the capitalist-agrarian division separate the leading opponents of ratification outside the convention. Patrick Henry, George Mason, and Richard Henry Lee were conspicuous leaders of the opposition in the agrarian South as were George Clinton, Melancthon Smith, and Elbridge Gerry in the mercantile North. Lee and Smith shared grounds for annoyance with a constitution which abolished the Continental Congress to which they had been elected. Henry and Clinton

were concerned for the sovereignty of the state governments,
for each of these two was the dominating political figure in
his own state.

A recent study by Forrest McDonald of the economic
origins of the Constitution—incomparably more thorough-
going than Charles Beard's classic work—has demolished all
the simple generalizations on the subject. The men at the
convention, with few exceptions, did not act consistently in
such a way as to further their own private interests. The
struggle in the ratifying conventions did not divide clearly the
West from the East, the creditor from the debtor, or the
agrarian from the merchant, while the ratifying conventions
themselves were more broadly based than has been generally
assumed. The boldest generalization which can well survive
McDonald's study is that the Constitutional Convention represented the dominant—but complex and mutually conflicting—
property interests of the nation, and that the resulting constitution was conservatively whiggish in its emphasis upon securing property rights and checking the power of popular assemblies. There remained the question of what kind of government
would result from this unprecedented union of federal
republics.

II

Among the unlooked-for political developments under the
new Constitution, perhaps the most unwelcome was the appearance of the two-party system. "There is nothing I dread
so much," John Adams wrote during the Federalist period, "as
the division of the Republic into two great parties, each under
its leader . . . . This, in my humble opinion, is to be feared as
the greatest political evil under our Constitution." Adams had
more reason than most to dislike political parties, but his
sentiments toward them were shared by all the leading political
figures of the time, including those masters of party organization, Hamilton and Jefferson.

Each of these two men thought of himself not as a party leader, but as a champion of rightly constituted government. Each thought of the other as the chieftain of a dangerous faction, subversive of good public order, a threat to the state. That was Jefferson's point of view when in his first inaugural address he said, "We are all Republicans; we are all Federalists." He meant that the Hamiltonian faction had been defeated, and that the country henceforth would be in the hands of a truly national government, not a party one. The bitterness of politics in the 1790's fed on this assumption that the fight was to the finish for permanent control of the nation. The assumption proved correct at the time, for the Federalists never recovered from their defeat in 1800. But it was not for the want of a role to play in national politics that the Federalists died out. They were destroyed by their own irreconcilable spirit, fortified by the suspicion of the two-party system which they shared with the conquering Jeffersonians. Two generations passed under the Constitution before Americans came to accept organized political parties as a regular part of constitutional government.

The Constitution itself had been cunningly contrived to play faction off against faction, but it failed to guard specifically against the rise of a two-party system, because nothing of quite that sort had been anticipated. In the famous tenth Federalist Paper Madison observed that the regulation of "various and interfering interests . . . involved the spirit of party and faction in the necessary and ordinary operations of government." Madison argued that these factions, which could be seen operating on the state level, would be multiplied on the national level and would be thereby rendered harmless. "The influence of factious leaders may kindle a flame within their particular states, but will be unable to spread a general conflagration through the other states." The idea of organized political parties playing a positive role in republican government was as alien to Madison's thought as it was to his contemporaries, and it remained alien to his thought through a long, successful life as a party leader.

In retrospect the division between Federalists and Republicans can be detected in the *Federalist Papers,* chiefly written by Madison and Hamilton. Although the co-authors worked effectively together, what they produced, as Herbert W. Schneider has pointed out, was actually two separate attitudes toward the Constitution. Madison's argument revealed the document as creating a balanced, limited government drawing its authority from the people. Hamilton defended it as the plan for an effective administrative organization, which would further the national interest and protect property against the injudicious political acts on the part of the states. These divergent points of view created no issues in the Convention, because Hamilton was in such a feeble minority position that he contented himself with announcing his position and standing aside while the convention as a whole worked out a plan alien to his views.

Hamilton described his own personal plan to the convention, without requesting that it be given formal consideration. He imagined a constitution modeled on the English government, short of the establishment of hereditary offices. The president, elected by electors who in their turn were elected by elected electors, would, like the King of England, reign during his lifetime, and he would have the power to appoint the governors of the states just as the King had the power to appoint the lords-lieutenants of the counties. He would have absolute veto power over federal legislation, and the governors would have the veto power in the states. The senate would be an American House of Lords, the members serving for life. The lower house would be an American House of Commons, elected by the people and wielding the power of the purse. Hamilton's one presentation of his ideas to the convention was "praised by everybody" but "supported by none," according to one delegate. Where Madison supported the Constitution

because it was to his liking, Hamilton supported it because it
was an improvement over the Articles of Confederation. Afterwards, as Secretary of the Treasury, he found himself in a
better position to make his influence felt.

As Secretary of the Treasury, Hamilton fashioned a clear-
cut program to strengthen the power of the central government
at the expense of the states and to secure Federal power by
attaching to it the interests of the mercantile community. A
vital part of his nationalist program was achieved with the
Judiciary Act of 1789, which created, in addition to the Supreme Court, circuit courts and district courts, paralleling
the state court systems. This was the initial instance in which
a significant ambiguity in the Constitution was resolved in
favor of the strong nationalists. Its importance to property
rights was not entirely appreciated until the nineteenth century and the rise of Chief Justice John Marshall, but Marshall's main ideas were all argued earlier by Hamilton. The
Judiciary Act won support from agrarian as well as mercantile
elements. It was Hamilton's economic program which at once
divided the nation along economic lines.

The political purpose of Hamilton's economic program
was to create a financial, commercial, and, if possible, manufacturing power whose interests would be served by supporting
the Federal government. He began with a bill for the assumption of state debts and the funding of both state and Federal
debts. The assumption measure served to shift the center of
interest for holders of state securities from the state capitols
to the national capitol; the funding measure served to retain
this attraction by perpetuating the debt. Hamilton next proposed a nationally chartered bank, privately owned except
for one-fifth Federal control. The institution was calculated
permanently to attach the interest of the investing classes,
while its great size and its government connections would
enable it to control the policy of state banks. Hamilton
next proposed, unsuccessfully in the face of both commercial

and agrarian opposition, a moderate protective tariff to encourage the development of manufacturing in America, while making it also dependent on the Federal government. Hamilton's tax policy followed the same political intent. Excise taxes on whisky and other products forced positive obedience from the people at large. When the common people submitted to these taxes, they submitted directly to the majesty of the central authority.

Hamilton based his policy on no faith in the superior nature of "the rich and well-born." He assumed that both rich and poor were driven alike by harsh passions of self-interest. He did not much care who made up the wealthy circle, and for himself he remained arrogantly honest and impoverished, while the men around him grasped at the windfalls which dropped plentifully during Hamilton's years in the government. The important point for Hamilton was the certainty that the financially wealthy group, however constituted, would be conservative, nationalist, and powerful, and that as a matter of self-interest it would use its power to protect a strong union and a stable society. These monocrats, as their enemies called them, would defend a solvent union against the landed gentry, who combined pretensions to provincial authority with a lofty and feckless attitude toward money matters in general and debts in particular. In England, after the Glorious Revolution, the Whigs had buttressed the authority of the crown by the creation of the national bank and the national debt, and in America Hamilton emulated the English example.

While conflict between the mercantile and agrarian interests was inevitable, it was Hamilton's militant partisanship which split the two interests into irreconcilable factions. He gathered in the support of the speculators by granting them opportunities such as they had never anticipated. The government securities from the first had been watered by more than half, and during the Confederation period they dropped to as little as 25 per cent of their face value. At first the merchants and shopkeepers hoped for little from Congress, and viewed their government paper as all but worthless. Within twenty-four hours of Hamilton's first financial report, however, the value of government securities rose 50 per cent, speculators ran to the woods to buy securities from the common people before the news spread, and Congressmen, about half of whom were probably holders of public securities, began to speak of assumption at par as the minimum requirement of honesty. In Congress, Fisher Ames, so William Maclay wrote in his journal,

> delivered a long string of studied sentences . . . . He had public faith, public credit, honor, and above all justice, as often over as an Indian would the Great Spirit, and if possible, with less meaning and to as little purpose. Hamilton at the head of the speculators, with all the courtiers, are on one side. This I call the party who are actuated by interest.

Hamilton's program drove into the opposition agrarian leaders who had been nationalistic supporters of the Constitution and the Judiciary Act. Both Madison and Jefferson had at one time favored empowering the government to establish a bank, and neither had been opposed to Federal assumption of the old state debts on some basis. Neither, for that matter, had given systematic attention to financial questions. Some of their planter-colleagues had, however, and the naked ruthlessness of Hamilton's program brought the landed interest at once to the political economy of such southern agrarian writers as John Taylor of Caroline.

The agrarians argued the injustice of enriching speculators at the expense of the nation, but beyond that they argued the evil of maintaining the debt for what amounted to purposes of political bribery. It should be paid off. They objected to the bank as a government-authorized monopoly which similarly would lend itself to political corruption. The government, they argued, should conduct itself like an honest business house and economize for the purpose of paying its debts. It should do so also as a useful exercise in self-limitation of powers. It should be beholden to no particular group in the nation and should be used to benefit no particular group, last of all the small speculating interest, as compared with the great farming majority.

When Hamilton's program divided the commercial North from the agrarian South, it also crystalized a long standing contrast in political outlook between New England and the southern states. New Englanders were proud of their township, county, and state governments, and of the complicated paraphernalia of government regulation, which the people themselves maintained for the good of the whole. They spoke glowingly of the "steady habits of New England, which habits were formed by a singular machinery in the body politic." But to the southern agrarian aristocrats, living as they did in comparative isolation upon splendid, self-sufficient estates, such complicated machinery of government seemed like the wheels and cogs of tyranny. The planters believed in centralized government for their own plantations; otherwise the best government was the one which governed least.

Defending their natural rights against Hamiltonian encroachments, the planter aristocrats placed themselves at the head of the popular party of the government, the Republican party. The planters themselves generally shared a deep distrust of democracy, though a few of them might view democracy sympathetically, as a purely theoretical proposition. Even Jefferson, among the most radical of the planters, took no serious practical interest in democracy. As Charles Beard said, it was a subject of only academic interest to him.

Despite this distrust of democracy, the planters shared important qualifications for popular leadership. They were farmers and debtors, and when they attacked the mercantile-creditor interest they spoke in the interest of the large majority of Americans, who were also farmers and very likely debtors. As befitted cultured gentlemen of the time, the planters were libertarian in their views. They argued as naturally in terms of rights and liberties as the Hamiltonians argued in terms of interest and privileges. And, as enemies of the existing Federal order, the planters attracted to their cause democratic elements which also opposed the government. In the interest of victory, the planters accepted political support where they found it; even the support, both distasteful and dangerous from the agrarian point of view, of the city mechanics.

Although the planter was a world apart from the city mechanic, he often found it expedient to court the mechanic's vote, and where the contest was close the aristocratic Federalists often allowed themselves to adopt the same popular tactics. Where elections were in doubt, both parties tended hastily to construct democratic party machinery on the local level, township primaries to elect delegates to county conventions, and township committees of correspondence. But the planters were at an advantage over the merchants in this struggle for the city vote. Living in the country, they could agitate for change, free of the fear of the mobs that such agitation might arouse. And even though they might live as lavishly as the city merchant, they displayed their wealth in the country, where it was not a constant affront to the struggling city mechanic. And if political agitation resulted in local democratic political reforms, that was the misfortune of the urban Federalists, not the rural Republicans.

"Jeffersonian Democracy," Charles Beard wrote,

> simply meant the possession of the federal government by the agrarian masses led by an aristocracy of slave-owning planters, and the theoretical repudiation of the right to use the Government for the benefit of any capitalistic groups, fiscal, banking, or manufacturing.

That was the view of the leaders of the movement; the movement itself took a somewhat different direction. What

Henry Adams said of John Randolph of Roanoke can justly be applied to Randolph's fellow Republican planters, that

> nonetheless was it true that between his Anglican tastes and his Gallican policy he was in a false position as he was also between his aristocratic prejudices and his democratic theories, his deistical doctrines and his conservative temperament, his interests as a slave-owner and his theories as an *ami des noirs,* and finally in the entire delusion which possessed his mind that a Virginian aristocracy could maintain itself in alliance with a democratic party.

III

The extra-constitutionality and novelty of the two-party system was sufficiently shocking in itself to eighteenth-century statesmen, but the evil was compounded by the violent revolutionary influences imported from France. On May 4, 1789, a month after the first Congress of the new Federal government took up its duties, the Estates-General met in France for the first time in 175 years. It was summoned to vote taxes for the King, who was finally bankrupted by the ultimate extravagance of having joined the American patriots in their war against the French enemy, England. Revolution swiftly followed, and Americans gave it an enthusiastic welcome; in fact took positive pride in it. They congratulated themselves that the more enlightened part of the Old World was taking a lesson from the New. At the outset this sentiment was general in America. But as the Revolution grew increasingly violent, American conservatives became increasingly critical. They read Burke's *Reflections on the Revolution in France,* and they became convinced that Burke, the old champion of the American cause, was right again. Americans began to take sides and argue heatedly about France. The argument remained largely academic until war broke out in Europe in 1793.

The French government opened the year 1793 with the execution of the King, followed shortly by a declaration of war against Great Britain, Holland, and Spain, and accompanied by an invitation to the peoples of Europe to rise up against their rulers. In November it announced the abolition of the worship of God and the organization of the Cult of Reason. Within a few days of the French King's execution Citizen Genet arrived in the United States as the new French minister to America. His orders were to make what capital he could of the fund of republican enthusiasm in America and of the military alliance of 1778, which still bound the United States to support France in war. Genet was greeted with enthusiastic mass demonstrations wherever he went, to the point where he became convinced apparently that he, rather than Washington, represented the will of the American people. He busied himself with projects to make American men and resources felt on the French side. His irresponsible conduct was acutely embarrassing to Jefferson, who finally requested the French government to relieve Genet of his duties.

To staunch Federalists, however, Genet was more than an embarrassment. He was the advance agent of a new American revolution of the lower classes, directed by the French government against liberty and property. And to complicate matters, there was the problem of that military alliance with France. American conservatives looked with horror upon the possible prospect of joining the red-handed Jacobin government against England, that ancient mother country, that noble monument to political and social stability, that extremely important investor in American land and American business, and by far the best customer America had in the world. American businessmen enjoyed five times as heavy trade with Great Britain as with France. Alliance or no alliance, the Federalists were on the side of England.

Fast on the heels of the French declaration of war there appeared in Philadelphia the first of those Democratic Societies which spread rapidly throughout the Union. Although less violent and more law-abiding than the old Sons of Liberty, these societies were disturbingly democratical in their behavior, and some of them functioned without the restraining influence of upper-class leadership. They were suspiciously similar in some respects to the revolutionary Jacobin clubs in France—they passed resolves in favor of the French Revolution and their members addressed each other as "Citizen"— and they made Citizen Genet's travels through America one long triumphal march.

Similar societies had been organized under aristocratic leadership to fight ratification of the Constitution. George Mason had accepted the chairmanship of such a society in Virginia and John Lamb had done likewise in New York. But the Democratic Societies five years later tended to draw their leadership from the less substantial citizenry or from the intellectuals, such as the members of the American Philosophical Society. The societies enjoyed strong support from the radical printers, Philip Freneau in New York, Thomas Adams in Boston, and Benjamin Franklin Bache in Philadelphia. More than forty such societies sprang up within two years of the French declaration of war, and they were concentrated in the cities and in the western areas. In New England six of the seven societies were located on the frontier. There were other societies of the plain people: mechanical societies in all cities, ultra-democratic Tammany Societies organized to combat the influence of the Cincinnati, and miscellaneous other organizations such as societies of the United Freemen. These cooperated cordially with the Democratic Societies.

In 1794 the Reign of Terror was at flood tide in France, and in that year farmers in western Pennsylvania demonstrated against the newly imposed excise tax on whisky. They raised liberty poles, they held mass meetings, and they rioted. Rioting spread to the western areas of other states. That was the extent of it. The violence lacked direction, and it failed to win support from the law-abiding and essentially middle-class Democratic Societies outside the region involved. The Philadelphia Democratic Society issued a resolution condemning the violence, in much the same spirit that the New York City Sons of Liberty had condemned the upstate New York rent rioters during the late colonial period.

Washington nevertheless was convinced that "the insurrection may be considered as the first ripe fruits of the Democratic Societies." Although he himself was a member of the Cincinnati, he did not suppose that anything could be "more absurd, more arrogant, or more pernicious to the peace of society, than . . . self created bodies . . . endeavoring . . . to form themselves into permanent censors . . . endeavoring . . . to form that *will* into laws for the government of the whole . . . . He authorized the summoning of a large militia and appointed Hamilton, as eager as ever for military glory, to lead the troops into battle. By the time Hamilton reached the scene the local authorities had stepped in, and there was no organized rebel opposition to attack. Cheated of his glory, Hamilton nevertheless charged ahead, making arrests and calling for "rigor everywhere."

Under the impact of Washington's opposition and of the absurdities of Genet, the rather flimsy Democratic Societies disintegrated. But the harsh suppression of the very little rebellion damaged the reputation of the administration, and the membership of the societies continued to work actively for the administration's overthrow in other organizations. At the same time, the whisky insurrection drove the frightened Federalists farther into reaction. John Adams long afterwards wrote to Jefferson:

> You never felt the terrorism of Shays' Rebellion in Massachusetts . . . . You certainly never felt the terrorism excited by Genet in 1793, when ten thousand people in the streets of Philadelphia day by day, threatened to drag Washington out of his house . . . . Market Street was as full of men as could stand by one another, and even before my door; when some of my domestics in Frenzy, determined to sacrifice their lives in my defence.

The French crisis continued through the election campaign of 1796, heightened by the administration's pro-British Jay Treaty and the growing danger of French retaliations. John Adams' distinguished career and popularity in Massachusetts made him the logical choice of the Federalists, despite the opposition of Hamilton. Jefferson, temporarily in retirement at Monticello, was the equally logical candidate for the opposition. Adams won by three electoral votes from a relieved Jefferson, who had observed on the eve of the election that public affairs had never worn so gloomy an aspect since the year 1783. Adams took office at a time when the unavoidable alternatives appeared to be a war with France—which would inflame the Jacobin mob—or a war with England, which would demolish the Federalist party. Hostile to the pretensions of both France and England, and at odds with both parties, Adams sent a commission to negotiate with France. The Commission, confronted by a demand for bribes preliminary to negotiation, refused the demand and reported this so-called X.Y.Z. affair to Adams. Adams forwarded the report to Congress. The news of the insult to American honor united the nation in patriotic anger against France. Adams found himself in the unaccustomed role of the national hero of the hour, as Congress prepared the nation for war.

The alien and sedition laws which accompanied the undeclared naval war with France were inspired by fear, necessity, and party advantage. In the early summer of 1798 Congress passed three laws regulating citizenship and the treatment of aliens, as well as one additional law defining sedition and authorizing imprisonment as a punishment. The first three acts were inspired by the fear of a possible new revolution in America and also by the clearly observable fact that recent immigrants generally voted Anti-Federalist. It was the Sedition Act, however, which drew the heaviest fire. The act authorized fines and prison sentences for "writing, printing, uttering or publishing any false, scandalous and

malicious writing or writings against the government of the
United States," or for bringing the President or Congress
"into contempt or disrepute." The alien and sedition laws
were popular Congressional measures, advocated originally by
neither Adams nor Hamilton, and Adams, touchy as he was
about criticism, did little to execute the new laws. Once the
measures were enacted, however, Federalist judges prose-
cuted Republicans vigorously for "seditious" criticism of the
government, and, despite repeated assertions by historians to
the contrary, as James M. Smith points out, Hamilton encouraged lively prosecution of the acts, except where they
interfered with foreign trade.

Then, at the moment when the Federalists appeared destined to win again in 1800 as the patriotic war party, Adams,
without consulting Congress or his cabinet, took advantage of
peaceful French inclinations to bring the war crisis to an
end. Shortly before his campaign for re-election, he arranged
a peaceful conclusion to the troublesome alliance of 1778.
The Federalists were deprived of their most attractive issue,
and Adams, "president by three votes" as he afterwards
testily referred to himself, lost to Jefferson by eight. Among
his last acts Adams made a number of hurried Federalist appointments to judicial posts, including the appointment of
John Marshall as Chief Justice of the Supreme Court. Defeated permanently on the national scene, as it turned out,
the Federalists held on in New England until after the War
of 1812, and then faded away. The judiciary, however, remained a Federalist stronghold well into the age of Jackson,
despite Jefferson's attempt to purge the court of those Federalists who were not serving according to his own interpretation
of the Constitutional qualification, "good behavior." Edged
into power by the slimmest of margins, and inheriting the consolidated Hamiltonian system, Jefferson set forth quietly upon
what he was ever afterwards pleased to call a republican
"revolution."

IV

The election campaign of 1800 was bitterly waged in an atmosphere of especial hostility and suspicion, created by the recent undeclared naval war with France and by the judicial harassment of Republicans. Supporters of Adams charged Jefferson with atheism, immorality, and disrespect for private property rights. If Jeffeson were elected, it was said, the guillotine would be raised in every town and blood would run in gutters. The Jeffersonians charged Adams with the intent to establish himself as King of the United States behind his monocratic retainers. Jefferson and Madison made capital of the alien and sedition laws by arranging for the passage of resolutions against them in the legislatures of Virginia and Kentucky.

Yet the campaign at this level appears to have influenced few electoral votes, and the Virginia and Kentucky Resolutions do not appear to have won Jefferson any votes at all, with the possible exception of one electoral vote in Virginia. Indeed, outside the state of New York President Adams in 1800 actually made modest but solid gains over his electoral votes of 1796. He retained the support of New England. He gained heavily in Pennsylvania, and he gained substantially in Maryland and North Carolina. Had the New York legislature remained in Federalist hands in 1800, as both Jefferson and Adams assumed it would, then the election of 1800 would have been a modest mandate for Adams, increasing his margin of victory to sixteen electoral votes. Instead the conservative leadership of New York lost control of the legislature for the first time since the Revolution. The legislature named twelve Jeffersonian electors, where in 1796 it had named twelve for Adams, and Jefferson, with his running mate Aaron Burr, was snatched from defeat and enabled to emerge narrowly victorious. All credit for this achievement was due to his brilliant partner, Aaron Burr, the inventor, so far as any one man can claim title to the invention, of the modern American political machine.

New York politics at the close of the eighteenth century was dominated by a few wealthy and influential families, mainly Schuylers, Van Rennsaelers and Livingstons, and by the military hero of the Revolutionary War, George Clinton. Under the guidance of these families New York had become a strong point of Federalism, the favorable field of operation for Alexander Hamilton, John Jay, Rufus King, and Gouverneur Morris. All the leading political figures in New York at the close of the century were Federalists except the Livingstons and Aaron Burr. The Federalists, in addition to controlling the legislature, had elected Jay governor by a large majority, while Hamilton's father-in-law, General Schuyler, had won the seat in the United States Senate from Burr. The fortunes of Burr and the Republicans were at a low ebb in 1800. It was then that Burr staged the supreme political triumph of his career.

Burr's strength rested in his control over the New York branch of the benevolent society of St. Tammand or St. Tammany. Originating among the troops in Pennsylvania, Tammany Societies were organized in various cities, taking their name from a Sagamore Indian and adopting Indian titles and ceremonies. Formed to counteract the activities of the Order of the Cincinnati, the Tammany Societies drew their membership from the common soldiers, and afterwards from the city artisans, mechanics, and small shopkeepers. Most of the societies died out by the end of the century, but the New York Wigwam continued actively under its Great Father, its thirteen Sachems, its Sagamore, its Winkiskee, and its Scribe. The founder, William Mooney, had been active in the New York Sons of Liberty, but until Burr, the New York Tammany Society had remained a non-political organization, devoted to strengthening the bonds of brotherhood and dispensing charity. Its membership was naturally Anti-Federalist by conviction, however, and under Burr's guiding genius it became the highly effective political machine it has remained ever since.

Starting from this position of strength among the poorer freeholders of New York City, Burr moved in 1800 to exploit the animosities existing between the rival great families. He persuaded a group of highly regarded men to run for the state legislature against the reigning Federalists. The list was headed by George Clinton, General Gates—persuaded to run because of his hatred for the Schuylers—and Brockholst Livingston, the only convinced Republican of the three. Then Burr put the Tammany Society in motion. Operating from a complete list of the voters in the city, including a description of the politics and personality of each, the members swept the city for the Republican ticket.

The somewhat Napoleonic Hamilton, amazed by the Federalist defeat in the city and foreseeing the possible consequences to his party nationally, advocated a *coup d'etat*. If Governor Jay would call the existing Federalist state legislature into session, there would still be time for it to return a slate of Federalist electors. Governor Jay would not. The new legislature therefore elected twelve Republican electors, and Jefferson won the presidency.

Hamilton conceded that his arch rival Burr deserved all credit for the victory. If the Federalists were ever to regain power, he argued, they would have to emulate the strategy of their opponents. Hamilton went so far as to draw up a plan for political machinery similar to Burr's Tammany Society, and in some areas where the forces remained evenly divided the Federalists did develop such machinery for a time. But such popular methods tended to outrage Federalist sensibilities, and it was two generations before American conservatives were brought to the point—in the log cabin and hard cider campaign of 1840—of going all out, root, hog, or die, to win the popular vote.

Chapter 7

**REPUBLICAN
AMERICA**

JEFFERSON'S first inaugural address is the classic document of eighteenth-century republicanism, with its faith in a libertarian society founded upon a self-reliant yeomanry and maintaining itself in perfect equipoise within the balanced government of the Constitution. Jefferson took the occasion to present "the essential principles of this government, and consequently those which ought to shape its administration."

> Equal and exact justice to all men of whatever state or persuasion, religious or political; peace, commerce and honest friendship with all nations, entangling alliances with none; the support of the State governments in all their rights, as the most competent administrations for our domestic concerns and the surest bulwarks against antirepublican tendencies; the preservation of the General Government in its whole constitutional vigor, as the sheet anchor of our peace at home and safety abroad; a jealous care of the right of election by the people—a mild and safe corrective of abuses which are lopped by the sword of revolution where peaceable remedies are unprovided; absolute acquiescence in the decisions of the majority, from which is no appeal but to force, the vital principle and immediate parent of despotism; a well-disciplined militia, our best reliance in peace and for the first moments of war, till regulars may relieve them; the supremacy of the civil over the military authority; economy in the public expense, that labor may be lightly burthened; the honest payment of our debts and sacred preservation of the public faith; encouragement of agriculture, and of commerce as its handmaid; the diffusion of information and arraignment of all abuses at the bar of the public reason; freedom of religion; freedom of the press, and freedom of person under the protection of the habeas corpus, and trial by

juries impartially selected. These principles form the bright constellation which has gone before us and guided our steps through an age of revolution and reformation.

Jefferson's republicanism breathed the old-fashioned whig spirit of John Locke. It comfortably retained from Locke the mutually contradictory tenets of majority rule and unalienable personal rights. Like Locke, Jefferson was able to incorporate this inconsistency in his beliefs, because while his conception of individual rights was vivid and specific, his conception of majority rule was hazy and general and not altogether distinguishable from the idea of the "common good."

Jefferson spoke for a passing age when he placed this overriding importance upon the liberty of the individual. The future was with those champions of majority rule who, at the time of Jefferson's inaugural, were making their influence felt most powerfully in the equalitarian society of the new West. By 1801 Vermont, Kentucky, and Tennessee had been admitted to the Union on a basis of equality with the older states, despite the fears of eastern conservatives. In Kentucky the radicals had fought against including a bill of rights in the state constitution, on the grounds that it was an undemocratic barrier to the will of the majority. In this the Kentucky radicals represented more truly than Jefferson did the spirit of American democracy in the generations to come. Jacksonian democracy was to prove far more alien to the political philosophy of Jefferson than was the Federalism of his old friend, and erstwhile political enemy, John Adams.

I

Of all Federal administrations in the nation's history, the first Jefferson administration governed least. Jefferson reduced the personnel of the government by half. He cut the army, stopped naval construction, eliminated most of the ceremonies of his office, removed excise, stamp, and land taxes, and still reduced the national debt. He wrote a friend that "the path we have to pursue is so quiet that we have nothing scarcely to propose to our Legislature. A noiseless course, not meddling with the affairs of others, unattractive of notice, is a mark that society is going on in happiness." Those first four years were a brilliant fulfillment of the promise of Jeffersonian republicanism. Except for the irresistible—but constitutionally questionable—purchase of Louisiana, Jefferson's government was as nearly a model of self-restraint, surely, as the world has seen. Society during those years, bucolic, peaceful, prosperous, and happy, presented a felicitous subject for a Jeffersonian idyl.

The system survived for one term only. Elected overwhelmingly for a second term, Jefferson was swept from his noiseless course by a world at war. In a valiant effort to avoid entanglement in the European struggle, he wielded stoutly the coercive power of the Federal government, laying down an embargo against European trade. He continued the embargo for fifteen months, until its impact upon the United States was everywhere apparent, in eastern ports filled with idle ships, southern wharfs piled up with bales of tobacco, and in farm foreclosures in the West. Jefferson's personal popularity survived the embargo, but his quiet system did not. Although the appearance of Jeffersonian republicanism was preserved for a full generation by the continuance in the President's office of eighteenth-century Virginia republicians, the principles which underlay Jefferson's first term were never revived.

These Virginia Presidents remained living images of the old-fashioned republican virtues, but they found it necessary to keep moving with the times. And even during that incomparable first Jeffersonian administration the Republican leadership found it impossible to remain immaculate amid the corruptions of power. In 1802 Jefferson wrote his Secretary of the Treasury, Albert Gallatin, that "The monopoly of a

single bank is certainly an evil. The multiplication of them
was intended to cure it; but it multiplied an influence of the
same character with the first . . . . Between such parties the
less we meddle the better." The next year he wrote Gallatin:

> As to the patronage of the Republican Bank at Providence, I
> am decidedly in favor of making all the banks republican by
> sharing deposits with them in proportion to the dispositions
> they show. If the law now forbids it, we should not permit
> another session of Congress to pass without amending it. It is
> material to the safety of republicanism to detach the mercantile
> interest from its enemies and incorporate them into the body
> of its friend.

Jefferson the political leader remained at odds with
Jefferson the political theorist, and increasingly so, as the
European war drove his government, in spite of itself, toward
more effective organization at the expense of his idea of
liberty.

The war and its aftermath drove the Jeffersonians to
accept the establishment of a second national bank, the
maintenance of a substantial national army and navy—even
at the cost of continuing the national debt—the adoption of
that protective tariff which Hamilton had championed unsuccessfully, and the admissibility at least of a huge public
works program of canal and road construction, to be financed
by Federal taxes—provided only that specific authorization
for such a program be obtained through a constitutional
amendment. The Jeffersonians had moved so far by the close
of Madison's second term that their demand for a constitutional amendment to authorize Federal internal improvements
was, said Jefferson, "almost the only landmark which now
divides the federalists from the republicans."

Monroe's first inaugural address reflected the change
wrought upon the Republicans by sixteen years of national
control. Monroe manifested little of that deep concern for
civil liberties and limited government which had characterized

the first inaugurals of Jefferson and Madison. On the contrary, he boasted to his fellow citizens that the United States had attained "the dimensions and facilities of a great power under a Government possessing all the energies of any government ever known in the Old World." He was not concerned lest the energetic operation of such great power might endanger the liberties of the people, for the government, he asserted, was also endowed "with an utter incapacity to oppress the people," presumably by virtue of its Republican leadership.

Still, although the Virginia dynasty did not fail to move with the times, the times did not allow these gentlemen to appear to their best advantage. Jefferson remained a powerful leader of his party in 1808, but his second term had been a disappointing anticlimax to so brilliant a public career. For his successor, this quality of anticlimax was more dismally apparent. Madison, the forceful statesman of the Constitutional Convention, became the unimpressive, wizened little war leader of 1812. "Our President tho a man of amiable manners and great talents," commented John C. Calhoun, "has not I fear those commanding talents, which are necessary to control those about him." The lack was especially damaging in Madison's case, called upon as he was to revive the Hamiltonian program which he had heretofore fought on grounds of political principle. The signing of the bank bill, in particular, required Madison to recant a belief which for a generation he had held with fervent conviction. He yielded, he said, to overwhelming pressure, "Public Judgement necessarily superceding individual opinion."

Monroe fared better than Madison, mainly by managing to achieve a lofty detachment from the vital domestic issues of the day. This veteran of the Revolutionary War, still dressed in the knee breeches and white-topped boots of the older time, plainly had become a sartorial and political anachronism. So completely removed was he from the realities of politics that he was re-elected almost by national acclaim during a time of bitter sectional controversy and during the worst economic depression in the nation's history. Monroe was hardly a political leader at all in 1820; he was rather a patriotic symbol, like the American flag. Actually few people— probably less than 2 per cent of the free population— bothered to cast a vote in that election. Political interest lay elsewhere, as political factions prepared for 1824, when the Presidency would be available at last to the aging younger generation.

In 1824 all of the leading candidates for the Presidency claimed to be of Jefferson's party, but none would have subscribed to the principles of Jefferson's first inaugural address. It was not merely that they accepted, with Jefferson, the need for a somewhat stronger and more expensive government, the need to foster trade and industry as well as agriculture, and the need in politics to compromise with fondly held principles. Beyond that they responded actively to changes in society which were forming the nation into a distinctly non-Jeffersonian democracy — equalitarian, majoritarian, demagogic irrational, and evangelical. In the generation that followed, the democrats, in the name of Jefferson, triumphed repeatedly over the opposition. Leadership of the party, however, passed from the Jeffersonian landed aristocracy of the South Atlantic states to new political leaders in the rising West. These new leaders did not speak for the quiet, ordered society, led by a responsible landed aristocracy and supported by a self-reliant yeomanry. They were the leaders of a new society obsessed, as Hezekiah Niles noted, with an *"almost universal ambition to get forward."*

The outlook of the enterprising American farmer-land speculator was a far cry from the stable, self-sufficient, independent yeoman of the Jeffersonian ideal. Jefferson, as Albert Jay Nock has said, never seemed aware that the prospect of getting an unearned dollar was as attractive to an agrarian

as it was to a banker. Jefferson's social system was founded
upon the hypothetical yeoman farmer who possessed steady
habits, was industrious, and yet was not so eager to advance
beyond the meagre fare of subsistence agriculture as to unsettle
society by speculative ventures. Jefferson rested his hopes for
a quiet, stable, republican society upon the open West, where
the yeoman farmer could find room to settle for the "thousandth and thousandth generation." But even as Jefferson
voiced this belief in his first inaugural address, the West was
busily unsettling the balance upon which rested the quiet
society of the Jeffersonian dream.

II

Spring was the time to move west for farm boys ready to
stake out for themselves. Older farmers with their families
moved west also. They sold their old homesteads and moved
on fifty or a hundred miles with some ready money, or perhaps
they just took what equipment they had and moved to keep
ahead of land officers and creditors. Footloose, shiftless men
and boys moved west to escape home, wives, debts, jail sentences, and the monotony of staying put. Bright young men
with eastern contacts or some capital or a few slaves or mer-
chandise or six weeks' training in a law office moved west
alert for the main chance to make their fortunes. The West
gave each of them a free chance, according to his liking and
according to his luck, against drought, fever, Indians, and
lawyers.

By the eve of the Revolution several thousand of these
migrants were across the Appalachian range, either near Pitts-
burg or in the western lands of Virginia and North Carolina,
by way of the Cumberland Gap. A generation later, in the
year of Jefferson's election, the census recorded 386,000 souls
living in the new West. Kentucky and Tennessee were sovereign states and Ohio was ready for admission to statehood.
In the next generation six more western states joined the Union

and the trans-Appalachian population rose to well over two million, mainly in the three states of Kentucky, Tennessee, and Ohio. The Federal reapportionment of representation in 1822 gave the new western states 47 of the 213 Congressmen and 18 of the 48 senators. Not only did the new West hold the balance of power between the conflicting regions of the seaboard; it possessed a greater voting population than either New England or the southern seaboard states, and, while about equal to the middle Atlantic states in Congressional strength, it held twice the representation in the Senate. The West was in the driver's seat and was ready to go.

Land speculation offered the hope of prodigious profits to men with political influence, but these hopes on the grand scale proved largely illusory. During and after the Revolution individual men such as Judge Symmes in Ohio and Judge Henderson in Kentucky acquired enormous tracts of land, which promised them immense wealth. They found this apparently easy road to wealth beset with obstacles, however. There was always much more land on the market than the purchasers could take up, and there were continual legal difficulties and unending opposition from settlers. Special cooperation from the Federal government was essential to success in such huge enterprises, and after the experience of Congress with the land companies in the Ohio Territory, such special assistance was no longer forthcoming. All of the grandiose schemes of the early years collapsed for the lack of any method of controlling land sales, leaving the field open to the many smaller speculators. It was success on this smaller scale which raised up innumerable westerners to positions of prominence in their own locality. When those men walked about, the eastern visitor Timothy Flint wrote, "it was with an air of solemn thoughtfulness upon their countenance as though wisdom would die with them." The great and fortunate land speculator and landholder, he said, was looked up to with as much veneration by the people as any partner in the house of Hope in London or Gray in America. These men emerged as the leaders of republican America in the West. Until the railroad age, the economic basis for power remained locally based.

The farm folk who made up the great mass of new westerners had bothered to learn little that was new in two centuries of frontier farming. There was not much they needed to know that had not been known since ancient times, so long as they were content to get along at the dead level of plain but ample subsistence. Most of them were wholly ignorant of the progressive farming methods widely practiced in England and Europe, and so long as the land was good and the roads were bad they might just as well remain ignorant. The frontier farmer needed only to be in fair physical condition, be inured to suffering and boredom, have a generally practical bent, and be a skillful hand with an axe. Entering the virgin forest, he followed the old routine. He turned his hog or two loose to feed in the woods while he made a clearing and raised a cabin. He ringed the surrounding trees and left them to die while he scratched the ground between with a hoe or a wooden plough, to plant mostly corn, but also oats, flax, and vegetables. Corn grew well everywhere. With improvements in inland transportation, corn made the upper Mississippi Valley into the richest meat-producing area in the world. The westerners soon caught the vision of a society which, connected to world markets by great internal improvements, would raise corn mainly for hogs; meanwhile corn remained the staff of life for the frontier farmer himself.

The average farm family at the turn of the nineteenth century owned its own farm, although there were very likely payments yet to be made on it. The family owned the cabin it had built as well as the various articles of furniture within. It probably kept several hogs and perhaps a cow or two and sheep. Sheltered in a one-room log cabin and clothed in homespun, the family might live moderately well with very few outside economic contacts. "There is no settler, however poor," observed the Duc de Liancourt, "whose family does not take coffee or chocolate for breakfast, and always a little salt meat; at dinner, salt meat, or salt fish and eggs; at supper again salt meat and coffee." The few outside purchases required for this standard of life were paid for in the Southwest in tobacco and, increasingly, cotton. In the Northwest the sale of hogs and whiskey was made possible by the corn crop. Corn, Albert Gallatin said, turned the American immigrant into a capitalist.

These farmers were the men who set the tone of western society. They were practical and self-reliant, ignorant and narrow-minded, restless and acquisitive, intolerant and equalitarian. The key to the western character lay in the word individualism. The western environment cut the pioneer to the pattern of the rugged individualist, capable of taking care of himself and subservient to no master. The western individualist was absolutely equal to his fellow citizens, in fact almost identical. His needs and desires being substantially those of his fellows, they seemed bound to be secured under the rule of the majority. Any sharp variation from the western standards of rugged individualism, if they survived the environment, were unlikely to survive western disapproval. Western society demanded conformity to an extent not seen in the seaboard societies.

The first of the western states, Kentucky, drew up its constitution and entered the Union in 1792. In one respect the constitution was distinctly more democratic than any that had preceded it. It declared that all free white male residents of full age were entitled to vote by secret ballot. In other respects it fell short of democracy. The lower house was elected directly and annually, but the upper house and the governor were elected indirectly through an electoral college. The governor was given a wide power of appointment, and the judges were elected for life terms on good behavior. Slavery was protected. No provision was made for public education.

Despite its broad franchise, the Kentucky constitution represented the victory of the comparatively conservative element, the large land-speculating interest, with its attendant lawyers, colonels, and slaveholders, against the radical democrats. These conservatives, good professing Jefferson Republicans, were not opposed to universal manhood suffrage, and they fought hard for an extensive bill of rights—which incidentally protected slavery from adverse legislation—against radical democratic opposition. They wished to see the administration of the government removed from the direct control of the people, however, and in this they succeeded also. An important key to their strategy was the appointment of local officers, including the justices of the peace, by the governor. The resulting constitution served its main purpose of protecting property and privilege from leveling enthusiasms.

The radical Kentucky democrats, drawing their program from the Pennsylvania constitution of 1776, fought for manhood suffrage, for abolition of slavery, a one-house legislature, the popular election of all local officials, and the omission of a bill of rights. Opposition to the bill of rights was founded partly on the protection such a bill would give to slavery as a form of private property. Partly, however, the radicals rejected it as an undemocratic restriction upon the will of the people. "And this," as Thomas P. Abernethy has said, "is the keynote of frontier democracy. It cared little for principles or for the rights of the individual. It wished to carry its point, whatever that point might happen to be at any given moment, by popular action . . . ." In Kentucky and elsewhere in the West, the radicals sought the winning of the unobstructed, authoritarian power of the majority. There, as elsewhere, they failed entirely to carry the day against the conservative republican principles of limited government with its specific safeguards for the individual. A struggle over the constitution led to a revision in 1799, which abolished the electoral col-

lege but imposed additional safeguards for slavery and retained the appointive power over local offices.

The Tennessee Constitution of 1796 advanced beyond
Kentucky in providing for the direct election of both houses
of the legislature and direct election of the governor, and in
providing that the justices of the peace be chosen by the assembly. The least democratic feature of the Tennessee constitution, and the target of the radicals thereafter, was the
life tenure of justices of the peace and the power invested in
the justices to appoint most local officers. Slavery was protected, and a system of taxation was instituted which bore disproportionately upon the small landowners.

In 1803, Ohio, where slavery was prohibited by congressional law, drew up a thoroughly democratic constitution.
The ballot was extended to all white male taxpayers resident
in the state for a year. Both governor and legislature were
popularly elected, and all town and township officers were
chosen annually by the people. Judges were chosen by the
legislature rather than by the governor, and the ballot was
used for all popular elections. The constitution concluded
with a bill of rights. The model for the Ohio constitution was
that of Tennessee; the removal of the undemocratic restrictions of the Tennessee constitution was clearly facilitated by
the absence of a slaveholding interest.

III

Republican America remained predominantly rural, and
there was little evidence, before the coming of the railroad,
to indicate that it would ever be anything else. Between 1810
and 1820 the proportion of people living in towns of more
than 2,500 actually declined slightly, the only decade in
American history from the taking of the first census in 1790
when that has ever happened. By 1820 the two principal cities,
New York and Philadelphia, each exceeded 100,000 in population. Baltimore had almost doubled its population in the

decade, to rank third among the nation's cities. The next ten towns ranged from Boston, with 43,000, to Norfolk, Virginia, with 8,500. Cincinnati, with a population of less than 10,000, was the nearest approach to a city throughout the new West. All of these cities, including Philadelphia and New York, were primarily commercial centers serving a rural America. Manufacturing, widely dispersed, still remained largely in the hands of the individual craftsmen. Industrial towns, such as Fall River and Lowell, were only beginning to make their appearance. The textile mills at Waltham, Massachusetts, organized by Boston merchants in 1813, were probably the first factories to pay wages regularly in money. The day of the industrialist was still in the future when Monroe stepped down from the presidency. As yet there was hardly more than a hint that a proletariat was forming itself in American cities.

Urban radicalism from the time of the Sons of Liberty had been middle-class radicalism, voicing the demands of the skilled mechanic and the small shopkeeper rather than the unskilled worker. It had struggled for middle-class objectives: the vote, easy credit, abolition of debtors prisons, free land, library facilities, and schools. Urban radicalism did not aim to improve the condition of a permanent working class, but rather to make such alterations in the system as would enable the industrious workingman to rise to a higher station. The unskilled workers, while profiting in higher wages from the growing demand for labor in the first decade of the nineteenth century, remained disunited and beyond the pale of political society. Occasionally there were violent outbursts from sailors in the towns or from workers on the canals, but of systematic organization or formulated program there was none. The first manifestation of a general labor movement did not appear until 1827, when wage earners in Philadelphia joined together as a class and crossed trade lines to pit their united strength against the employer class of the city. Even then the workingmen directed their strength toward the achievement of general, political, social, and economic reforms rather than reforms which would benefit them as a class.

Among the skilled workers, some division of interest between the master craftsman and his journeyman employees was becoming evident. Except in isolated cases the wages of skilled workers did not advance as rapidly as those of unskilled workers, and mechanics' associations occasionally exerted themselves to correct the situation. The printers in Philadelphia struck successfully in 1786 for higher wages, and the carpenters of that city struck for a twelve-hour working day five years later. A number of strikes occured during the first decade of the nineteenth century, involving particularly tailors and shoemakers. Such strikes carried the risk of jail sentences, however, and the maintenance of wages was by no means the central purpose of the trade associations. These were organized chiefly as benevolent organizations, often enrolling master craftsmen and journeyman employees alike, to provide unemployment, sickness, and death benefits. Although the antagonism between master and journeymen was inevitable, a clear, sustained division of interest did not manifest itself in Republican America.

At the summit of society there were very few men of really large fortunes. Such fortunes as existed were founded on commerce, banking, and trade. Of great merchant kings there were really but two, both of whom began life as poor boys in Europe: John Jacob Astor of New York and Stephen Girard of Philadelphia. Others, like William Gray of Boston and Alexander Brown of Baltimore, no doubt also had some claim to such a title. As a whole, however, the merchants who controlled the business world were to be described as well-to-do, not so far above the common run that they could maintain themselves as a separate class. They possessed no distinctive badge to set them apart from the ambitious mechanic, the owner of the small shop, the master craftsman, or the young man who rather arbitrarily set himself up as a lawyer or a politician. The well-to-do complained that the common people were getting above themselves, dressing according to the fashion and driving carriages, but there was nothing to be done about it. In colonial times laws might be passed prohibiting the lower orders from dressing like their betters, but in Republican America that sort of legislation was no longer possible. On the other hand, many an affluent merchant still lived above his store and husbanded his wealth by plain living. Under the republican form of government, only money was a permanently effective basis for class distinctions, and in Republican America there were too few distinctively rich men to form an exclusive aristocracy purely on that basis.

IV

One entirely fortuitous circumstance, the decline in immigration for two generations after the Revolution, was of critical importance to the forming of democratic institutions in America. From the Revolution to the Civil War the national population continued to increase by about one-third every ten years. From a nation of just under four million in 1790 it increased to just under ten million in 1820 and to seventeen million in 1840. In this the national population simply maintained the rate of acceleration which it had followed with remarkable consistency since the mid-seventeenth century. Unlike the population increases for the preceding century and for the century that followed, however, those for two generations after the Revolution were not accounted for to any considerable extent by immigration. European immigration fell to a minimum during the French Revolutionary and Napoleonic wars. It rose slowly from 8,000 in 1820 to 23,000 in 1830. Thereafter it rose rapidly to an annual average of more than 200,000 prior to the Civil War and to an annual average of about one million in the decade before the First World War. The subsidence of this stream in the decade after 1776 was an accidental circumstance which sapped the strength of the American aristocracy, at the moment when America was forming its national society.

Unrestricted immigration to America was always a powerful force for class consciousness and class exploitation. The traditional view of America as the land of welcome for the masses of the world has served to clothe the naked fact of ruthless exploitation. One-fifth of the population in 1790 had come from Africa in chains or was descended from others who had. Many had been forcibly transported to America from English prisons. A much larger group—the indentured servants—came to America in a state of bondage. The redemptioners came more willingly, perhaps, and with a greater hope of freedom upon arrival; still they came because they had to, and they faced the probable prospect of entering into a temporary condition of involuntary servitude upon arrival. Beginning in the 1840's, the Irish fled to America for their lives, penniless and defenseless, and every advantage was taken of their helpless condition. The story was repeated on larger scale after the Civil War. The immigration restriction laws of the 1920's brought an end to three centuries of commerce in human lives which always had worked to sap the vitality of the democratic spirit.

So long as heavy immigration continued it provided a soft cushion for aristocracy. The immigrant peasants, born into an old-world feudal tradition, carried their servile habits to America, where they accepted menial positions as fitting to their lowly station in life. Trained to know their proper place and helplessly ignorant of American language and custom, they tended to make excellent servants, as the older Americans did not. New immigrants formed a subordinate foreign class in American society, looked down upon by native Americans, rich and poor alike. This universal American feeling of superiority to the new immigrants broke the logic of an equalitarian society and accustomed Americans to think in class terms. The number of servants in a household became an index to position in society. By the close of the nineteenth century, unlimited immigration threatened, in conjunction with the rise of great fortunes, permanently to stratify American society. In the twentieth century, immigration restriction helped to avert this stratification; in the early nineteenth century the temporary subsidence of immigration helped to destroy the existing aristocracies, wherever slavery was prohibited.

The needs of aristocracy required a constant stream of fresh immigrants, for the children of immigrants repudiated the old world standards of their parents. In common with other native Americans, they made woefully bad servants. "Europeans," Hezekiah Niles wrote,

> especially Englishmen, settling in the United States, who lived decently at home, have a universal complaint to make about the "impertinence of servants," meaning chiefly *women* and girls hired to do housework . . . . These girls will not call the lady of the house *mistress* or drop a *curtesy* when honored with a command; and, if they do not like the usage they receive, will be off in an instant, and leave you to manage as well as you can . . . . These girls who behave as they ought, soon get married and raise up families for themselves. This is what they *calculate* upon, and it is this calculation that makes them "saucy."

Until the resumption of heavy immigration, the servant problem obliged even the wealthy to get on with little help, by European standards. "No country of the same wealth, intelligence and civilization," noted Tench Coxe, "has so few menial servants (strictly speaking) in the families of persons of the greatest property."

The American tendency toward bigness weakened aristocracy in Federal and Republican America as it had once weakened imperial authority in British America. So long as good cheap land remained easily available, increases in the native-born population served to lower the political center of gravity. This democratizing power of numbers was multiplied by the accompanying westward advance of society, always moving the geographical center of political power farther from the old, established, Atlantic seaboard communities and keeping society everywhere in a constant state of readjustment to new conditions.

The incalculable vastness of America, largely unexploited and but sketchily explored, guaranteed continuing commotion in American society. In 1800 the United States, with a population of about five million was territorially the largest nation west of Russia; three years later it more than doubled its size. Its immensity worked upon the imagination of Americans, dissolving the standards of social, economic, and political exclusiveness. Against this rising landowning population, this constantly unsettling westward movement, this abundance of opportunity, and this growing reverence for bigness, aristocracy—dignified, select, refined, and stable—was helpless to maintain itself before the public as the pattern of American leadership.

Chapter 8

THE TRIUMPH
OF DEMOCRACY

THE national democratic revolution was overdue by almost a decade in 1828. Most of the state governments had by then capitulated to the people. Badly eroded before the War of 1812, aristocratic state politics collapsed everywhere, outside the seaboard South, beneath the successive waves of postwar nationalism and postwar depression. For the second time in as many generations, the farm boys of America defended their nation against British regulars. With the Second War for Independence the ordinary people everywhere became convinced past argument that the republic belonged to the people who had defended it, and that the republic was great because the people were great. The air was filled with the tall stories of veterans, the buoyant arguments of land speculators, the commotion of the westward advance, and the noises of patriotism. Then came the panic of 1819. Stung by bankruptcy, foreclosure, and unemployment, the ordinary people rose to demand the services of their state governments. Wherever the vote was denied them they demanded that as well. In 1824 they moved on to claim the national government for the people. Cheated of victory by Congressional manipulation, they pressed forward to victory with Jackson's election in 1828.

The advent of democracy, long dreaded by the politicians of Federal and Republican America, proved less serious to most established political fortunes than many had anticipated. It obliged the dynasty of Virginians to give way to more popular figures, mainly from the new West, and it necessitated the development of party organization to an extent never before seen in the world. Parades and picnics became important. But the leading politicians of the Republican period, who had fought the democratic advance almost to a man, adjusted themselves to the new situation, once it was upon them. The political manipulators found, not that their control had been broken by the spread of democracy—even though they lost some power, notably in the selecting of presidential candidates—but that they were required to master new techniques in order to retain power. The people had created a new political atmosphere by 1828, and the people thereafter became the main factor in the politician's calculation.

I

Universal white manhood or taxpayer's suffrage was substantially the rule in all of the new states created under the Federal government except Louisiana and Mississippi. Among the original thirteen states, it was substantially the rule by the eve of the War of 1812 in New Hampshire, Pennsylvania, New Jersey, Maryland, North Carolina, and Georgia. It existed in South Carolina also, but under conditions which rendered it innocuous to the ruling group. In the rest of the original states property qualifications remained. In a few of them these qualifications survived the democratic nationalism of the postwar period. In Virginia they survived until 1850, and in Rhode Island until well into the post-Civil War period. But the years after the War of 1812 saw striking victories for the principle of popular rule in three populous states: Connecticut, New York, and Massachusetts. The same period saw the admission of a half dozen new states, under constitutions based upon white manhood suffrage. These six years were therefore decisive in the history of popular rule in America. After 1821 the few states which retained property qualifications remained anachronistic deviations from the accepted rule.

Connecticut conservatism was the victim of an unhappily

timed anti-nationalist movement, the Hartford Convention, summoned in 1814 to consider what separate course New England might take with respect to the locally unpopular war against England. At a moment when the war—wretchedly waged by the Republican administration—threatened America with defeat at English hands, Connecticut Federalism directed the anti-war opposition from a position of apparent strength. Secure in the "steady habits" of its citizenry and the authority of its established church, the Connecticut Federalist leadership conducted the Hartford Convention in a more moderate spirit than had been anticipated. Unfortunately for its success, the convention concluded its deliberations at the same time that the news of Jackson's victory at New Orleans and the favorable peace treaty of Ghent spread through the country. Under the circumstances, the representatives sent by the convention to Washington, D. C. decided not to present their demands, but the damage was done.

Deserted thus unkindly by their own special providence, the Connecticut Federalists bowed to the inevitable. They did not seriously resist the call for a state constitutional convention in 1818, and, rather than fight democracy to the death, they cooperated, hoping only to exert a moderating influence. They were not altogether unsuccessful in this. The reformed franchise stopped just short of manhood suffrage, being extended to men who served in the militia or paid a state tax or held a freehold estate valued at seven dollars. The Congregational Church was disestablished. That was inevitable. And religious tests for officeholding were abolished. The separation of the legislative, judicial, and executive branches was effected, the judicial and legal systems were reorganized, and a more equitable tax system was instituted. When the deed had been accomplished, the Federalist party of Connecticut condemned the new constitution officially and, attempting to make a political issue of the matter, passed out of existence.

The Federalists in Connecticut's neighboring states, New York and Massachusetts, had been a degree less aggressive in their opposition to the war, but they were not spared in the hour of triumph. If the ruling groups in those states could have withstood the force of triumphant nationalism, they were unable to withstand the outraged popular sentiment which followed the panic of 1819. Unexampled wretchedness swept the nation, and nowhere more fiercely than in the national metropolis of New York. Bank failures and business foreclosures discredited the whole crew of speculators who, it was charged, operated the state government in their own interest. Artisans and skilled craftsmen lost from a fourth to a half of their business. Pools of unemployment widened in the cities in a way that had never before been seen. Pauperism spread frighteningly, quickly outstripping the slender resources of the existing charitable institutions.

Somebody was to blame. It did nothing for the ordinary man to be told that he was the helpless victim of an international depression; that he would be obliged to wait until conditions in England righted themselves sufficiently to permit a return of prosperity in America. Fury could well be vented upon the United States Bank, which was indeed generally viewed as the chief villain in the piece. The state governments were closer to hand, however. Where the people controlled the state governments, they demanded popular aid; where the state governments were in the hands of oligarchies, the people demanded control.

In New York a longstanding opposition to the Council of Appointment sparked the movement for constitutional revision. Set up by the state constitution of 1777 to limit the power of the governor, the five-man council controlled appointments to fifteen thousand public offices. In the hands of DeWitt Clinton, this council had become the basis for a spoils system which centered tremendous power in the hands of a few men. Temporarily out of power, the anti-Clinton

Tammany Society in 1818 demanded a state convention to revise the system for making political appointments. Governor Clinton delayed for a year, while depression conditions spread through New York. When he finally agreed to a convention, the Tammany Society pressed for more thorough-going reforms, including abolition of the Federalist-dominated Council of Revision, a governmental agency also created by the 1777 constitution, which possessed the power to veto popular legislation. Clinton's efforts to postpone the convention helped to produce an overwhelming majority of anti-Clinton Democrats—110 to 16—among the delegates elected for the convention.

Not all the men of wealth and station in the convention opposed themselves to democratic reforms. Daniel D. Tompkins, Vice-President of the United States, former governor of New York, and president of the convention, was the "farmer's boy" who long had been an advocate of democratic reforms. The convention included also General Erastus Root and the wealthy democrat Peter R. Livingston, both of them aggressive champions of radical reform. It included advocates of such limited reform as the practical politicians of the Tammany Society thought desirable. These men did not, after all, wish to see that system radically altered within which they had learned to operate profitably. The most influential spokesman for this school of thought, and probably the most influential man in the convention, was Senator Martin Van Buren. Among the stalwart conservatives the leading spokesman was James Kent, chancellor of the state.

The Council of Revision and the Council of Appointment were past hope, and they were abolished by unanimous vote. The main struggle developed over abolition of the property qualification. "I am not," said Chancellor Kent,

> prepared to annihilate all distinction and cause all to bow before the right of universal suffrage. This democratic principle cannot be contemplated without terror. We have seen its career

in Europe . . . . Universal suffrage jeopardizes property and
puts it into the power of the poor and the profligate to control
the affluent . . . . The poor man's interest is always in opposition to his duty, and it is too much to expect of human nature
that interest will not be consulted.

It was to no avail. The majority of the convention was
out of harmony, not only with Chancellor Kent, but also
with Senator Van Buren, who, while favoring certain reforms,
was opposed when it came to extending the vote, to "cheapen-
ing this invaluable right."

General Stephen Van Rensselaer, the wealthiest man
in the state, was agreeable to taxpayers' suffrage, but he opposed the desire of the majority to extend the vote to non-
taxpayers simply because they worked on the roads or served
in the militia. Against General Van Rensselaer it was argued
that his limitations would exclude most of the men who had
served under him during the war. In New York as elsewhere
such voting restrictions had become, since the war, an offense
to the patriotic spirit. President Tompkins spoke for the
majority when he declared that property was but one of the
rights, and by no means the most important one, which governments were instituted to protect. According to the Declaration of Independence, Tompkins said, civil society was formed
to protect life, liberty, and the pursuit of happiness, rather
than the pursuit of property. In this spirit the convention gave
the vote to all adult white male residents of the state who
had lived in the state one year and who had paid taxes or
served in the militia or worked on the highways. On one
point, it was the conservatives who fought successfully for
a broadening of the suffrage against the opposition of the radicals. They secured the vote for all adult male Negroes
who owned a freehold worth $250 and paid a tax upon it. The
conservatives and the radicals both reasoned that the wealthy
men of the community were in a position to gain these votes.

Democratic reforms continued inexorably in New York
during the next generation. In 1826, following a state refer-

endum, the remaining restrictions on free white manhood suffrage were abolished. In the same year the office of justice of the peace was made elective. The office of mayor of New York City became elective in 1833, and the principle was extended to all the cities of the state six years later. In 1845 the property qualifications for governor and state senators were finally abolished.

Massachusetts, in the meantime, had subjected John Adams' constitution of 1780 to the same criticism, and had altered it along similar lines. Adams himself was on hand at the Massachusetts convention of 1820 to repeat the old arguments in favor of property qualifications, and he was sustained by conservatives of the new generation, notably Daniel Webster. "Life and personal liberty," Webster told the convention,

> are, no doubt, to be protected by law; but property is also to be protected by law, and is the fund out of which the means for protective life and liberty are usually furnished . . . . The disastrous revolutions which the world has witnessed; those political thunderstorms and earthquakes which have overthrown the pillars of society from their very deepest foundations, have been revolutions *against property.*

The substantial falsity of this assertion concerning the French Revolution did not prevent it from being widely believed, and it prevailed upon the convention in Massachusetts, as it did in New York, to the extent of limiting the privilege of holding office as governor or state senator to property holders. Meanwhile, amid the foreboding pronouncements of Adams, Joseph Story, and Webster, the convention extended the vote to all adult, white, male taxpayers.

In both Massachusetts and New York the defenders of property qualifications consistently had the best of the debate. The democratic reformers could not meet the argument that voting was a privilege and not a right. If voting were a right, they were asked, then why deny it to women, Negroes, and Indians? Since the democratic reformers were almost universally opposed to extending the vote to these elements of the population, they were obliged to make their defense, not on generous grounds of democratic theory, but on such narrow grounds as taxpayers' and militiamen's and road workers' rights. Nevertheless, they were sustained by the democratic spirit of the times, and although they may have lost the arguments, they won the decisions in both states.

II

So far as the western farmers were concerned, the panic of 1819 may well have been the severest depression ever to be experienced before or since. Later depressions found most farmers in possession of the title to their own lands. In 1819 most western farmers were still in the process of making payments on their land, and the panic faced them with the prospect of mass eviction. In Tennessee they found their spokesman in Felix Grundy, who pushed through the legislature various relief measures, including a bill establishing a state loan office to tide the debtors through the depression. In state after state the debtors grasped control of the government as they had not done since the depression days of the Confederation. When the Bank of Kentucky suspended payments, the legislature passed a stay law and established a new bank, authorized to issue bank notes to the amount of three million dollars. At the same time, the legislature voted a mere seven thousand dollars toward establishing the bank, a sum sufficient to pay for the printing of the notes. Any creditor who refused to accept the new paper might be forced to wait two years for a settlement of his bills. "Stop laws—property laws—replevin laws—stay laws—loan office laws—the intervention of the legislature between the creditor and the debtor," Senator Thomas Hart Benton later wrote, "this was the business of legislation in three-fourths of the States of the Union—of all south and west of New England."

Historians and economists have generally attacked these relief measures as irresponsible and ineffective. Other reforms of more permanent significance, however, received a decisive impetus during the depression. Most important among these was the reform in laws concerning the crime of indebtedness. Imprisonment for debt was still generally practiced at the time of the War of 1812, despite the movement which had developed against it during the Revolutionary era. It remained the most widely hated and feared aspect of the still medieval American penal codes, and it was the first to be generally reformed. New York in 1817 exempted from imprisonment debtors who owed sums less than twenty-five dollars. Of almost two thousand debtors imprisoned in New York City at the time, more than one-third had been jailed for debts of less than that amount. New Hampshire and Vermont passed similar laws a year later. Pennsylvania and Kentucky abolished the prison sentence for women debtors. Then Kentucky in 1821 abolished the sentence of imprisonment for debt in all cases, except where the intent to defraud could be shown, and in the next generation state after state followed suit. The great age of humanitarian reform was still a decade and more in the future, but the panic of 1819 served to reorient the thinking of many to a more humanitarian point of view.

Conservatives everywhere were horrified at the leveling economic legislation of the depression period, and party struggles divided sharply along debtor-creditor lines. The debtors, for their part, saw villainy everywhere among the creditor classes, and they saw the very incarnation of villainy in the Bank of the United States. The most obvious immediate cause of the panic had been the contraction of credit by the United States Bank, inevitably followed by a run of failures among flimsy state banks. In the midst of farm foreclosures and business failures, the branches of the U. S. Bank were gathering in large amounts of property. In Cincinnati the bank actually acquired a large part of the city in house lots, hotels, business firms, warehouses, and iron foundaries. Although the bank survived the popular hostility for the time, much of the sentiment was created which supported Jackson a decade later in his fight against the bank.

Nationally the depression produced no outstanding leader, and no really significant piece of legislation, except the Land Act of 1820. The depression had no effect whatever on the unopposed re-election of President Monroe, and Monroe, for his part, all but ignored the depression in his second inaugural address. As his second administration progressed, prosperous times returned to the nation, and the panic was not an issue in the election of 1824. It was in this apparently placid atmosphere that the Richmond Junto of Virginia and the Albany Regency of New York set about, following Monroe's re-election, to select the next presidential candidate and see to his election.

III

Beginning with the Jefferson-Burr collaboration of 1800, the selection of President and Vice-President for twenty years had regularly been made by a few gentlemen from Virginia and a few gentlemen and machine politicians from New York. In Virginia the Richmond Junto was organized during Jefferson's first administration, to control the state for the Republican party. It was started by the editor of the leading Republican newspaper, Thomas Ritchie; the leader of the Virginia bar, Spencer Roane; and the dominant banker of the state, John Brockenbrough. A secret organization, its activities were never divulged. But they appear to have resulted in a comprehensive political control of the state, and—with the aid of New York allies—in the authority to select the chief executive of the nation every four years.

In New York Burr fell out of favor with Jefferson and the Junto when it appeared that he had tried to displace Jefferson as President in 1800. The Tammany Society, however, tended faithfully to follow the lead of the Junto. New York was torn by political battles in the first quarter of the century, and on several occasions the New York-Virginia alliance seemed at an end. In 1812 New York's DeWitt Clinton opposed Virginia's James Madison, and in 1816 New York's Daniel Tompkins moved to unseat Virginia's James Monroe. Nevertheless the connection was maintained, and the threat from outside interference in 1824 did not seem great. New England had yet to emerge from the shambles of disrupted and tainted Federalism. The populous state of Pennsylvania had suffered such violent political battles and such a collapse of party discipline that no politician survived in a sufficiently strong position to receive united backing as a favorite son. Pennsylvania was overwhelmingly Republican, and, with the South and West, it had habitually followed the New York-Virginia lead. In New York Martin Van Buren, with the Tammany Society behind him, dominated the state through a tightly knit group of important politicians known as the Albany Regency.

In 1824 the Junto and the Regency were in good agreement as to Monroe's successor. He was to be the then secretary of the treasury, William H. Crawford, and Van Buren among others did not doubt that Crawford would win the office. It was true that he faced a host of rivals, including Henry Clay, John C. Calhoun, DeWitt Clinton, John Quincy Adams, and Andrew Jackson. As late as fall of 1823, none of them seemed to have a serious chance of upsetting him. He was in his own right a skillful political manipulator, to whom many Congressmen and state politicians were beholden, and he enjoyed the united support of the king-makers. Even if he did not receive a majority of the electoral votes, he would be among the top three candidates to be presented to the House of Representatives. At that stage his popularity and power in Congress would place him in the Presidency, barring some unforeseen accident.

There was an unforeseen accident. A year before the election Crawford was striken by paralysis. Immobile, almost

blind, and not entirely in possession of his senses, he was reduced to a campaign consisting of a series of hopeful medical
reports. Even so, he still won sufficient electoral votes, prin-
cipally in New York, Virginia, North Carolina, and Georgia,
to qualify for election by Congress. By that time his helpless
condition had placed him beyond consideration. Meanwhile
Pennsylvania, the South and the West, refusing to accept a
complete invalid, had deserted the reigning coalition to vote
for the old hero of the Second War for Independence,
Andrew Jackson.

In the campaign of 1824 Crawford's competitors, differ-
ing from him in no important respect on political issues, were
hard put to it to discover talking points during the campaign.
These men were so little divided in political policy that Adams
and Calhoun both indicated their willingness to run on the
same ticket as Jackson, although Adams was unwilling to
accept the inferior position. Crawford was the chosen candidate of such Old Republicans as Nathaniel Macon and John
Randolph of Roanoke; yet Crawford's political views were
closer to those of Adams and Clay than to those of Macon and
Randolph.

Bereft of clear political differences, the candidates eagerly
grasped the anti-caucus issue and argued it for all it was
worth. Crawford was the man to beat, and Crawford was
the man upon whom the Richmond Junto and the Albany
Regency planned to bestow the nomination of the Congressional caucus. For a generation Federalists and Republicans
had permitted their party members in Congress to select
their respective candidates for the Presidency. The system
was extra-constitutional, but so was the whole party system.
The Congressional caucus system was attacked partly on the
grounds of unconstitutionality, but mainly on the grounds that
it was undemocratic. For want of a better political issue such
aristocrats as Adams and Calhoun, obtaining sanction for their
own candidacies through state caucuses, pressed the fight

against the Congressional caucus. So hot did the issue become, that when Congress met to nominate Crawford, only sixty-six members attended out of a total of 261 Congressmen, and the system was never again resorted to. It was replaced by the nominating convention, originated by Pennsylvania in 1824. Following the Pennsylvania example, state nominating conventions were widely called before the Presidential election of 1828, and four years later the national convention finally established itself.

It is sometimes argued that the substitution of the nominating convention for the caucus was an apparent reform which actually left the power of Presidential appointment little disturbed, in the hands of the leading professional politicians. Such has not been the case, as party leaders from Henry Clay to Robert Taft found out to their sorrow. The development of the nominating convention took control out of the hands of the national party leaders and placed it in the hands of party leaders on the state and local level. In some cases, as in the case of Jackson, the nominating convention placed control in the hands of the people themselves. This contrast between the caucus and the convention presented itself strikingly in the first nominating convention, the Pennsylvania convention of 1824, which stampeded for Andrew Jackson, against all the expectations of the professionals.

Andrew Jackson as a political force was a shocking surprise to the most seasoned professional politicians in 1824. Van Buren, who afterwards was quick to become the director of Jackson's political machine, was at the time unable to take Jackson seriously as a political contender. It was true that Jackson had moved easily and successfully in Tennessee politics, but he was a backwoods politician who did not fit the aristocratic mould of the Presidency. It was also true that from the time of Monroe's re-election Jackson was everywhere talked about as a possibility by the common people.

Practical politicians still were reluctant to treat him seriously. The people, after all, did not make the nominations. This line of reasoning changed almost overnight. It was impossible to misread the meaning of the Pennsylvania convention.

In Pennsylvania, unlike New York, party organization had all but collapsed with the disintegration of the Federalist party. Local issues and local patronage failed to maintain party discipline, either on the level of village faction or of gubernatorial contests. Pennsylvania was therefore not a promising field for machine organization, and Crawford did not trouble himself to develop an organization there. He noticed Jackson's popularity in the state, but he reasoned that Jackson would fail to get the nomination of the Congressional caucus, and that his popularity accordingly would avail him nothing. Adams had no hope of gaining Pennsylvania's votes, and he wasted little effort in the state, but Clay and Calhoun were more optimistic and more enterprising. The anti-caucus sentiment in Pennsylvania was everywhere evident, and expert political opinion tended to the view that Calhoun would be the beneficiary of this sentiment.

The demonstrations for Jackson became increasingly frequent and increasingly riotous, but they were directed by no important political figures in the state. Lacking any really powerful political champions, Jackson, in order to announce his willingness to run in the state, was reduced to making his views known in a letter to a tavern keeper who represented a pro-Jackson group in Harrisburg. George M. Dallas, shortly to become a good Jacksonian, was impatient with those who were taking the Jackson demonstrations seriously. "Some exertions," he wrote, shortly before the meeting of the state nominating convention, "should be made to inspire those who are unnecessarily drooping beneath the outcry in favor of Jackson. My own convictions remained unshaken that the excessive popularity of the General is merely apparent—is an effervescence that can accomplish nothing."

Initiated on the recommendations of members of the state legislature, the Pennsylvania nominating convention was at first supported by the friends of Crawford and Calhoun and opposed by those of Jackson—so completely did all sides misjudge the outcome. The state legislators were to act as delegates for those counties which failed to elect special delegates, and the Jacksonians feared that this provision would place the nomination in the hands of the professional politicians. It was only when the counties began to elect delegates that Jackson's prodigious political strength became apparent and the "eleventh hour men" among the practical politicians began to scramble to his side. By the time the delegates had been elected, the issue had been settled far past doubt. The first order of business following the election of officers was the nomination of Jackson. A motion to substitute Crawford was defeated 123 to 2. A motion to make no recommendation was defeated 120 to 5, and Jackson's nomination was passed 124 to 1. In the general election Jackson received 35,929 votes. Adams proved to be his closest competitor with 5,436 votes.

In 1824 the presidential electors were chosen by the people in all of the twenty-four states except Vermont, New York, Delaware, South Carolina, Georgia, and Louisiana. Jackson won in New Jersey, Maryland, Pennsylvania, and North Carolina among the eastern states. In the West he won in Tennessee, Indiana, Alabama, Mississippi, and Louisiana, while losing to Clay by a few hundred votes in Ohio. The popular vote cast for Jackson approximately equaled the combined votes cast for Adams and Clay or the combined votes cast for Adams and Crawford, but he fell short of a clear majority over his three competitors by about fifty thousand votes, while winning only 99 of the 261 electoral votes. Calhoun, meanwhile, having bowed before the Jacksonian storm and accepted the nomination for Vice-President, was elected by a clear majority.

The names of Crawford, Jackson, and Adams were presented to the House of Representatives for a vote, Clay having been edged out of third position by Crawford. Adams, receiving the support of Clay in Congress, won on the first ballot. Clay afterwards became Adams' Secretary of State, and Adams was hardly in office before the next Presidential campaign was under way, waged chiefly on the issue of an alleged "corrupt bargain" between Adams and Clay, by which the people had been robbed of their first choice for President.

IV

John Quincy Adams' main historical function as President was the same as his father's had been before him: to facilitate the transition to democracy by a stern abstention from the vulgar mechanics of politics, so necessary to the maintenance of political power. Unlike his father, John Quincy Adams in 1828 did not have an even chance of re-election. Still he might have avoided the landslide defeat he sustained, had he not exhibited such an iron unconcern for the politics of loaves and fishes. Adams made no concessions to the politics of democracy, and the politics of democracy rewarded him accordingly.

The author, shortly before his election as President, of a brief history of political parties in America, Adams was apparently quite unaware of the nature of party politics as it was developing in the twenties. He thought of parties purely as the manifestation of "a struggle for political principles, for sectional interests, and for individual men." Of these, only sectional interests provided a permanent basis for party division. Individual men died, and political principles changed with the times. Since America had become universally republican in principle, parties could be expected to disappear when the nation was not torn by sectional controversy. Indeed political parties had died in America with the close of the War of 1812.

The collisions of opinion upon the principles of government had lost all their asperity and much of their ardor, the results of the French Revolution had disappointed the enthusiast of democracy, and the Republican administration had adopted and practiced upon most of the principles which they had strenuously contested while the government was in Federal hands.

This was the situation as it presented itself to Adams when he assumed office in 1825. "If there have been those who doubted whether a confederated representative democracy were a government competent to the wise and orderly management of the common concerns of a mighty nation," he declared in his inaugural address,

> those doubts have been dispelled. . . . Ten years of peace, at home and abroad, have assuaged the animosities of political contentions and blended into harmony the most discordant elements of public opinion. There still remains one effort of magnanimity, one sacrifice of prejudice and passion, to be made by the individuals throughout the nation who have heretofore followed the standards of political party. It is that of discarding every remnant of rancor against each other, of embracing as countrymen and friends, and of yielding to talents and virtue alone that confidence which in times of contention for principle was bestowed only upon those who bore the badge of party communion.

Adams looked upon himself as a Patriot President, just as had Washington and John Adams a generation earlier. There is little evidence, as E. Malcolm Carroll has written, that he understood what was clear to many at the time, that a new period of intensely partisan politics was about to begin.

Under harsh partisan attack almost from the moment he assumed office, Adams steadfastly followed the course outlined in his inaugural address. He broke with his chief political supporters, Clay and Webster, over the disposal of patronage. They were eager to reward the administration's friends and punish its enemies, but Adams, despite strong indications that Postmaster General John McLean was using the patronage of his department in the interest of Jackson and Calhoun, permitted McLean to retain his position on the grounds that he was a competent postmaster general. "Mr. Adams," the rising national political boss Thurlow Weed later wrote, "during his administration, failed to cherish, strengthen, or even recognize the party to which he owed his election; nor as far as I am informed, with the great power he possessed did he make a single influential friend."

Daniel Webster and Henry Clay protested against Adams' unwillingness to use the office to build up the party. "Henceforward," Clay wrote in 1827, "I think that the principle ought to be adhered to . . . of appointing only friends to the Administration in public offices. Such I believe is the general conviction in the cabinet." The othermindedness of Adams in these matters was one of the main reasons why the creation of an effective successor to the Federalist party was delayed until after the election of 1832. By then, Adams' repudiation at the polls had removed him from political leadership, bringing forward the willing political manipulator Clay as the leader of the anti-Jackson faction.

While Adams was holding to his Washingtonian ideals, the motley opposition to the administration moved aggressively and comprehensively to create the political machinery necessary for victory. After the election of 1824, Van Buren, the erstwhile Crawford man, set himself the task of achieving a Crawford-Jackson union which would work for the election of Jackson in 1828. The Adams-Clay combination all but dictated the opposing combination which Van Buren sought. In addition Van Buren welcomed the supporters of Calhoun into the new political grouping. The purpose of the new coalition was victory, pure and simple. It was, as Mosei Ostrogorski wrote,

> in American history, the first example of a national party created not to give shape to ideas, but to form a conquering army, that is to say, on an essentially mechanical basis. It had there-

fore to look for its main support to a powerful organization in
the country. Van Buren set to work to provide for this want
with an exceptional competence acquired by a long apprentice-
ship in his native State, which had early developed the arts of
the politician.

Van Buren applied his organizational skill to three separate spheres of politics, the United States Senate, the political machinery of New York, and the state capitols of the
nation. In the Senate, an opportunity presented itself with
the irrelevant question of whether to send representatives to
the Panama Congress in 1826. At the outset this was a small
matter and seemingly noncontroversial. Adams himself was
no enthusiastic champion of the Panama Congress. The heat
of the arguments appeared in retrospect to have been quite
artificially created. The debate ranged to such subjects as
the institution of slavery and the frightful character of slave
insurrections. It produced sharp exchanges between Senators
and the President, and it confirmed the Calhoun faction in its
opposition to the administration, joining it to the Crawford
faction. "Although nothing to that effect was then said,"
Van Buren later wrote,

> there was also an obvious concurrence in opinion between us
> that opposition to so prominent a measure of the Administra-
> tion could not fail to lead to an ultimate union of efforts for its
> overthrow. This followed and from that period to the election
> of Gen. Jackson there was a general agreement in action be-
> tween us.

Van Buren cultivated the attentions of the Richmond
Junto, with a view to bringing the New York-Virginia alliance
to the support of Jackson. His success in this attempt was
followed by an extended tour of the southern states, where
Van Buren presented himself as a steadfast friend of state
sovereignty and southern rights. He was embarrassed in his
efforts by the rivalry between Crawford and Calhoun. He
overcame this difficulty by concealing from Crawford his
fixed intention to support Calhoun for the Vice-Presidency.

Meanwhile, Crawford's political strength naturally declined with the decline in his physical strength.

The most difficult problem facing Van Buren was that of securing the support of his own New York for Jackson. There Van Buren and the Albany Regency had suffered a severe defeat with DeWitt Clinton's election as governor in 1824. Van Buren set himself the task of uniting the Clinton men with his own anti-Clinton Tammany Bucktail party. Clinton's Vice-Presidential ambitions presented an obstacle which might not have been overcome, had Clinton not died several months before the state nominating convention met. As it turned out, New York gave twenty electoral votes to Jackson in 1828, where it had given but two in 1824.

The driving force behind the new party was, of course, that popularity of Jackson's to which the professional politicians had been until lately so indifferent. Jackson's popularity was politically negotiable among a wide variety of groups, because it was not connected with any policy. In the West Jackson was a frontier democrat; in the South he was a southern planter, although the Richmond Junto continued to eye him dubiously and later dropped him completely. In the East he was a farmer, a nationalist, and a representative of the common man. Above all, he was everywhere the hero of New Orleans, where, as one member of the House of Representatives said, he led the "farmers of the country triumphantly victorious over the conquerors of the conquerors of Europe." He was the living embodiment of the triumphant new democratic nationalism.

It has been pointed out, notably in the writings of Thomas P. Abernethy, that Jackson, himself, in the course of a long political career, never associated himself with the democratic movement until he was thrust at its head by other men. Beginning as a poor boy, Jackson had risen rapidly to the station of frontier aristocrat. Acquiring wealth in land and slaves, he also acquired political and military positions, almost

casually, as fitting the role he had assumed of aristocratic leadership. The panic of 1819 found Jackson bringing
lawsuits against scores of debtors and stoutly opposing the
relief programs championed by Felix Grundy. In the state
elections of 1821, Jackson fought the democratic candidate William Carroll, who as governor, inaugurated an era
of broad democratic reform within the state, a brand of
reform later known as "Jacksonian Democracy." Had Jackson campaigned in 1828 on the basis of his past political
record, the results of the election might have been different.

Jackson's past politics had little bearing on the election. As John Ward has pointed out, Jackson was elected,
not as a politician, but as the symbol for an age. If he lived
the life of an aristocrat, it was not in the manner of the old
seaboard aristocracy. Jackson was by nature a man of the
people, who never became fussy about class distinctions. If
he had risen well above the general level in economic station,
it only demonstrated the superiority of the American system,
which rewarded ability and industry. As a westerner he shared
the popular distrust of the eastern monocracy, even while
representing the creditor interest in Tennessee politics. In
the eyes of Jackson and the American people, wealth was not
a rebuke to the ideal of equality. "When one starts poor,
as most do in the race of life," Abraham Lincoln later said,
"free society is such that he knows he can better his condition. . . . That is the true system." Jackson, in the eyes of
most Americans, was a heroic product of that system.

In religion Jackson accepted naturally the self-righteous,
fundamentalist emotionalism of the popular evangelical revival, whereas the intellectual John Quincy Adams rejected
it in disgust. Jackson, from his own point of view as well
as from the point of view of the people, was the average
man drawn larger than life. Jackson entered the campaign
of 1828 with no program whatever, where Adams campaigned
on the basis of clearly enunciated aims, including the institut-

ing of a moderate protective tariff and extensive internal improvements to be financed out of Federal funds. From the standpoint of interest, Pennsylvania, perhaps more than any other state in the Union, ought to have been attracted by the Adams program; yet in 1828 Pennsylvania went two to one for Jackson. The majority of American voters in 1828 cast their ballots, not for a program—as Adams thought they ought to have—but for an emotional ideal. Abernethy has charged that Jackson simply identified democracy with his own personality, that he might have said in a paraphrase of Louis XIV's statement, "I am democracy." And so, for most practical political purposes, he was.

In 1834 Adams confided to his diary an account of American party politics which contrasted sharply with the history of American parties he had written in 1822.

> Caucuses, County, State, and National Conventions, public dinners, and dinner-table speeches two or three hours long constitute the operative power of electioneering; and the parties are working-men, temperance reformers, Anti-Masons, Union and States-Rights men, Nullifiers, and, above all, Jackson men, Van Buren men, Clay men, Calhoun men, Webster men, and McLean men, Whigs and Tories, Republicans and Democrats, without one ounce of honest principle to choose between them. . . . There are five or six candidates for the seccession to the Presidency, all of them demagogues, and not one of them having any consistency of system for the government of the Union . . . .

With this new politics of democracy Adams would have no part. Not so the politicial associates who were to lose power with his defeat in 1828. In New York the administration's most capable supporter was Thurlow Weed. Destined to rival and then surpass Van Buren as a national political manager, Weed found himself grievously balked by the stiff-backed idealism of the President. Weed traveled to Washington in 1825 to show Adams how political conditions in New York might be turned to the account of the administration.

Upon finding that the "suggestion did not interest" Adams, Weed did what he could on his own to strengthen the anti-Jackson forces in New York. He found his opportunity in the emotional frenzy which followed the mysterious disappearance of one William Morgan in New York in 1826.

Morgan, a member of the Masonic order, was alleged to have been kidnapped and murdered by Masons to prevent his revealing the secrets of freemasonry. His disappearance took place in an area of upstate New York swept by the excitement of evangelical revivalism. Committees were formed to investigate the matter and the incident swiftly developed into a popular anti-Masonic movement which spread to other parts of the Union; a movement which opposed all secret orders as anti-democratic and which absorbed the excitement and emotional energy of revivalism. Politically the movement seemed promising to the anti-Jackson forces, since Jackson was himself a prominent member of the Masonic order. Weed moved at once to capitalize on the development, and he was joined by such rising political leaders as Thaddeus Stevens of Pennsylvania and William H. Seward of New York. The Anti-Masonic party continued into the election of 1832, where it ran its own candidate and polled a meager thirty-three thousand votes. The extent to which it contributed votes to Adams in 1828, or whether it helped him at all, is impossible to judge. It was the most hopeful expedient available to Weed in the face of Jackson's great popularity, and it was a step in the realignment of political forces according to emotional loyalties rather than "any consistency of system for the government of the Union."

The result of the campaign, which in the final weeks reduced itself to exchanges of slanderous vituperation, was a landslide victory for Jackson. With approximately 56 per cent of the popular vote, Jackson won in the electoral college 178 to 83. In all states but South Carolina and Delaware, the electors had been chosen by the people rather than by the state legislatures, as originally had been almost universally the case. Adams won in New England and divided the vote with Jackson fairly evenly in New York, Maryland, Kentucky, Ohio, Louisiana, and Indiana. Elsewhere he lost by heavy margins. In Tennessee he lost by twenty to one.

The election brought to the Presidency a man who, at the age of sixty-two, was broken in health. It was doubted that he would live out his term of office. If he did, it was generally assumed in political circles, he would remain merely titular President, to be manipulated by the professionals who had conducted his campaign. Jackson's campaign, from the first, had been managed by others with little more than his passive consent. He had been willing clay, as James Parton wrote, in the hands of a few friendly potters. Until his defeat in 1824, by what he was convinced had been a corrupt bargain, Jackson had seemed almost indifferent to his own candidacy. After Adams' election by Congress, Jackson's heightened interest appeared to be little more than a personal desire for vengeance against Adams and Clay. Once in the Presidency, however, Jackson gathered into his hands the authority of the office, augmented by his own great popularity. The first President to be elected by the people, he became in his own eyes the special guardian of the people by the divine right of majority assent. In the view of conservatives he became the dreaded demagogue, that fearful threat to republican insitutions which the founding fathers, through the contrivance of the electoral college, had so carefully defended against.

Chapter 9

JACKSONIAN
DEMOCRACY

JAMES PARTON concluded his biography of Andrew Jackson with an equivocal reflection.

> Respecting the character of Andrew Jackson and his influence, there will still be differences of opinion. One fact, however, has been established: during the last thirty years of his life, he was the idol of the American people. His faults, whatever they were, were such as a majority of the American citizens of the last generation could easily forgive. His virtues, whatever they were, were such as a majority of American citizens of the last generation could warmly admire. It is this fact which renders him historically interesting. Columbus had sailed; Raleigh and the Puritans had planted; Franklin had lived; Washington fought; Jefferson written; fifty years of democratic government had passed; free schools, a free press, a voluntary church had done what they could to instruct the people; the population of the country had been quadrupled and its resources increased ten fold; and the result of all was, that the people of the United States had arrived at the capacity of honoring Andrew Jackson before all other living men.

That, as Parton said, is the fact that renders Jackson historically interesting. He personified the American idea to the American people as no other President until General Eisenhower. "Other men are lenses through which we read our own minds," Ralph Waldo Emerson wrote in *Representative Men*. Among all of America's Presidents these two generals emerge as Emerson's "representative men."

Jackson was the visible sign of the people's triumph. His inauguration is remembered, not for what he said, which was very little and to no clear point, but for the motley crowd of farmers and mechanics who obtruded themselves upon a ceremony which formerly had been reserved for gentle folk. Traveling by horse and by foot over roads made all but impassable by the spring rains, these common people converged on Washington by the thousands, some of them coming as far as five hundred miles for the occasion. Muddy and unmannerly, they crowded their way, uninvited, into the post-inauguration reception, threatening to reduce the White House to shambles, until they were diverted by tubs of punch hastily carried out to the White House lawn. They announced their sovereignty to the world.

There were hostile observers who found this inauguration of democracy disgraceful and fittingly so. As Alexis de Tocqueville noted, many Americans of wealth, position, and education privately despised democracy. Publicly, however, these men were compelled to accept the prevailing democratic shibboleths. Privately they might be guided by sensible and decorous religious conventions; publicly they were obliged to conduct themselves in such a way as to give no offense to the prevailing mores of the evangelical religions. They might profess to despise a society which made money the naked measure of social position, but the southern gentleman who disdained the counting house sometimes found his place in society pre-empted by his overseer. And however much certain rich men might despise the democratic process, the age of Jackson taught them the hard lesson that if they desired the political power to which they felt their position entitled them, they would have to go to the people to get it. As a class the aristocracy had become separated from the national character, which was democratic.

I

What followed Jackson's White House reception was anticlimax. The nation, awaiting the outcome of the Jacksonian revolution, waited in vain for any startling political changes. It turned out that Thomas Jefferson had disturbed himself unnecessarily over the possiblity of a Jacksonian *coup d'etat* against the republic. The new President and his chief lieutenants thought of themselves, not as political innovators, but as good, safe Jeffersonians, whose duty it was to safeguard the people against dangerous centralizing tendencies in the national government.

The Jacksonians pledged themselves to reduce government personnel and introduce other economies to the end that the national debt be paid off, the government freed from the grasp of the money power, and the burden of taxation be lifted from the people. The Constitution should be strictly construed to the end that the states be protected in their rights from the encroachments of Federal power. The Federal government should always act in the general interest; never in the interest of a special group.

Where Jackson departed from the Jeffersonian tradition, the difference was often largely a matter of style. Where Jefferson believed that a good government was one which operated so quietly as to go almost unnoticed, Jackson acted on the principle that a good democratic government ought to trumpet forth in the name of the people now and then. Where Jefferson, fearing the city mobs, placed his reliance upon those "who labor in the earth," Jackson presented himself as the spokesman for the workingman as well as the farmer. In practice, however, the two men followed very similar policies toward those who labored in the shops and mills. The Jeffersonians had eagerly made common cause, both with the urban radicalism of the Democratic-Republican societies, and with the urban political machinery of the Tammany Society. Jackson, on the other hand, while drawing political strength from these same elements, showed no marked interest in the problems which were peculiarly those of the city worker. It was his successor, Van Buren, who set out to secure the workingman's vote by adopting measures, notably the ten-hour working day, which were demanded by urban workers particularly, rather than by the laboring classes as a whole. Most Americans were still farmers in Jackson's day, and most of the laborers in whose name Jackson spoke were those who labored in the earth.

The most startling novelty to occur during Jackson's first year in office, his defense of the spoils system, was, at the time, largely academic. Concerning the inevitable redistribution of political offices which accompanied the change in administrations, Jackson presented an aggressive defense on democratic grounds. Rotation in office, he said, freed the nation's government from control by an entrenched bureaucracy. To argue that public offices should remain in the hands of those trained by experience to perform them was to call democracy itself into question. "The duties of all public offices are, or at least admit of being made, so plain and simple that men of intelligence may readily qualify themselves for their performance." Jackson's defense of the spoils system shocked those who were prepared to be shocked by anything that this plebeian President said, and certainly it was a world apart from Jefferson's idea of a natural aristocracy. In practice, however, Jackson showed considerable restraint in his redistribution of the patronage. The turnover in personnel was roughly comparable to that which had taken place under Jefferson. After Jackson, President Van Buren, who, of course, inherited an administration he himself had helped to staff, made only eighty removals. It was not until the forties that the spoils system really came into its own.

No part of the Jackson administration has been so widely and uncompromisingly denounced by historians as Jackson's defense of the spoils system; yet, as Carl Russell Fish pointed out, the system was essential to the very existence of democracy. Some citizens there no doubt were who would exert themselves politically with no thought of patronage, but they would be exceptional. The people as a whole could be expected to play an active and effective role in the maintenance of their governments only through political parties which could keep discipline based upon the expectations of future rewards. In the Old South, Fish noted, democracy, in terms of a broad suffrage, existed everywhere by the eve of the Civil War, but it existed without elaborate party organization and without the spoils system, and the aristocracy did not find it difficult to control the state governments.

There remained a further basic difference between Jeffersonian republicanism and Jacksonian democracy: Jackson rejected the Jeffersonian idea that government was a necessary evil and by its very nature an abridgement of liberty. "There are no necessary evils in government," he declared. "Its evils exist only in its abuses. If it would confine itself to equal protection, and, as Heaven does its rains, shower its favors alike on the high and the low, the rich and the poor, it would be an unqualified blessing." Jefferson, with his generation, feared the tyranny of the majority. Jackson supposed that the nation was secure against tyranny so long as it was under majority rule. As the first President literally to represent the popular will, Jackson conceived of himself as the embodiment of the majority, and in its name the special guardian of the Constitution.

It was in his emphasis upon the sovereign will of the majority that Jackson departed farthest from Jeffersonian republicanism. While Jefferson, with John Locke, had viewed sovereignty as residing in the will of the majority, those two political philosophers of the enlightenment had proceeded from the original assumption that men were endowed by their Creator with inalienable rights, and that the purpose of governments was to secure them in these rights. What was to be done if the majority asserted its sovereignty for the purpose of depriving individuals of their inalienable rights? Locke did not meet this problem, but there can be no doubt as to how he would have resolved it. For Locke and for Jefferson the whole purpose of society was to secure the liberty of the individual. For Jackson this was not the case. The individual already was sufficiently secure in his rights, protected by common law, by the first nine amendments to the Constitution, by the balance of powers within the Federal government, and by the balance of powers between the Federal and the state governments. These arrangements, devised by America's "sages and patriots," were accepted by Jackson as "sacred." At the same time, all of these arrangements together did not entitle the individual to flaunt the will of the majority. For Jackson, and for Jacksonian democracy, those citizens who opposed the will of the majority were the enemies of democracy, and, the sacred principles of the Constitution aside, they should be treated accordingly.

Jacksonian democracy demanded social as well as political conformity to the will of the majority. The man who differed from his neighbors publicly in matters of dress, speech, morals, or religion risked a tarring and feathering, and rightly so. The history of Joseph Palmer is a case in point, though no doubt an extreme one. Palmer, an eccentric Massachusetts farmer, was "Persecuted for Wearing the Beard," as his gravestone testifies. Palmer wore a full beard during the Age of Jackson, at a time when it was customary to go about cleanshaven. This defiance of accepted convention was more than the democratic community of Fitchburg, Massachusetts, could tolerate. Palmer's physician told him to shave; that he was spreading disease. Ministers labored to bring him out of his waywardness, and the minister of his own church attempted to prohibit him from receiving communion. When argument did not suffice, Palmer was set upon by men of the town, who attempted to shave him forcibly.

When some of his assailants were injured in the struggle, Palmer was jailed on charges of unprovoked assault. Refusing to pay his fine, he remained in jail, where the jailer and the prisoners attempted unsuccessfully in their turn to force him to shave. He remained in jail for a year, until unfavorable publicity resulted in his release. A temperance man, abolitionist and advocate of a wide number of reforms, he moved on to help Bronson Alcott found a utopian community, Fruitlands. To Alcott and the Transcendentalists, Palmer's brand of crusty individualism was a vital part of American democracy. That was not the view of the democratic majority, however. To the majority, the ideals of democracy called for identification with the community and conformity to the accepted social and moral code.

Amid the fierce sectarian struggles of the period, Jacksonian democracy demanded at least an outward show of conformity to Christian belief. Jefferson, a religious liberal, understood religious liberty as including the right to be a professing atheist. Jacksonian democracy did not join him in this view. The nation accepted the doctrine of separation of church and state necessarily, in the face of the fact that no sect was sufficiently dominant to establish itself against the competition of rival sects. But the view that an atheist could be a good American was not widely held. Jackson personally accepted the principle of religious liberty as part of the sacred order of things. That was not to say that he was ever quite easy with it. On Sunday mornings, Parton relates, Jackson would say to his guests, "Gentlemen, do what you please in my house; *I* am going to church. Among Jackson's advisers there were religious liberals and outright materialists, but the religious views of these men were suffered, rather than gladly tolerated, by Jackson and by Jacksonian democracy.

II

Jackson's first administration was a democratic pageant; his second was a democratic crusade. Until the veto of the bank bill late in his first term, Jackson led a party without a political program of its own, and it was no doubt the deep desire of his political lieutenants that he avoid ever arriving at a program. Jackson had been elected by high-tariff and low-tariff men, by broad nationalists and states-rights men, by inflationists and hard-money men, and by friends and foes of internal improvements. Under such circumstances the interests of the party seemed best served by doing as little as possible about anything.

Jackson, himself, seemed to think that he possessed a political program and, furthermore, that he had presented it to the public in his first annual message to Congress. The message contained no specific recommendations concerning domestic legislation, however, and it led to the passage of no bill. The Peggy Eaton episode was by far the most important event of Jackson's first three presidential years, when the chivalrous President used the full weight of his office to defend the wife of his friend the Secretary of War, John Eaton, against the snobbery and aspersions of Washington society. The event was important because it contributed to the political break between Jackson and Vice-President Calhoun, the husband of Washington's leading socialite. As the most important event to follow the democratic revolution of 1828, however, the Eaton episode was significantly lacking in ideological import.

Second in importance to the Eaton episode during those years was the Maysville Road bill veto, which placed Jackson in opposition to Federally financed intrastate internal improvements, on grounds of both economy and constitutionality. Jackson broke no new political ground with the veto, however. He merely reaffirmed a principle established by several of his predecessors. Nor did the veto commit Jackson to any very clear policy in the field of internal improvements, for subsequently he signed other very similar measures, on the grounds that they were national rather than local in scope, and the Federal internal improvements program did not diminish during his administration. Not even his chief Whig opponent Henry Clay could find in Jackson's vigorously worded veto a campaign issue for 1832. Jackson's treatment of the tariff question was similarly vague, cautious, and middle-of-the-road. He signed both the tariff of 1832 and the compromise tariff of 1833, but neither of them was passed as an administration measure. They were associated rather with his presidential rival Clay. They hardly could serve to separate the Jacksonians from their political opponents.

Had Jackson not been presented by Congress with a bill rechartering the United States Bank in 1832, he would have entered the campaign for re-election as little involved in any real political issues as he had been four years earlier. As it happened, Nicholas Biddle, director of the bank, called for a new charter four years before the expiration of the existing one. Biddle and Congressional leaders, knowing Jackson's hostility to the bank, reasoned that political considerations would force Jackson to sign the bill, if it were presented to him before the election. Jackson returned the bill to Congress with what has remained the most famous veto in American history, and he launched an attack which continued throughout his second term, serving, more than any other circumstance, to crystallize the national political forces at last into two separate organized political parties of Whig and Democrat.

In vetoing the bill Jackson followed his own private convictions. Typically, the veto for him was as much a private matter between himself and Biddle as it was a matter of political principle. "The bank is trying to kill me," Jackson told Van Buren, "but I will kill it." As Richard Hofstadter writes, the challenge aroused the dueling instinct in Jackson. The glove was thrown down, and Jackson picked it up—and instinctively in the name of the people and against the forces of wealth and privilege. The bank war made Jackson the hero of radical democrats, many of whom had shown little previous enthusiasm for the old hero of Horseshoe Bend. In American financial history the bank bill veto was a disastrous error which committed the nation for a century to the least serviceable banking system of any major industrial nation in the world. In the history of American democracy it was a heroic attack by the people's President against the bastion of wealth and privilege. With the bank bill veto Jacksonian democracy at last went into action on a national scale.

Jackson's veto was vigorously forthright in style, and electric with ideology.

> It is to be regretted that the rich and powerful too often bend the acts of government to their selfish purposes. Distinctions in society will always exist under every just government. Equality of talents, of education, or of wealth can not be produced by human institutions. In the full enjoyment of the gifts of Heaven and the fruits of superior industry, economy, and virtue, every man is equally entitled to protection by law; but when the laws undertake to add to these natural and just advantages artificial distinctions, to grant titles, gratuities, and exclusive privileges, to make the rich richer and the potent more powerful, the humble members of society—the farmers, mechanics, and laborers—who have neither the time nor the means of securing like favors to themselves, have a right to complain of the injustice of their Government.

This line of argument, although it represented the dominant economic radicalism of democratic America, was neither novel nor peculiar to American democratic thought, except in its aversion to titles and its pointed concern for the farmers, mechanics, and laborers. With those exceptions, the statement might well have been presented more than two centuries earlier amid loud cheers to that Elizabethan House of Commons which in 1601 successfully forced the Queen to rescind certain chartered monopolies.

Considering the strength of the anti-monopoly spirit in English tradition, the wonder is that the spirit emerged so late in American history and remained relatively so impotent. Part of the reason no doubt lies in the fact that almost all of the American colonies came into existence as state or private monopolies, and that colonial and frontier conditions necessitated a large measure of government supervision. Then, once independence was won, the American people tended to the view that they controlled their own governments and therefore had little to fear from the monopoly-creating power. The United States began life with a long-established tradition of government economic regulation to the minutest detail, including government-chartered local monopolies over a wide variety of economic activities.

The Bible of economic liberalism, Adam Smith's *Wealth of Nations* was published in the same year that Jefferson wrote the *Declaration of Independence*. The *Wealth of Nations* was the economic declaration of independence for the British businessman, who went on to win England to free trade over the opposition of the landed interests during the second quarter of the nineteenth century. Jacksonian America, meanwhile, experienced a somewhat similar struggle with the sides roughly reversed. The landed interests of the Cotton Kingdom won a partial victory for free trade over the opposition of the tariff-minded business community. Economic liberalism, in the sense of free trade, was never accepted by the American businessman, and, if it was accepted privately by Jackson, he did not advocate it as President.

Jackson did place himself at the forefront of the anti-monopoly fight with his bank bill veto, but he did so in a highly qualified manner. The veto lashed out at the principle of monopoly itself, but specifically it was an attack upon a national, as opposed to a state, monopoly. Indeed one of Jackson's arguments against the bank was that it infringed upon the rights of the less powerful banks which had been chartered by the states. The monopolistic state banking interests fully appreciated this argument, as their strong support of Jackson indicated in 1832.

The truth is that even in the heyday of Jacksonian democracy the anti-monopoly spirit, although it dominated one wing of the Democratic party, did not triumph in the nation. As the industrial revolution progressed, the scope of government regulation widened, and the chartering of government monopolies of banks as well as of bridges, canals, turnpikes, and then railroads, continued. These monopolies brought criticism, but they were nevertheless accepted as the most expeditious means of exploiting the resources of the nation. The nearest approach to the triumph of liberal capitalism in the age of Jackson was the passage of uniform laws of incorporation in various states, giving any group an equal chance to enter a field of economic activity—banking for instance—providing it fulfilled the general requirements of the law. In the pre-Civil War period, however, most corporations continued to operate under special charters.

In the meantime, the Jacksonian Supreme Court handed down a series of decisions, most notably the Charles River Bridge case, attacking the vested interest of old chartered companies, where their assertion of monopoly rights interfered with the rights of the community, in a country "free, active, and enterprising, continually advancing in numbers and wealth." To spokesmen for vested interest, the Charles River Bridge case was a Jacobinical attack upon the rights of private property. Actually it was a sensible decision which, as Charles Warren has written, encouraged "all business men who contemplated investments of capital in new corporate enterprise and who were relieved against claims of monopoly concealed in ambiguous clauses of old charters."

The notion that economic liberalism emerged hand in hand with political liberalism in America outside the planting states is absurdly false, as recent studies of Massachusetts, Pennsylvania, Georgia, and Missouri make abundantly clear. In each of these states down to the Civil War the governments engaged themselves vigorously and un-self-consciously in regulating, financing, and even administrating, a bewildering variety of economic activities. "Massachusetts observers," wrote Oscar and Mary Handlin, "conceived of the beneficent hand of the state as reaching out to touch every part of the economy." The Locofoco movement in attacking monopolies was not proposing *laissez faire*. The Locofocos accepted government control, and they did not oppose government support for private enterprise. They simply wished, as Jackson said, to live under a government which would "shower its favors alike on the high and the low, the rich and the poor." Jefferson the Physiocrat was an advocate of *laissez faire,* and he was joined in this doctrine by other southern planters, who wished to be let alone on their lordly plantations. The doctrine did not fail altogether to win its converts in the North as well, especially in academic circles, but it was no significant part of Jacksonian democracy. Its strength remained with the broadcloth party of southern Whig planters.

In one respect, however, Jackson was curiously Jeffersonian in his economic views. A successful career as lawyer, land speculator, and merchant had failed to win him away from the ascetic policy of hard money. To the enterprising America of Jacksonian democracy banking institutions were absolute necessities. The railroad age was unthinkable without the existence of extensive credit; yet Jackson, with the left wing Locofoco Democrats, was opposed to all banks. Metallic currency was the only honest currency. Bank notes were means by which the wealth produced by labor was syphoned off to the financial manipulators—the monocrats. Jackson favored the entire elimination of banking institutions, and he was joined in this wish by certain of his leading advisers and supporters, including Thomas Hart Benton, Roger B. Taney, and Van Buren. Their views, as Bray Hammond has written, "belonged with an idealism in which America was still a land of refuge and freedom rather than a place to make money," the land of Jefferson's golden dream, where commerce and industry would remain the handmaidens of agriculture, in a nation of self-sufficient farmers.

Upon this subject Jacksonian democracy was divided, however, and so were Jackson's lieutenants. Among his closest advisers Jackson counted men who had been closely connected with state banks and who represented the more enterprising wing of the party. These easy money Democrats, especially the state banking interests, disliked the United States Bank, not on hard money grounds, but on grounds that the bank imposed a restraint upon their own lending activities. They wished to destroy the bank to free themselves from all central control. Facing the election of 1832, Jackson worded his veto in such a way as to commit himself to neither wing of his party. The veto made no criticism of the state banks or of banks as such, and it suggested no alternative to the United States Bank. It straddled the issue so successfully that Jackson entered the campaign with the enthusiastic support of both the hard money men and the state banking interests.

Jackson's policy toward the bank during his second administration reflected the ambivalent character of his political following. Upon his re-election Jackson struck at the bank by removing Federal funds and distributing them among "pet" state banks. The banks were requested not to use the funds for speculative purposes, but nothing was done to enforce the request. The banks naturally followed their inclinations, and a rapid extension of credit ensued. At the same time, the national debt was paid off, and Congress enacted the Jacksonian policy of distributing the surplus revenue among the states, thus further accelerating the inflationary tendency. Then, during his last year in office, Jackson reverted to his hard-money principles with the Specie Circular, requiring specie payments for public land, and helping to trigger the panic of 1837. The panic broke upon the country several months after Jackson went into retirement in the Hermitage.

Inheriting the panic as well as the concerted animosity of the dominant economic interests of the nation, Jackson's successor, Van Buren, moved unsuccessfully to settle the crisis according to hard-money principles. An independent treasury would be established to hold government funds where they could not be used for speculative purposes. Against the hard-money program of Van Buren the business interests struggled without final success until the Civil War, when southern secession gave them the opportunity to pass new laws authorizing the establishment of banks under a uniform national charter.

Within the Jacksonian ranks the bank war revealed the fundamental conflict between the Jeffersonian ideal of the simple, virtuous, agrarian society and the democratic reality of an acquisitive society which could call upon its government to assist in the exploitation of a continent. Senator Benton indignantly declared that he "did not join in putting down the Bank of the United States to put up a wilderness of local banks." It did not matter. His old-fashioned intentions were powerless to alter the fact. In attempting to make democratic practice conform to Jeffersonian theory he was attempting the impossible. Democratic America believed with Abraham Lincoln that "it is best for all to leave each man free to acquire property as fast as he can," and the motto for democratic governments was, "boost; don't knock."

III

"Our party as at present organized," wrote the Whig politician Thurlow Weed in 1834, "is doomed to fight merely to be beaten. . . . The longer we fight Jacksonianism with our present weapons, *the more it won't die!* . . . With Clay, Webster, or Calhoun, or indeed any man identified with the war against Jackson and in favor of the Bank, or the Bank's shadow, the game is up." Twice the anti-Jackson forces had lost the Presidential election by a landslide, and at the time Weed wrote they faced almost certain defeat again, barring a completely unforeseen eventuality or else the adoption of new tactics. In 1836 against Van Buren the Whigs attempted to defeat the newly established democratic process by creating the kind of election which the founding fathers had intended always to happen, but which had happened only once, in 1824. They attempted, by supporting favorite-son candidates, to deprive Van Buren of a clear majority of electoral votes, and so to throw the election into the House of Representatives. Failing this, they nominated a military hero in 1840 and rode to victory on the crest of a popular majority. American democracy completed its triumph in 1840, when the party of wealth and station, interested in nothing so much as victory, put aside its squeamish dislike of democracy and went after the popular vote.

Created in 1834 out of the bank war and the South Carolina nullification crisis, the Whig party was essentially a coalition of the National Republicans of John Quincy Adams' administration and the broadcloth party of southern gentlemen. From the point of view of economic self-interest the southern cotton planters probably had less reason to oppose Jackson than they had to oppose the northern and dominant wing of their newly created patry. They were offended, however, by the vulgar equalitarianism of Jacksonian democracy and by the spirit of assertiveness it engendered in the leathershirt class in the South. They resented the arbitrary authority which Jackson assumed in the name of the people, especially his highhanded way with Congress. And, however much southern planters outside South Carolina might disapprove of the attempted unilateral nullification by that state of a federal law, they were nevertheless sensitive to any attack upon the principle of state sovereignty, and ever more so as the slave states came to assume a distinctly minority position in the nation. Outside the Carolinas—each of which operated according to political laws of its own—the southern planter class, conservative in its views and extremely considerate of property interests, joined forces with the substantial classes in the North. Taking the name Whig, as the opponents of "King Andrew I," this coalition of northern high-tariff nationalists and southern free trade states-righters did what it could to combat the party of popularity.

The coalition was made possible by a softening of the lines of National Republican doctrine and by the party's repudiation of John Quincy Adams. Under Adams' leadership the party had defended the United States Bank and had called, additionally, for secure tariff protection and active encouragement of manufacturers. Adams had envisioned a mighty expansion of internal improvements under Federal direction. He had envisioned an orderly sale of western land in such a way as best to utilize the nation's natural resources and raise funds for further national development. He had favored a system of taxation which would curb speculation and distribute the national wealth more equitably. He may be credited with being a prophet of the twentieth-century democratic national state; he cannot be credited with being a competent statesman for his own time. Adams' program, while containing much that was of interest to northern businessmen, was far too austere in its disregard of the profit motive to arouse full-throated enthusiasm in any quarter. His lack of interest in the machinery of politics compounded the offense in the eyes of his professional political supporters. With his defeat in 1828 he was dropped at once, and much of his program was dropped with him. As Adams himself wrote in his diary, "My own system of administration, which was to make the national domain the inexhaustible fund for progressive and unceasing internal improvement, has failed . . . it has been undisguisedly abandoned by H. Clay, ingloriously deserted by J. C. Calhoun, and silently given up by D. Webster . . . ."

Under Clay's leadership the National Republicans supported a moderate tariff, a program of internal improvements as extensive as seemed politically practical, and a program of public land sales which would supply funds for internal improvements, prevent the precipitous fall in land values, and perhaps also serve to check the westward emigration of the working-class population from the East. So mild a program as this presented no clear points of contrast with the Jackson administration. It did tend to conciliate the southern gentlemen, who, although opposed generally to tariffs and taxes, and not entirely trustful of northern banks, were closely associated in all of their business dealings with northern manufacturers, bankers, and merchants. And as cotton became increasingly important to the American economy, the southern planter became increasingly confident—and with reason—that northern capitalism could be brought to terms with King Cotton.

The bank issue in 1832 had roused the business community of the North and brought enthusiastic support to Clay's candidacy. Unfortunately for Clay and the National Republicans, it was the enthusiastic support of a distinct minority of the nation. The Whig coalition in 1834 failed to create a majority for the party of wealth and talents, and it lost the party its unity of purpose. The 1836 Whig strategy of splitting the vote among favorite sons was a strategy all but dictated by the lack of cohesion among Whigs. It failed of its purpose, however, and further it tended to discredit the Whigs, as a party openly attempting to frustrate the will of the majority.

By 1840 control of the Whig party was passing into the hands of younger politicians, Thurlow Weed and William H. Seward in New York, Thaddeus Stevens in Pennsylvania, and Tom Corwin in Ohio. The careers of these men had been checked by a series of national defeats in the hands of democracy. They were more than ready to join the democracy and win national offices, and for this purpose the election of 1836 had produced one hopeful omen. Wherever General William Henry Harrison had been run by the Whigs, his candidacy had stirred excitement among the people. Long out of the political limelight and associated with no political issues, Harrison was best remembered for his part in the Battle of Tippecanoe, where in 1811 he had managed to avoid defeat at the hands of the resourceful Indian warriors. With no more than this to recommend him, Harrison had won more than half a million votes. Harrison and some of the younger Whig politicians remembered this impressive showing while the panic of 1837 broke upon the nation, discrediting the Van Buren administration. Amid rent riots and bread riots, rising unemployment and business failures, the Whigs gathered their strength behind Harrison in the 1840 convention. Amid extravagant praises of the unhappy Presidential aspirant Clay, and after repeated balloting, the old war hero Harrison nosed out the old war horse Clay. The convention then nominated the Virginia aristocrat John Tyler for the Vice-Presidency, in what at the time was considered a nominal concession to the southern Whigs. The convention adjourned without drawing up a platform.

In the campaign that followed, the leading spirit was Thurlow Weed, the first of the national political bosses. Weed had already done much to prepare himself for the campaign with his work in the Anti-Masonic party, where he had gone after the vote of the common people through highly effective irrational appeals to their emotions. In the campaign of 1840 the Anti-Masonic element had been absorbed into the Whig party, and, as Robert G. Gunderson has pointed out, the coalition brought the Whigs some invaluable new political assets: a rural following, a political vocabulary attuned to the popular ear, and above all a semblance of democratic spirit until then quite foreign to the party. Weed and likeminded party leaders determined from the beginning to apply these popular, irrational, emotional techniques on a national scale and to mobilize the wealth of the nation behind them. An executive committee composed entirely of Congressmen was formed to direct the campaign nationally, and innumerable additional committees on the state, county, and local levels were rapidly organized. Campaign contributions were levied upon the well-to-do on such a scale as to arouse in Horace Greeley the fear that they would "drive our rich men out of politics."

All that remained was an issue upon which to base the campaign, and this the party managers found in an article in the *Baltimore Republican*. There the suggestion was made that Old Granny Harrison, as the Presidential aspirant was called by his opponents, could be very easily and cheaply disposed of without all the expenses of a campaign. "Give him a barrel of Hard Cider, and settle a pension of $2,000 a year on him, and my word for it, he will set the remainder of his days in his Log Cabin, by the side of a 'sea-coal' fire and study moral philosophy.'" Omitting the damaging charge that their candidate was a student of moral philosophy, the Whig politicians grasped the rest of the statement as an issue entirely sufficient to their purposes. They launched a nation-wide circus performance, working endless variations on the theme that their candidate was a man of the people, born and living in a log cabin and content to drink hard cider. There were many slogans in addition to the immortal "Tippecanoe and Tyler too." There were the ubiquitous log cabins constructed as local campaign headquarters. There were monster mass meetings, harvest-homes, conventions, and picnics. There were many special songs and poems and campaign songbooks. There was Tippecanoe Shaving Soap, Harrison and Tyler neckties, and the manufacture of Old-Cabin Whiskey by a firm, the E. C. Booz Distillery, which, itself, achieved a permanent place in the national vocabulary as a result of the campaign.

A whole new school of political stump speakers emerged, led by Davy Crockett, the Coonskin Congressman; John Bear, the Buckeye Black Smith; and Abe Lincoln, the Railsplitter. Older, formerly more dignified politicians put on old clothes and got into the act. The southern aristocrat and classics scholar, Hugh Swinton Lagaré, put on a coonskin hat and toured five states on what had by then come to be known as a "slang-whanging expedition." Even Harrison, that dignified, aristocratic, country gentleman, whom the professionals would have preferred to see stay at home, moved about the country giving long, meaningless speeches in which he referred from time to time to his log cabin background. In vain did the Democrats protest that Harrison had been to the manner born, while Van Buren was in true fact a poor boy who had made good. Van Buren, the people were told, lived in a palace, drank champagne, ate out of gold spoons and wore slippers, and the Whigs got their point across. They got out the vote in an unprecedented manner, with a more than 54 per cent larger turnout than in the campaign of '36. They won by a slender margin, even though the loser Van Buren received 400,000 votes more than he had gained in the previous campaign.

Following his election, Harrison was brought forward by the Whig politicians to deliver an inaugural address which he had written by himself, despite Daniel Webster's protests. Harrison, it appeared from his inaugural, wished, as John Adams and John Quincy Adams had before him, to become a Patriot President after the model of George Washington. "All the influence that I possess," he said, "shall be exerted to prevent the formation at least of an Executive party in the halls of the legislative body." He would select his aides from among the most capable members of society, and he hoped that his administration would be such as to bring an end altogether to the contest of political parties. A month later, exhausted by the furious onslaught of office-seekers, President Harrison died of pneumonia, and his place was taken by Vice-President Tyler, states-rights advocate, opponent of the tariff, and enemy to any Whig scheme for the reconstitution of a national bank. After a fruitless struggle to force the northern Whig program through Congress over Tyler's vetoes, the Whigs in Congress caucussed and wrote their President out of the party. The northern Whigs had been poorly rewarded for their exertions, but they had learned at last how to make Presidents in democratic America.

Part III

BROTHERHOOD

Chapter 10

DEMOCRATIC
RELIGIONS

ORGANIZED Christianity probably exerted less influence upon American society during the first generation of independence than at any other time in American history. It was during this reign of "infidelity"—the spread of religious liberalism among the upper classes and of "nothingism" among the common people—that America established its independent political institutions and organized its Federal government, and it was during this period that the principle of the separation of church and state was won, by men who opposed the pretentions of organized religion to divine authority. Consequently, when, in the early nineteenth century, American society was converted to the religions of the Great Revival, the spirit of American society assumed a character never intended by the founding fathers and was, itself, forced to work within a secular framework it would never willingly have devised.

The masses of the American people in the early nineteenth century gave their allegiance to a different God than the God of the Enlightenment. Theirs was the religion of evangelism, accepting the literal word of the Bible, worshipping the God of Wrath, accepting the total depravity of man, and viewing human progress single-mindedly in terms of the mysterious process of personal salvation. Amid this emotional and anti-intellectual torrent, upper-class, literate America retained the religious tradition it had inherited from the eighteenth-century Enlightenment. Though in some quarters its religious outlook took on the emotional and irrational coloring of the Romantic Movement, it nevertheless remained closely akin to the moderate Deism of the founding fathers.

American democracy was therefore interpreted most arti-
culately, by its social philosophers and literary men, in terms
of religious liberalism and the deification of the individual,
while the main spiritual energy of democracy was created by
the evangelism of the revival meeting, with its insistence upon
social conformity. The religious spirit of American democracy
was compounded of these antagonistic liberal and evangelical
religious currents. In important respects they were obviously
incompatible with one another; yet they were never entirely
separable, and, as Reinhold Niebuhr has pointed out, they
shared many common attributes. Together they preached the
good moral life. Each believed in the perfectibility of man.
Each was convinced that America had been especially chosen
by divine providence for a special world mission. Each worked
in its own way for an American millennium. America belonged to both, and neither was entirely easy with the other.

I

The founding fathers were of the opinion that faith in revealed religion, when it opposed itself to reasonable evidence,
was an unhappy relic of barbarism. The diffusion of knowledge, they hoped, would serve to dissipate the superstitions
which surrounded Christianity. Then all good men would join
in enlightened worship of the Creator, whose glorious works
were revealed to man's rational senses in the visible wonders
of the Newtonian universe. Their God was the benevolent
and reasonable Creator, not the wrathful mysterious God of
the prophets. They viewed with genteel distaste all manifestations of what the age of John Locke had called "enthusiasm"—religion based upon irrational and emotional
appeals to faith. Not all the founders, of course, shared this
distaste, but most of the leading figures did, including Washington, Adams, Hamilton, Franklin, Mason, Madison, and
Jefferson.

These men were not professing Deists. Most of them continued to remain nominal members of the locally established church as a matter of good form. They were not anti-Christian or anti-clerical. They considered it unkind, unwise, and intruding upon the rights of others to criticize another man's religion. They distrusted all doctrinaire assertions in the field of religion, but they believed in the existence of God, the creator of the universe, and they also believed, with Voltaire, that if there were no God, it would be necessary to invent him. Franklin spoke for this utilitarian aspect of their religion when he remarked, in reference to a Deist friend who had failed to repay a debt, that Deism might be the true religion, but that it was not very useful. Jefferson distrusted church organizations for the same reason that he distrusted all large organizations. They were potential instruments of tyranny. But he did not question the need for organized religion in a republican society. "Can the liberties of a nation be thought secure," he asked, "when we have removed their only firm basis, a conviction in the minds of the people that these liberties are the gift of God?" He did not suppose it possible.

Deistical beliefs spread quietly during the eighteenth century among upper-class members of the Anglican Church in all the colonies. Liberalism in religion continued to characterize the southern ruling groups well into the national period. Although they avoided religious contests, they permitted liberalism and irreligion to flourish in the colleges where their sons were trained. The University of Virginia was organized by Jefferson on a secular basis. Transylvania College, the oldest college in the Old Southwest, remained a center of religious liberalism until the mid-twenties, when its Unitarian president, Horace Holley—though supported by the affluent classes in Kentucky—was forced to resign by pressure from the Kentucky Presbyterians. Thomas Cooper, a contentious Unitarian, became president of South Carolina College in 1821, and he remained president until 1834, to train the future leaders of the Confederacy in the more radical religious doctrines of the Enlightenment.

In Massachusetts there emerged, in contentious company with the Great Awakening and Edwardian Calvinism, an anti-Calvinistic liberalism which was readily adopted by the better class of Bostonians. Under the leadership of Charles Chauncy of First Church and Jonathan Mayhew of West Church, the Unitarian movement was already well advanced in Eastern Massachusetts by the eve of the Revolution, with its belief in the unity of God, the subordinate nature of Christ, the categorical denial of predestination, and the salvation of the individual through moral character rather than through divine election. The well-to-do in New England as elsewhere saw little in their own gracious lives to convince them of the doctrine of total depravity, and they had too great a respect for their intelligence to follow the word of the Bible where it contradicted science and common sense. They placed their faith in supernatural rationalism, the belief in a rationally ordered Newtonian universe, comprehensible to man's intelligence so far as man was able to observe its operation.

Despite attacks from orthodox Puritans, liberalism was able to develop openly in Massachusetts, because the Congregational system of church government left the individual church memberships free to practice their religions according to covenants of their own devising. It was also true that the original New England Puritans had in some respects prepared the way for nineteenth-century Unitarianism with their softening of the predestinarian aspect of Calvinism, with the independence they allotted to individual congregations, and with their own ready, confident acceptance of Newtonian science. Those early Puritans had also accepted supernatural rationalism, arguing only that it was necessarily to be supplemented by special miraculous revelation of God's will. Religious liberals in Massachusetts, for their part, did not deny the validity of revelational knowledge, but they were inclined to avoid notice of it. They preached in the spirit of John Adams when he wrote Jefferson, "Had you and I been forty days with Moses on Mount Sinai, and admitted to behold the divine Shechinah, and there told that one was three and three one, we might not have had courage to deny it, but we could not have believed it." Science had replaced religion as the highest source of truth.

The election of a Unitarian as professor of religion at Harvard College in 1805 precipitated a critical struggle within the Congregational fold, and there followed the establishment of a distinct Unitarian Church in the next generation. The Universalist Church, established simultaneously in New England, worshipped a God of Love, who would finally restore the whole of mankind to holiness and happiness. The Unitarians and the Universalists, William W. Sweet has written, were in fundamental agreement, the Unitarians insisting that man was too good to be damned, and the Universalists maintained that God was too good to damn mankind. Universalism tended to draw its converts from a lower economic class than did Unitarianism, winning many converts from the Baptists.

The Quaker gentry of Philadelphia, like the genteel Boston Congregationalists, pursued their devotions in a highly civilized atmosphere, unmarked by poverty and untrammeled by hierarchical discipline. And the Quakers, as opposed to the Boston Congregationalists, from the first had been innocent of orthodox beliefs based on the literal word of the Bible, beliefs which had served to check the humanitarian impulse in the New England Puritans. From early colonial times, the Quakers devoted themselves to the service of humanity, and in the age of Jackson the Quakers together with the Unitarians moved forth with astonishing force to achieve what they considered to be the national destiny of individual freedom and happiness. Among the Quakers, John Greenleaf Whittier, Lucretia Mott, Susan B. Anthony, Neal Dow, Angelica and Sarah Grimké became national figures in the championship of libertarian and humane causes. Among the Unitarian clergy Theodore Parker and William Ellery Channing wielded a powerful humanitarian influence upon educated people throughout the North, while Joseph Tuckerman became the great champion for the cause of philanthropy, Dorothea Dix for decent treatment of the insane, and Horace Mann for the cause of public education. Often moved by a thoroughly Puritanical zeal for moral righteousness, these religious liberals sought reforms for the sake of giving mankind a better life in this world, rather than for the sake of preparing it to meet its maker in the next.

Quakers and Unitarians, in common both with religious liberals of other non-evangelical churches and with freethinkers and atheists, together comprised that small minority within Jacksonian America which actually championed the doctrine of the separation of church and state as a positive good. But for the vast majority of church members—the Methodists, the Baptists, the Congregationalists, the Presbyterians, and the many smaller sects—the doctrine of separation of church and state was never anything other than a necessary evil. It was a necessary evil which each individual sect was obliged to bear, because none was in a position to force its own particular doctrines—the true doctrines—upon the rest of the nation. Had any one evangelical sect achieved a position of potential ascendancy over the others, there can be hardly a question that it would have renounced that blasphemous doctrine of religious liberty. While the liberal, literate minority glorified religious liberty as a cardinal tenet of American democracy, the democratic majority gave it grudging, opportunistic acceptance.

II

All religious denominations suffered during the reign of infidelity which accompanied and followed the Revolutionary War. Anglicanism was associated with treason, and disestablishment of the Anglican Church resulted in its rapid decay.

Even those dissenting churches which the war liberated suffered by its consequences. "The war," wrote a Baptist minister, "though propitious to the liberty of Baptists, had an opposite effect upon the life of religion among them . . . persecution was more favorable to vital piety, than unrestrained liberty. . . ." Even at Yale College, in the heart of Congregational orthodoxy, according to one student, "an aspiring, ambitious youth hardly dared avow his belief in the Christian religion."

Under the impact of the French Revolution, independence from Christian orthodoxy became an article of political faith for American radicals. The abolition of Christianity in France and the establishment of the Cult of Reason was reflected in America in a rising enthusiasm for Deism in Democratic-Republican clubs and mechanics associations. It became altogether clear, as a Connecticut gentleman pointed out, that "infidels in religion are apt to be Democrats." Against this alliance between infidelity and political radicalism American conservatives rallied to the support of the churches in Federal America. Washington — himself an indifferently poor churchgoer—became alarmed at the possible consequences to society of the decline in religion. "Let it simply be asked," he said in his Farewell Address, "Where is the security for property, for reputation, for life, if the sense of religious obligation desert the oaths which are the instruments of investigation in courts of justice?" Alexander Hamilton had never been noted for pretentions to piety. Faced with political defeat at the hands of the Deistical Jeffersonian Republicans, however, Hamilton commenced to think about the possibilities of forming a Christian political party to stem the tide of Jacobin radicalism, with its alleged threat to private property.

Hamilton's New York, lorded over by aristocratic religious liberals, was an unlikely state for such a party. Massachusetts, its ruling class also Federalist in politics and liberal in religion, was just as unsuited to such a political program.

The political leadership of Connecticut, however, was both politically Federalist and spiritually orthodox. Unlike the churches of Massachusetts, those of Connecticut had submitted to group control by the terms of the Saybrook Platform of 1708. Consociations of congregations had been organized to maintain unity in matters of church doctrine, while the ministers of the colony had joined themselves into associations for the same purpose. Unitarianism, as a consequence, had hardly penetrated Connecticut at the close of the eighteenth century. In Connecticut during the Federal period the alliance between political and religious orthodoxy found its leader in Timothy Dwight, president of Yale College.

Dwight, as Vernon Parrington wrote, was "a walking repository of the venerable Connecticut *status quo*," but not even Connecticut and Timothy Dwight were entirely immune to the changed spirit of the age. Without denying the doctrine of election, these clergymen yet contended that Bible reading, praying, and church attendance might have some effect upon one's salvation. Against the opposition of the old guard they encouraged revivals in order to heighten religious zeal and increase church attendance. Throughout, however, they emphasized obedience to civil and religious authority.

Within Connecticut Dwight and his colleagues were wholly successful in their efforts to revive the spirit of old religion. In 1816, the year before Dwight's death, the Fairfield County Bible Society could declare that "The present has been emphatically called the age of Bibles and Missionaries. The atheism of Voltaire and his associates, is gone down, almost with their dust to the grave. The blasphemies of Paine are remembered only to be abhorred." Nor was Connecticut satisfied to put its own house in order. In 1798 the Connecticut Home Missionary Society was formed to bring true religion to the wild society of the new West. In the view of the Connecticut clergymen, theirs was the twin mission of spreading Calvinism and Federalism among the infidel Republicans of the West. "The happiness of the rising generation," the Society declared in its preamble, "and the order and stability of civil government are most effectively advanced by the diffusion of religious and moral sentiments through the preaching of the gospel."

The Connecticut missionaries wrought mightily, and especially in the field of higher education they made a lasting mark upon the West; yet they fought a losing fight. The spread of Congregationalism was not at all commensurate with the volume of the westward movement of New Englanders alone. Although Congregationalism thrived in many areas of the West, it remained primarily a New England religion. The best hope of the eastern conservatives, Connecticut Congregationalism failed to dominate western society and failed also to bring Connecticut Federalism in its train. Eastern advocates of steady habits and property rights received the answer to their prayers, not from the activities of their own church, but from other, newer sects, mainly the Baptist and Methodist, which overwhelmed Congregationalism to become the truly national religions of democratic America.

Among the old established eastern religious denominations the Presbyterians were in the western missionary field earlier than the Congregationalists and proved more successful in establishing themselves throughout the nation. In the late 1780's Presbyterian missionaries from Hampden-Sydney and Washington Colleges in Virginia moved across the Appalachians to bring religion to the West. In 1801 a Plan of Union was arranged between Congregational and Presbyterian churches to unite in western missionary work.

In this arrangement the advantage lay with the Presbyterians who gained membership from the resulting "Presbygationalism." At the same time, they suffered from this plan doctrinal and organizational difficulties which left them rent by faction to a greater degree than any other frontier religious sect. Under any circumstances, neither Presbyterianism nor Congregationalism was destined to become the national religion of democracy. Both were too closely associated with the aristocratic doctrine of election. The insistence of both upon a formally trained ministry limited them to a distinctly eastern and elite ministry, ill at ease and distrusted in western society. They proved no equal match for the Baptist farmer-preacher and the Methodist circuit rider, men of the western world, talking in language the West understood, and preaching a way to salvation open to all men equally. It was the Baptists and Methodists pre-eminently who lighted the flame of the Great Revival, that main spiritual energy of democratic America.

The tremendously rapid rise of the Baptist Church in the early ninteenth century was due, in the opinion of William Warren Sweet, to the simplicity of its doctrine, the democracy of its organization, and its ability to extend itself without great administrative apparatus. The distinctive dogma of the Baptist Church lay in its belief in adult baptism. Like the Congregationalists, the Baptists lacked the cohesive force of a central organization; unlike the Congregationalists they had lacked also the advantage of state support. More than any other important religious denomination in the United States they relied upon the zeal of the individual member and of the individual church. Their experience opposed them bitterly to state control of religion and to the entire idea of an educated elite ministry.

Choosing their preachers from their own numbers, the Baptists argued out their own doctrine and cared for their own souls. At monthly meetings attended by all members, the individual churches meted out discipline to erring members, punishing members for dishonest business dealings, harmful gossip, adultery, and other misconduct. Religious disputes within Baptist congregations resulted in the splitting away of dissenting groups and the multiplication of varieties of

Baptist sects. Quarreling among themselves, the Baptists united in their opposition to the Presbyterians and Methodists, and united with the Presbyterians and Methodists in their struggle for the moral regeneration of society. By the close of the Republican era they ranked with the Methodists as by far the most popular of the Protestant denominations in America.

The sweeping success of Methodism demonstrated again that rising American democracy prized equality above liberty. The Methodist Church, unlike the Baptist Church, was highly centralized and rigidly authoritarian in its administrative structure, and the Baptists attacked the Methodists vigorously on those grounds. Violent struggles went on ceaselessly within the Church also, resulting in numerous schisms and in the development of new sects. Nevertheless the highly centralized organization, far from alienating the common people, enabled the Church, injured during and after the Revolution by its Loyalist leadership, to spread rapidly in the nineteenth century. For, while the Methodist Church was authoritarian in its organization, it was thoroughly equalitarian both in doctrine and in the conduct of its ministry. It stressed freedom of the will against predestination, and it stressed the responsibility of the individual for his own salvation. On the local level much of the responsibility for organizational matters rested with lay members of the church, while the ministry itself was recruited from among the people it served, without requiring an esoteric training in theology. The anti-intellectual bias was never as pronounced in the Methodist Church as it was in the Baptist, however, and after 1816 candidates for the ministry were obliged at least to take a course of readings.

The camp meeting was the great agency of the evangelical churches, especially the Methodist Church, for saving souls and winning churchmembers. Thousands of people gathered together for days at a time to sing hymns, drink in the exhortations of the preachers, and work themselves up to the experience of salvation. To the westerners living among the lonely terrors of frontier life the horrid descriptions of hellfire and damnation touched a responsive cord. The frenzies of revivalistic emotion produced peculiar reactions —talking in tongues, barking, jerks, running, jumping, and passing out. Such excesses were discouraged by church leaders, and yet it was impossible to draw the line between the true experience of salvation and the fraudulent experience marked by emotional excesses. The test of salvation came later, after the heated confession of sins, in the orderly life of moral earnestness which characterized the soul truly saved from the burning pit.

By mid-century the Methodist Church included a membership of more than a million, while the Baptist Churches were not far behind. Protestant church membership had risen from 365,000 in 1800 to 3,500,000. In comparison to the total national population, the victory appears somewhat less impressive. Only about one-seventh of the non-Catholic population was made up of churchmembers, compared to present-day membership, technically at least, of more than one-half. However, the great majority of modern churchmembers are not required to undergo the religious experience of personal salvation or to believe in the literal word of the Bible and the literal existence of a Hell where souls burn in torment. They are not obliged to confess their sins before the congregation of their neighbors or to submit to the scrutiny of the church members into the affairs of their daily lives. The majority of the people meanwhile quickly accepted the standards of the evangelical churches, even if they did not all equally experience the inner compulsion to moral earnestness.

The swiftness of the reformation in the rural areas of America was breathtaking. Six years after the start of the gold rush in California the Protestant ministry forced an anti-saloon measure upon the state and, while failing to win the state as a whole, actually secured a majority in its favor throughout the gold mining country. The majority of settlers had not joined churches in the gold mining country, but they had accepted the standards of the churches, even though they may not personally have lived by these standards.

By the time of Jackson's election the Great Revival had established its dominion. "Religion in America," Alexis de Tocqueville wrote, "takes no direct part in the government of society, but it must be regarded as the first of their political institutions; for if it does not impart a taste for freedom, it facilitates the use of it. . . ." Tocqueville found it hard to believe that many Americans were not hypocritical in their attitude toward religion. "But the revolutionists of America are obliged to profess an ostensible respect for Christian morality and equity, which does not permit them to violate wantonly the laws that opposed their designs. . . . Thus while the law permits the Americans to do what they please, religion prevents them from conceiving and forbids them to commit, what is rash or unjust." Religion had succeeded, as eastern conservatives hoped it would, in imposing morality and stability upon society. In the process, however, religion developed an equalitarian zeal which helped to level the standards of aristocracy.

III

American literalists and liberals alike believed in the perfectibility of man. Liberals subscribed to the faith that man could redeem himself through his own good nature, if he were freed from ignorance through educational reform and if his environment were reformed to permit the development of his natural capacity for goodness. Orthodox Christians, for their part, read in the books of Daniel and Revelations of the coming millennium, when Christ would return to earth and, with his saints, rule for a thousand years. A belief that the millennium was almost at hand lent a special urgency to the mission of the evangelical religious leaders.

They must hurry to rid the world of sin, through the instrument of personal salvation, in time to prepare society for the second coming.

Millennialism, based upon a literal interpretation of the Bible, received learned support during the early nineteenth century from such academic leaders as the presidents of Yale, Rutgers, and Union Colleges. As the century wore on, however, millennialism lost its currency in academic circles, even among the supposedly orthodox. "If we can visualize a stratigraphical chart of the American intellect," wrote Dixon Ryan Fox,

> we can see this idea dropping through one social layer after another. In one decade it has largely left the academic stratum and in another it is well through that of the general educated class. Soon it is seen most conspicuously among such folk as the Mormons and the Millerites. Now and again some shred may be discerned lingering in the upper layers; one sees it in the *Essay on the Millennium* of the President of Dartmouth in 1854 and in the writings of some men of collegiate training who thought Napoleon III would probably turn out to be the Anti-Christ. But the course of the mass of it seems steadily downward.

Nevertheless, throughout the first half of the nineteenth century the idea of the achievement of millennial glories upon earth continued to inspire with zeal men who were no longer disposed to argue a literal belief in the second coming.

The great energies of the evangelical sects were spent upon the regeneration of mankind which would prepare the world for the second coming. The temperance and abolitionist movements were impelled by this fundamentalist theological spirit. As far as philanthropy for its own sake was concerned, the evangelical sects generally preached that charity was a Christian duty. At the same time, it seemed to members of these churches that charity was a rather weak and perhaps not altogether wise gesture. They preferred to attack the problem at the root, by bringing all men to the life of earnest moral striving. Once the souls of men had been saved, the superficial signs of social disorder would vanish.

This line of reasoning is evident, for instance, in the annual reports of the New York Society for the Prevention of Pauperism for the years 1818 to 1824. On the basis of its observations during these years the society listed the causes of pauperism as: 1) ignorance, 2) idleness, 3) intemperance, 4) want of economy, 5) imprudent and hasty marriages, 6) lotteries, 7) pawnbrokers, 8) houses of ill fame, 9) gambling houses, and 10) the numerous charitable institutions of the city. The leading causes of pauperism, in the view of the society, all stemmed directly from moral weakness on the part of the pauper. At a time of primitive medical techniques and sanitation methods, when the cities in particular suffered periodic epidemics of disease, ill health did not suggest itself to this society as one of the chief contributions to pauperism, nor did accidental misfortune of any other kind. These ills were basically moral rather than social. Christian charity demanded that these souls be kept alive; yet charity in turn only increased pauperism. The one true cure was the reformation of the moral character of these paupers through religious instruction and example. Therefore, while the evangelical sects found themselves necessarily involved in charitable activities, they reserved their enthusiastic efforts for the establishment of churches, of home missionary societies, and of tract societies, to root out the evil rather than attend to its manifestations.

American literalists and liberals were one in the faith that God had entrusted Americans with a special mission to extend Christian goodness through the world. There was infinite disagreement as to the exact nature of the special mission, but the hand of God was almost universally seen to be working through American history. The unfolding of God's plan had been the main theme of Cotton Mather's history of the New England churches. In the next century it remained the main theme of the Jacksonian Democrat George Bancroft's history of the United States. What other explanation was sufficient to account for America having been reserved as virgin territory through the centuries, until the reformation of Christianity in Europe produced a society fit to found a new Christian order? Even American atheists were brought to the conclusion that America was especially blessed by fortune and had, as a consequence, a special mission to lead the world away from error. They yielded to none in their zeal to achieve the millennium upon the chosen ground of American soil.

Clearly America was blessed by God over the nations of Europe. Still, in the colonial and early national periods men continued to have doubts concerning God's intentions. The early Puritan leaders were obsessed with the fear that the blasphemies of those who disagreed with them would bring God's vengeance upon all the residents of the New Zion. In the secular atmosphere of Revolutionary and Federal America the hand of God was not seen so clearly by religious leaders. Those who were most concerned to see God's plan in American life were not altogether able to trace its outlines in the election of Jefferson as President. "I do not believe," wrote Thomas Robbins of Connecticut in 1800, "that the Most High will permit a howling atheist to sit at the head of this nation!" The election of Jefferson, although it might accord in some quarters with the designs of the benevolent Creator of the universe, was to New England orthodoxy a mysterious and ominous portent.

The event which galvanized the whole nation into a firm belief in God's special favor was the battle of New Orleans at the close of the War of 1812. The battle followed upon three years of indecisive, vacillating struggle, which had been marked by national disunity and by numerous igno-minious defeats. The United States had appeared to be at the point of hopeless disintegration, not by force of powerful invading armies, but through internal weakness and simple inability to defend itself against such motley forces as Britain was able to spare from the Napoleonic conflict. Then came news simultaneously of peace based upon unexpectedly favorable terms and of a miraculously overwhelming victory against the British at New Orleans. The American republic suddenly and incredibly emerged from the struggle in a blaze of glory to vindicate the principles of republicanism against the attack of Old World monarchy. Federalist New England, at the very moment when it was considering the advisability of withdrawing from the nation altogether, was swept along in the rush of patriotism which followed the news of the victory and the peace.

To explain so miraculous a turn of events it was not sufficient to deal merely in such matters as diplomacy and military tactics. "The God of Battles and of Righteousness took part with the defenders of their country, and the foe was scattered as chaff before the wind," a Congressman told the House of Representatives. The result would point to Europe the moral that "It is only necessary that we judiciously employ the means which God and Nature have bountifully placed at our disposal." In New Orleans after the battle, the Abbé Guillaume Dubourg, at the suggestion of General Jackson, chanted a Mass in thanks for victory. "Immortal thanks," the abbé declared, "be to His supreme majesty, for sending us such a gift of his bountiful designs! A gift of that value is the best token of the continuance of his protection—the most solid encouragement to us to sue for new favours." To which the most fervent hatred of Catholicism could hardly have enjoined a Baptist or a Methodist from saying Amen. In the period that followed, as John Ward writes, "the people of the United States were predisposed to find God's special favor in nearly every passing event."

The triumphant conclusion to the war ushered in a period of perfervid nationalism, when it was generally supposed that

God was working through the people of the United States to make a new nation more nearly according to His designs than any of the Old World nations. A virtuous republic was His aim, and His instrument was the common man. Nationalism, evangelicalism, and democracy fused together in the new American crusade. The nation was caught up in a common sense of mission which each American might interpret according to his own fashion. Even Robert Owen, Englishman, atheist, and opponent of the institutions of marriage and private property, found in the national spirit the embodiment of his desires. "The United States," he declared, "but particularly the States west of the Allegheny Mountains have been prepared in the most remarkable manner for the New System. . . . In fact the whole of this country is ready to commence a new empire upon the principle of public property & to discard private property." Met with sharp struggles in his colony of New Harmony, Owen was soon under bitter attack from the press and pulpits of the nation for his views on religion and marriage. Yet, despite the fury and volume of these denunciations, the Owenites, in common with participants in other such unpopular projects, remained convinced that they represented the true cause, or at least one of the true causes, for which God or fate had been preparing the American nation. Amid bewildering diversity of aims and opinions, this sense of spiritual destiny bound together the triumphant American republic, especially outside the slave states, in the years after the War of 1812.

Chapter 11

THE AMERICAN
MISSION

W HEN in the Course of human events," declared the American revolutionists, "it becomes necessary for one people to dissolve the political bands which have connected them with another . . . a decent respect to the opinions of mankind requires that they should declare the causes which impel them to the separation." The patriots were alive to the fact that they were acting out a drama before a world audience. Three generations later the citizens of democratic America were no less conscious of this audience. Theirs was the nation which had been conceived in liberty and dedicated to the proposition that all men are created equal. Theirs remained the special mission of testing whether such a nation could long endure. Providence, Andrew Jackson told his countrymen in his farewell address, had chosen Americans as "the guardians of freedom to preserve it for the benefit of the human race."

In fact democratic America demonstrated a downright *in*decent respect to the opinions of mankind. It became the universal complaint of foreign travelers that Americans everywhere made nuisances of themselves with their endless fishing for compliments. Was not America the freest nation on earth? Were its people not the happiest and healthiest to be found anywhere? Was not its government the model upon which all other governments ought to reform themselves? Was such a thriving energetic society ever known in other places and other times? Foreigners could not escape these embarrassing questions, nor were they permitted to answer them in the negative. They could only bide their time until, returning to

England or Europe, they might revenge themselves in that book about their American travels, a revenge which was the sweeter for the wide sales such books commanded in America.

Most Americans, actually, were content to preserve freedom for the human race simply by making their own way in the free America they found about them. To the extent that they experienced any positive missionary zeal it was most apt to be the zeal to "extend the area of freedom" into rich adjacent lands at the expense of Mexico and the British Empire and in this way achieve America's "manifest destiny." There remained innumerable Americans with other missions, involving not only the preservation and possibly the extension of freedom, but the perfecting of it as well. The multifarious enthusiasms of these idealists produced a kaleidoscope of innovation and reform in democratic America.

But always there crouched that one gross, shocking offense against freedom, Negro slavery. However much these various reformers would have liked to go on tending their own fires, they could not escape this volatile issue. That old, original, confident democracy of Young America did have a manifest destiny, which, after a generation of distracting change, it faced at last.

I

Americans were alive to the fact that the downfall of their democracy was hopefully awaited by the ruling classes of Europe, and that the hopes of the common people of Europe rode upon the continued success of free American institutions. In truth America's consciousness of its own importance in European eyes greatly exceeded the fact of it. What happened in America did always interest Europeans, but it never could be made to seem entirely relevant to Europe's own affairs, in the way Americans thought it ought to be. The American Revolution aroused excited speculation in France in the years before 1789, and it encouraged French radicals to assert their own natural rights. Yet the advice of the American minister to France, Thomas Jefferson, seemed to the French revolutionists who gathered in his drawing room strangely out of harmony with their own purposes—too cautious, too conservative, too little governed by clear-cut theoretical principles. The fact of American democracy encouraged the English Whigs who were fighting for political reform in 1832, and, largely through Tocqueville's writings, it influenced European liberalism throughout the next generation. Yet it remained for Europeans an exotic experiment which could not be applied to the cribbed and crowded Old World. Throughout the nineteenth century, Russian reformers and revolutionists of all colors eagerly collected writings and rumors concerning the wonderful United States and its radical political system. But their America remained hardly less distorted than the *Amerika* of Franz Kafka, who wrote his fantastic novel because "I know the autobiography of Benjamin Franklin, and I always admired Walt Whitman, and I like the Americans because they are healthy and optimistic."

Americans sometimes talked as though they had a positive mission to win the whole world to democracy, but as a nation they never acted upon the thought. They cheered the French Revolution as a victory for American principles of liberty, and radicals among them organized pro-French Democratic-Republican clubs. Their enthusiasm was so boisterous that Citizen Genet believed he could win the American people to active aid in the French war against England. Quite to the contrary, within four years a chauvinistic America cheered on an undeclared naval war against France instead.

The Greek Revolution in the 1820's aroused the American sense of democratic mission once more. Jefferson was fired with enthusiasm. John Adams declared that his "heart beat in unison with the Greeks." Greek relief committees were organized. Individual American volunteers joined the Greek army, and Congress discussed ways in which the weight of American opinion might be made effective on the Greek side. But upon second thought America contented itself with President Monroe's vague statement that "The citizens of the United States cherished sentiments the most friendly in favor of the liberty and happiness of their fellowmen on that side of the Atlantic." The occasion for the statement was the enunciation of the Monroe Doctrine, greeted in America with universal enthusiasm, reaffirming the isolationist policy of Washington, Adams, and Jefferson. "In the wars of the European powers in matters relating to themselves," Monroe declared, "we have never taken any part, nor does it comport with our policy to do so."

The European revolutions of 1848 again momentarily aroused the spirit of democratic evangelism toward Europe, and the Federal government itself so far overstepped the isolationism of the Monroe Doctrine as to send an emissary to Hungary while the Hungarian revolution was still in course, "in impatience for the downfall of the Austrian monarchy," as the Austrian *charge d'affaires* complained. But with the failure of the revolutions of 1848 Americans once again quickly and easily gave up Europe as past hope of redemption.

There remained, in addition, a rather small number of people who thought that America had the mission to bring peace to all the world. In 1815 two peace societies, very likely the first of their kind anywhere in the world, were organized, one in New York by the wealthy Presbyterian merchant, David Low Dodge, and the other in Boston by the Unitarian minister, William Ellery Channing. In 1828 the movement was revived under the leadership of William Ladd with the organization of the American Peace Society. Following Ladd's death in 1841 the cause was taken up by Elihu Burritt, the "learned blacksmith." The movement maintained an impressive honorary membership and issued much literature, but, except among the Quakers, it appears to have received the devoted attention of only a handful of people. Joel Barlow in 1787 had supposed that "the example of political wisdom and felicity, here displayed, will excite emulation throughout the kingdoms of the earth, and meliorate the condition of the human race." It was chiefly in this sense that Americans understood their duty to the world. American democracy continued to pose as the model of freedom, but the kingdoms of the earth, still enmeshed in decadent feudalism, were plainly lost to wisdom and virtue.

However it was really Europe, rather than the whole world, to which America addressed its isolationist policy. Asia, although no doubt an unpromising area for the extension of democratic institutions, at least was not lost to Roman Catholicism, as was most of Europe. Latin America, on the other hand, although irrevocably Roman Catholic, had nevertheless thrown off monarchical control. More important, both Asia and Latin America, unlike Europe, were areas where America might make its political and social influence felt. In the thirties and forties American evangelical churches sent missionaries to India, China, Hawaii, and the South Sea Islands to bring Christian American civilization to the Orient in the name of the brotherhood of man. In the western hemisphere, meanwhile, America assumed the responsibility, in theory if not in practice, of defending the newly established American republics against possible designs of the Concert of Europe. By the Monroe Doctrine the United States pledged itself to make the Americas safe for republican institutions.

Some Americans, among them Henry Clay, appeared to have been sincerely roused by the vision of a western hemisphere united by common adherence to the republican principles of freedom. John Quincy Adams, the chief architect of the Monroe Doctrine, had no such illusions. He wished simply to keep Europe out of the Americas so far as possible and to open Latin America to American influence and to American trade. He did not suppose that Latin America was fitted for democratic government; nor did most other Americans. The actual extension of freedom, Americans became convinced, could be accomplished only by the expansion of the free American people themselves. By the forties Young America had merged its democratic missionary zeal with the immensely attractive notion that the manifest destiny of American democracy was to extend itself, by conquest if necessary, throughout North America.

The idea of extending freedom by means of the westward migration of American pioneers was not always a rationalization for territorial aggrandizement. Jefferson had envisioned a westward movement to the Pacific Coast which would people the continent "with free and independent Americans, unconnected with us but by the ties of blood and interest, and employing like us the rights of self-government." At the turn of the nineteenth century the idea of an actual transcontinental republic had seemed too farfetched to warrant consideration. It was feared by many that the original thirteen states already comprised too large an area to be governed successfully under republican institutions, not to speak of the problem of maintaining a continental republic. The acquisition of Louisiana Territory in 1803 seemed to many—particularly to many New England Federalists—to foreshadow the subversion of the Constitution and the disruption of the republic.

A generation of westward advance and of new statemaking served to dissipate these fears, even among New England conservatives. By 1824 even Edward Everett, the pattern of Boston gentility, believed that the indefinite extension of freedom had been made practicable.

> . . . by the wise and happy partition of powers between the national and state governments, in virtue of which the national government is relieved from all the odium of internal administration, and the state governments are spared the conflicts of foreign politics, all bounds seem removed from the possible extension of our country, but the geographical limits of the continent.

By the decade of the thirties, writes Albert K. Weinberg, every apprehension of incompatibility between democracy and the geographical extent of America had disappeared, and Americans were accustoming themselves to the idea of a continental democracy.

By the forties the nation was aggressively alive to its manifest destiny. Texas was an independent republic clamoring to be admitted to the Union. To the west California, rich with possibilities, was but loosely held in Mexican hands, and the Mexicans were doing almost nothing to settle and develop it. Oregon country was undergoing the bracing influence of American settlement, and the United States had some color of claim to that territory as far north as Russian Alaska. But merely technical arguments did scant justice to the American claims. Canada itself, the only nation in the Americas still "shackled" by monarchy, was destined to be freed from British "enslavement," by the force, not of legal claim, but of destiny. To the south Cuba would fall to America as naturally as ripe fruit from a tree, and if it did not fall of itself, then it would be picked. America would make honest payment to Spain, declared three American diplomats in 1854 in their "Ostend Manifesto," but if Spain should decline to sell, "then by every law human and divine, we should be justified in wresting it from Spain." American filibustering expeditions did what they could in an informal way to bring Central America as well into freedom's orbit.

In the absence of the slavery controversy these would perhaps not have been unrealizeable assertions. It seemed to Tocqueville that "At a period which may be said to be near,— for we are speaking of the life of a nation,—the Anglo- Americans alone will cover the immense space contained between the polar regions and the tropics, extending from the coast of the Atlantic to those of the Pacific Ocean." At the time he wrote, there were probably few Americans who would have cared to take issue. Manifest destiny served to annex to

the prodigiously acquisitive appetite of Young America and
to its romantic nationalism wide realms of American idealism.
It conjured up visions of the expansion of democracy, the conversion of Catholics and heathens to true Christianity, the defense of the western hemisphere against the designs of Old
World monarchy, and the opening of land for settlement
by independent freeholders to the thousandth and thousandth
generation.

But in the thirties and forties the prospect of a tropic
Caribbean empire of slavery rose insistently in northern minds
and mocked these ideals. John Quincy Adams, as Monroe's
Secretary of State, had pursued vigorously a policy based upon
"the idea of considering our proper dominion to be the continent of North America." By the forties he was still defending
America's manifest destiny to move northward to the arctic
circle, but he was no longer so certain of America's moral
right against the claims of Mexico to the slaveholding Republic of Texas. The enemies of slavery could not prevent
the acquisition of Texas. They could not prevent the Mexican
War and the march to the Pacific, but in the fifties America
stood deadlocked against itself, half slave and half free, face
to face at last with that destiny which it had vainly attempted,
by ignoring, to avoid.

II

Idealistic Americans, in the meantime, devoted themselves
to the achievement, within the nation's expanding boundaries,
of a democratic and Christian millennium. Although the idea
of an imminent last day of judgment had lost its authority
among the upper classes, it remained a vital force with evangelical churchmembers, and in the forties it became the basis
for a new religion, Seventh Day Adventism. And though
upper-class reformers did not strive in the expectation of a
second coming, they nevertheless did retain a holy vision of
the coming millennium, when society on earth would have
perfected itself.

"We are all a little wild here with numberless projects of social reform," Emerson wrote Carlyle in 1840. "Not a reading man but has a draft of a new Community in his waistcoat pocket." At a convention in Boston of the Friends of Universal Reform, Emerson found "Madmen, madwomen, men with beards, Dunkers, Muggletonians, Come-outers, Groaners, Agrarians, Seventh Day Baptists, Quakers, Abolitionists, Calvinists, Unitarians, and Philosophers—all came successively to the top, and seized their moment, if not their hour, wherein to chide, or pray or preach or protest." There were phrenological enthusiasts who would achieve the social millennium by moulding children's heads in such a way as to eliminate mental evils and foster socially benign thought processes. There were others who would harness mesmerism or animal magnetism or phrenomagnetic manipulation or the principle of "amativeness" to the perfection of society.

These were a few of the dregs produced by what Alice Felt Tyler has called "freedom's ferment." They did not result from the impact of democracy upon the ignorant and gullible common man so much as they represented the impact of democracy upon the gullible, upper-class, idealistic intellectuals. "The astounding thing about almost all of the quackeries, fads and movements of the past hundred years in America," wrote Gilbert Seldes, "is that they were first accepted by superior people, by men and women of education, intelligence, breeding, wealth and experience. Only after the upper classes had approved, the masses accepted each new thing." It is also true that the great humanitarian reforms of the age were chiefly upper-class responses to democracy, which the masses came but slowly to support. Social idealism among the uneducated classes concentrated itself chiefly upon combating sin through the propagation of the Gospel and through the temperance and anti-slavery crusades. The educated classes did not avoid these crusades, but they found scope for a wide variety of additional enthusiasms.

There was Sylvester Graham, who believed that dietary reform would create the perfect society. Others caught Graham's vision. Ladies' Physiological Reform Societies did what they could to propagate Grahamism. Graham boarding houses sprang up, and the use of Graham bread and Graham crackers became common. But it is not to be supposed that Graham and his followers were narrowly dietetic in outlook. They believed they had found the straight road to the millennium. Dietary reform Graham declared, "lies at the foundation of all others" as the basis for the general reform of society. Allied with the Grahamites were the hydropaths, who borrowed the water cure from Germany and applied water internally and externally in great quantities to achieve the bodily perfection which would lead to the perfection of society.

There was Amelia Jenks Bloomer, the dress reformer whose name, like Dr. Graham's, remained to enrich the English language. Mrs. Bloomer advocated for women, in the interests of health and freedom of action, the wearing of a short skirt over loose trousers gathered at the ankles. Idealistic American women braved the ridicule of society to emancipate their sex from costumes which were uncomfortable and unhealthful vestiges of women's supposed inferiority to men. Anti-corset societies exacted pledges from women not to wear certain categories of undergarments. Nor did the Grahamites, the hydropaths, and the Bloomerites strive in vain. As Richard Shryock has noted, their millennium was finally achieved in America with a vengeance. The time came when persons who were known to take three baths a week were not held up to derision, when interest in diet was viewed as sensible, and when ladies' dress reform passed beyond the wildest imaginings of the Victorian female radicalism of democratic America. If the result was not clearly a better moral order, few American men or women would deny that it had been worth the fight.

Dress reform was a major phase of the democratic struggle for women's rights, which reached an unimpressive climax in 1848 in the Woman's Rights Convention at Seneca Falls, New York. There the leading feminists of the day, including Lucretia Mott and Elizabeth Cady Stanton, drew up a declaration of the equality of women with men. They demanded legal equality and, amid some dissent, the right to vote. They were signally unsuccessful on both counts in their own lifetimes. The advanced legal position of American over English women was inherited from colonial times and was not extended. In 1860 the jurist David Dudley Field could still declare:

> A married woman cannot sue for her services, as all she earns legally belongs to the husband, whereas his earnings belong to himself, and the wife legally has no interest in them. Where children have property and both parents are living, the father is the guardian. In case of the wife's death without a will, the husband is entitled to all her personal property and to a life interest in the whole of her real estate to the entire exclusion of her children. . . . If a husband die without a will, the widow is entitled to one-third of the personal property and to a life interest in one-third only of the real estate. . . . The father may by deed or will appoint a guardian for the minor children, who may thus be taken entirely away from the jurisdiction of the mother at his death. . . .

From colonial times women had been admitted to the business life of the community, and it was common for a widow to assume the role of her deceased husband as editor of a newspaper or head of a business. This continued to be the case in Jacksonian America. In the area of higher education, the women's rights advocates won some important gains. With the opening of Troy Female Seminary in 1819 the principle was asserted that women could usefully be trained in fields of higher education. With the opening of Oberlin College to women in the thirties, the principle was asserted that women and men could be educated on a basis of equality.

The widespread extension of this principle, however, awaited the rise of the state universities following the Civil War.

Among the brightest and most fleeting manifestations of social idealism in democratic America were the Utopian communities, which appeared profusely and lived briefly, amid hostile surroundings, and vanished with hardly a trace. The most famous such community in the 1820's, New Harmony, was founded by the English manufacturer and Utopian socialist Robert Owen. Cordially welcomed in America by a respectful Congress and an admiring nation, Owen soon brought himself under bitter attack for his outspoken criticism of religion and of the institution of marriage. New Harmony, meanwhile, suffered almost at once from internal antagonisms. Attacked from within and without, the experiment collapsed, bringing financial ruin to Owen, after a long and incredibly successful business career.

A generation later a number of new Utopian experiments were undertaken in accordance with theories developed by the French socialist, Francois Fourier. Like Owen, Fourier envisioned a social system which was the very negation of individualistic American democracy in its belief in the evils of free competition, and the very negation of American evangelical morality, based as Fourierism was on the theory of the social benevolence of unrestrained human passions. Yet it was in America, the new land of unbounded optimism, and not in France, that Fourierism found its most active adherents, often among men who were thoroughly unsympathetic to the equalitarian politics of the Jacksonians. Its most effective champions, as Arthur M. Schlesinger, Jr., has pointed out, were such upper-class whiggish intellectuals as Albert Brisbane, Park Godwin, and Charles A. Dana.

Brook Farm, the most famous of the Utopian communities, was unsuccessful even by comparison with other contemporary experiments. It gained its fame from the distinction of some of its members. Hawthorne joined briefly,

while Emerson, Bronson Alcott, Margaret Fuller, and Theodore Parker were all to some extent associated with it. The
community lasted but three years in its original form and
disbanded completely several years after that. A second attempt participated in by Alcott, the community of Fruitlands,
owed what brief success it enjoyed to the inclusion among
its members of one able and industrious farmer—he of the
beard, Joseph Palmer. Of all these experiments the most successful was the Oneida Community, directed for thirty-two
years by John Humphrey Noyes. Its dissolution was finally
brought about through outside opposition to its system of
multiple marriages; not through internal dissention.

More successful than any of these were the Shaker and
the Rappite communities, which were religious movements
rather than social experiments. One such religious community, the Mormon state of Deseret, was permanently successful. The secular social experiments all failed, however,
and so far as they influenced American democracy they did
so by the completeness of their failure, which confirmed
America in its faith in individualism, if such confirmation
were needed.

III

More sober and enduring manifestations of upper-class
reforming enthusiasm appeared in the expansion of that
humanitarian spirit which had made its first general appearance in the Revolutionary era. In democratic America
the humanitarian spirit was aroused chiefly by the novel and
ominous consequences of industrialization, urbanization, and
ever increasing immigration, mainly from impoverished Catholic Ireland. In attacking the resulting conditions of crime,
pauperism, slums, insanity, intemperance, and ill health, the
humanitarian reformers were forced to struggle, not only
against a hostile American opinion, but also against some
of their own most ingrained American ideals. These new
immigrants crowding into city slums were a vast swarming

offense to the democratic ideal of America as the land of
opportunity for all who would put an honest hand to the
plow. They were an offense against the Protestant ideal of
America as the last best hope for a Christian civilization. Few
of the humanitarian reformers of the day could emancipate
themselves from an unwavering faith in the efficacy of self-
help and from the conviction that slum conditions were
founded upon the viciousness of slum-dwellers rather than
upon the environment of a rankly expanding industrial society.
Consequently the achievements of the humanitarians were
most impressive in areas—notably the area of popular education—where the ideal of self-help was a practical guide, and
were least impressive in meeting the problem of urban poverty,
where the ideal of self-help was so often exasperatingly
irrelevant.

Robert M. Hartley, who served for more than thirty years
as secretary of the New York Association for Improving the
Condition of the Poor, was the most important single figure
in American philanthrophy in the middle of the nineteenth
century. Yet Hartley brought to his great labors a Christian
compassion unsupported by any sympathetic understanding
of the problems facing the impoverished. Concerning the
"debased poor" he declared, "They love to clan together in
some out-of-the-way place, are content to live in filth and
disorder with a bare subsistence, provided they can drink, and
smoke, and gossip, and enjoy their balls, and wakes, and
frolics, without molestation."

In Boston the Unitarian ministers William Ellery Channing and Theodore Parker denounced the ill treatment of the
poor. Parker defended the poor aggressively against the aspersions of the comfortable Christian classes. "Some city missionary," he declared, "may dawdle the matter as he will; tell
them it is God's will they should be dirty and ignorant, hungry,
cold and naked. Now and then a poor woman starving with
cold and hunger may think it true. But the poor know better;

ignorant as they are, they know better." Parker's suggested solutions—chiefly organized charity—nevertheless remained woefully inadequate to the problem he described.

To the criminal classes the humanitarian reformers brought relief from many barbaric cruelties, as well as stricter discipline than formerly. Removal of the sentence of imprisonment for debt, begun during the panic of 1819, continued apace during and after the panic of 1837, supported by the full force of Jacksonian democracy. Capital punishment became limited to the crime of murder in certain states, and sentiment was growing to abolish it altogether, in defiance, even, of Mosaic Law. Such punishment as branding, cropping of the ears, and the public flogging of half-naked women were being removed from the penal codes and had already become exceptional in democratic America. The old practice was largely discontinued of ducking women convicted of being "common scolds." In 1829 the practice was discontinued in Massachusetts of tattooing upon each convict the words "Massachusetts State Prison." Public executions, formerly held as a deterrent to crime, were discontinued in one state after another, mainly on the grounds that they actually served as sadistic carnivals for the vicious classes.

With reform in the penal codes went widespread reform in prison systems as well. The old Connecticut copper mine prison closed down, and similar expedients were abandoned elsewhere. Prisons accepted the services of chaplains. The sexes were separated, and the health of the prisoners was cared for through proper food and exercise. Among the most influential prison reformers was Elam Lynds, the supervisor of the model prison, Sing Sing, where a separate cell was provided for each inmate, and a regime of long hard labor was instituted. The prisoners, who congregated together during working and dining hours, were kept from organizing prison breaks by a discipline of systematic terrorizing. Lynds believed that prisoners should be "tamed" with the lash. A second influential system was that developed in Pennsylvania, where the key to success was solitary confinement. Each prisoner worked and lived in an isolated cell, where he could receive only official visitors during the entire period of his sentence. These two alternate systems became patterns for prison reform in many American states by the eve of the Civil War.

Comparing the two main systems, the official French investigators of the American prisons, Tocqueville and Beaumont, were of the opinion that "the Philadelphia system produces more honest men, and that of New York more obedient citizens." They were struck at the same time, by the contrast between American penal theory and American democratic theory.

> To sum up the whole on this point it must be acknowledged that the penitentiary system in America is severe. Whilst society in the United States gives the example of the most extended liberty, the prisons of the same country offer the spectacle of the most complete despotism. The citizens subject to the law are protected by it; they only cease to be free when they become wicked.

Abolition of corporal punishment made headway in democratic America, and experiments were made with the merit system.

Treatment of the insane was transformed in a more generous spirit, chiefly under the leadership of Dorothea Dix, the Unitarian daughter of a religious fanatic. On the basis of two years' systematic inspection of the treatment of the insane in Massachusetts, she presented a memorial to the state legislature describing the cages in which the insane were kept, the cellar closet in which one madwoman was confined and the universal practice of chaining the insane and whipping them into silence. This lurid description brought in a bill enlarging and reforming the state asylum. In the years following, Dorothea Dix toured the United States presenting evidence which resulted in the construction of hospitals for the insane and the removal of the insane from ordinary prisons, in many states. In an area where self-help was so obviously out of the question, she received enthusiastic cooperation from humanitarians everywhere.

In democratic America the humanitarian spirit found its most congenial outlet in the struggle for free public education. Universal public education stood squarely upon the equalitarian ideal of a free and equal chance for all in life, It met the Jeffersonian demand for that enlightened citizenry, necessary to the maintenance of republican institutions. It answered the desire of the evangelical churches to give every soul the ability to read the Bible. It met the need of the rising business community for a literate population to fill the swelling ranks of white-collar workers. So basic was the requirement of free public education to democratic American society, the wonder was that the struggle for educational reform was such a long and hard one.

In the deep South no comprehensive systems of public education had ever been seriously contemplated, while the upper South could boast only rudimentary and haphazard school systems, to the eve of the Civil War. Except for those southern classes who could afford tutors and private schools, the population of the deep South remained densely illiterate at the eve of the Civil War. In the Northwest, provision for public education had been made in the land ordinance of 1785, but it had rarely been acted on in good faith. New England remained by far the most literate section of the nation, but with the decline in theological control the public school system in New England had fallen into decay.

The New England states took the lead in the thirties under the leadership of Horace Mann in Massachusetts, followed by Henry Barnard in Connecticut and Rhode Island. Against stalwart opposition from property and sectarian interests, these humanitarians erected school systems which became the models eventually for similar systems throughout the nation. Horace Mann, like Dorothea Dix the rebellious victim of a starkly Calvinistic childhood, remained a Puritanical Unitarian throughout his life. The purpose of his crusade for education was to bring a moral regeneration to the secular life of his state. Mann insisted that such a moral regeneration was essential to the continued existence of a Christian republic, and it was therefore the common duty of the community to support it.

Mann subjected himself to bitter, continuous attacks from conservatives, for his contention that "the property of this commonwealth is pledged for the education of all its youth, up to such a point as will save them from poverty and vice, and prepare them for the adequate performance of their social and civil duties." Even more violent was the sectarian opposition, which denounced Mann for his determination to limit religious instruction in public schools to the reading of the Bible without comment. Evangelical ministers denounced him as well for his opposition to corporal punishment in the schools, sorting as it did with Mann's infidel belief in the "native purity of children," as one minister expressed it. A zealot for his cause, Mann won the day in Massachusetts. He won over the majority of the people in the state, and by the eve of the Civil War the majority in the North accepted, in theory at least, the principle that basic education at the public expense was an American birthright.

The victories for free public education in the North were the crowning achievements of the humanitarian crusade in democratic America. More than any other reform of the age, including the extension of the suffrage, they expressed the American democratic demand for a free and equal start in life. Thereafter, almost everyone agreed, the individual was on his own, to make what he would of his career. If he failed, it behooved Christian souls to extend charity to him, but society as an organization owed him nothing. Some humanitarian preachers might argue rhetorically that it did, but only a few uninfluential radicals went so far as to propose that society accept systematically the burden of these failures. Democratic America continued to treat paupers, including the aged poor, not as evidence of defects in the social order, but as the poor which we always have with us, the consequence of that moral weakness inevitably to be found among some individuals. Except as warnings to the young or as objects of good works, they remained with the prisoners, outside the democratic system.

IV

It was a comparatively small band of reformers who had dedicated themselves to such causes as education, child welfare, treatment of the insane, and reforms in the treatment of criminals and paupers. Most of these reformers were also abolitionists and prohibitionists, however, and in these crusades they were joined by the militant hosts of the evangelical churches. Many a Methodist, Baptist, Campbellite, or Millerite was fired with the mission to free human souls while at the same time little concerned for the mere bodily welfare of his fellow man. The main force of evangelical reform worked for the moral regeneration of society, both to win individual souls to salvation and to prepare America for the coming millennium.

Nor was any important distinction made as to relative importance between the prohibitionist and the abolitionist campaigns. From the religious point of view slavery and drink were "twin evils," two aspects of the same thing, two great deterrents to a moral society and to the harvesting of souls. The drunkard and the slave were equally in a state of bondage, deprived of the free will necessary to work out their salvation. Christ would not return to earth, many millennarians believed, until drunkenness and slavery had been cleansed away.

The temperance movement in its early days was directed toward the goal of universal personal abstinence, first from hard liquor, and increasingly from all alcoholic beverages. It attempted to convert to sobriety a nation used to heavy drinking and to many drunkards. Drunkenness was widespread even among ministers in the first quarter of the nineteenth century, and increasingly it came to be viewed as the chief obstacle to the conversion of souls. A generation of unsuccessful efforts to redeem the drunkard enrolled thousands of religious men and women in the temperance crusade and turned them increasingly toward the goal of legally enforced prohibition rather than universal voluntary abstinence.

The first major landmark in the history of prohibition was the passage of the Maine prohibitory liquor law in 1846. The evangelical reformers immediately deserted the generation-long temperance campaign for the new fight for state-wide "Maine laws." Legislative successes followed swiftly. Prohibition was enacted in Massachusetts, Vermont, Rhode Island, and the Territory of Minnesota in 1852, Michigan in 1853, Connecticut in 1854, and New York, New Hampshire, Delaware, Indiana, and the Territory of Nebraska in 1855. In that year the corresponding secretary of the American Temperance Union stood, as he thought, upon the threshold of universal victory. "The North will give up, and the South keep not back; and men in other countries are already hailing and welcoming this as one of those moral revolutions which occur, under God, in the course of ages, to root out sin and sorrow, and usher in millennial glories."

As events proved, 1855 was the high water mark of the prohibitionist movement until the twentieth century. By that year the anti-slavery movement had leapt into national prominence, absorbing the energies of thousands of men who formerly had devoted themselves chiefly to the cause of temperance. Slavery as a national political issue forced itself before the nation, disrupted the very churches themselves, and made itself, for the moment, the main object of immediate concern for American society. The foes of social evil turned from the struggle to limit the freedom of the American drinker and concentrated their forces in the struggle to win the freedom of the American slave.

The rise of the abolitionist movement in the Jacksonian era closely paralleled the rise of the temperance crusade. On January 1, 1831, William Lloyd Garrison issued the first number of the *Liberator*. Garrison dedicated his paper to immediate abolition, and he declared, "I am in earnest—I will not equivocate—I will not excuse—I will not retreat a single inch—and I will be heard." He was never widely heard in the North, where the *Liberator* struggled to maintain a circulation of a few thousand, but he acquired a large audience in the South, where extracts from the *Liberator* were widely reprinted in newspaper columns. He remained an uncompromising agitator, rather than the spokesman for any practical abolitionist program. His personal following remained small in the North, even in New England, and his incendiary language served to antagonize many anti-slavery men and to divide the movement. His influence, which was tremendous, was largely felt within the slave states. There he was accepted increasingly as the spokesman, not only for the organized abolitionist movement, but for the Northern opinion generally.

The real nerve center of the abolitionist movement—and later the birthplace of the Anti-Saloon League—was Oberlin College in Ohio. Oberlin breathed the spirit of the most influential revivalist preacher of the age, Charles G. Finney. Finney had emerged out of the "burnt-over district" of upstate New York, the seed bed of Millerism, Mormonism, spiritualism, and Perfectionism and the training ground for a host of revivalist reformers. The emotional violence as well as the vast success which accompanied Finney's preaching had brought him in conflict with the leading figure of Connecticut Congregationalism, Lyman Beecher. Finney had carried all before him. "Beecher's own fastidious people," as Constance Rourke wrote, clamored for him. He ranged through

New England arousing a prodigious awakening and freighten-
ing the propertied classes, which wished revivalism to be moderate and controlled.

Beecher later moved to a larger field of activity, as he
supposed, by accepting the presidency of Lane Seminary in
Cincinnati, but within a year he was swarmed under by the
radical evangelism of Finney's followers, with its reckless disregard for orthodoxy or even good social order. The Lane
student body, under the leadership of a disciple of Finney,
Theodore Weld, mobilized itself in the anti-slavery cause
with such force as to alienate financial supporters of the seminary. Beecher, who, according to an old friend, had "without
being aware of it, not a little of the old Connecticut prejudice
against the blacks," attempted unsuccessfully to find the middle position between the trustees and the students. Weld led
a mass exodus to the then hardly existent college of Oberlin,
which, opening its doors to all comers regardless of race or
sex, won Finney from the Broadway Tabernacle in New York,
and set itself to training the leaders of the abolitionist movement within the northern churches.

Weld found a powerful partner in a southern gentleman
and former slaveholder, James G. Birney of Alabama and
Kentucky. Others followed Birney out of the South, and
together this coalition launched a campaign to awaken the
conscience of the North to the sin of slavery. The Lane rebels
began their work with a parting word to Beecher and the
Lane trustees.

> Sirs, you have mistaken alike the cause, the age and the
> men, if you think to intimidate by threats. . . . Slavery, with its
> robbery of body and soul from birth to death, its exactions of
> toil unrecompensed, its sunderings of kindred, its baptisms of
> blood, and its legacy of damning horrors to the eternity of the
> spirit. . . . The nation is shaking off its slumbers to sleep no
> more.

Working first through the American Anti-Slavery Society,
these abolitionists directed a propaganda campaign, which the

South met by blanket censorship. Northern opinion, angered by the abolitionist threat to the security of the Union, lashed out in editorials and mobilized in mobs. The propaganda continued to do its work, directed briefly from the House of Representatives by old, irascible John Quincy Adams, who stood forth in the name of free speech against the southern opposition to the reading of abolitionist petitions. In the meantime, the panic of '37 all but bankrupted the American Anti-Slavery Society, and in 1840 it passed into receivership in the hands of Garrison.

In that year the anti-slavery men launched themselves in politics with the Liberty party, a premature venture which won its candidate, Birney, an unimpressive seven thousand votes. Weld opposed such political action, arguing that it limited the effectiveness of the abolitionist campaign within the northern churches; and the main campaign continued in the forties along the lines laid down by Weld. From first to last, as Dwight L. Dumond has written, the churches were the forums, preachers the most consistent and powerful advocates, and the sin of slavery the cardinal thesis of the new social philosophy; a sin, as the British abolitionist Charles Stuart said, which was a sin twice over, for "its gross idolatry of a white and its atrocious abhorrence of a colored skin!"

The phase of the campaign which Weld directed won its battle in 1844. In that year the two great popular religions of Protestant America met the issue head on and both split apart. The Southern Baptist Church and the Methodist Church, South, separated and organized on pro-slavery principles. The parent bodies in the North reformed themselves to unite in the anti-slavery mission. In that year Birney's Liberty party won 62,000 votes, and, by defeating the Whigs in New York, threw the election to the expansionist James K. Polk. Polk, in turn, launched the nation upon an expansionist program which at last presented the abolitionists with a practical political program. In 1854 they helped to organize the Republican party upon the issue, not of abolition, but of prohibiting the extension of slavery in those territories acquired during Polk's term of office. Upon that issue they forced democratic America to undertake the dangerous mission of formulating a policy toward slavery. "Nothing short of miracles, constant miracles, and such as the world has never seen," Weld had declared,

> can keep at bay the two great antagonist forces. . . . They must drive against each other, till *one* of them goes to the bottom. *Events,* the master of men, have for years been silently but without a moment's pause, settling the basis of two great parties, the nucleus of one slavery, of the other freedom.

Chapter 12

SLAVOCRACY

CASUALLY accepted as a useful addition to free and indentured labor, Negro slavery thrived to shape the culture of the South in the eighteenth and nineteenth centuries. It shaped southern speech, manners, morals, and religions. It fostered a southern strain of gentility and a southern strain of brutality. At a time when the North boasted of its equalitaritarianism, slavery fixed southern society in clearly marked classes of slave, poor white, yeoman, squire, and lord. At a time of rapid industrialization in the North, the weight of slavery deterred industrial development in the South. Slavery created a national political issue which consolidated the South against the northern majority. It created southern national aims, southern expansionist ambitions, a southern constitutional theory, and a southern view of the nature of man and the purpose of society. The Confederacy was a slavocracy, its distinctive character created out of the consequences of its peculiar institution.

I

Mid-summer in 1619, several weeks after the meeting of the first representative assembly in Virginia, a Dutch ship put into Jamestown with a cargo of enslaved Africans, twenty of whom were sold to colonists. The Africans proved manageable, as the native Indians had not, and they became a permanent part of the colony's labor force. Six years later there were twenty-three Negroes in the colony, three more having been purchased, one having died, and one having presumably been born—although neither the law nor local opinion was at the time clear on the point—into the peculiar condition of perpetual servitude. By mid-century the number of Negroes had increased to about three hundred.

Gradually, over a forty-year period, the laws of Virginia adapted themselves to the institution, and legislation was passed encouraging its increase. By 1671 there were two thousand slaves in the colony together with six thousand indentured servants. Early in the eighteenth century the ratio of Negros to whites stood at two to three. The Negro population continued to increase more rapidly than the white down to the close of the American Revolution, when slaves may for a time have been in the majority. Then, with the collapse of the tobacco crop, the trend reversed itself. By the eve of the Civil War Virginia's five hundred thousand slaves made up about one-third of her population. She remained the ranking slave state in the South, but the states of the deep South all were on the verge of overtaking her in the size of their slave populations.

In South Carolina, Negro slave labor was introduced at once, and by the second decade of the eighteenth century the slaves in the low country of the state far outnumbered freemen. The stoop-labor in hot, humid, malarial rice fields under the eye of hired overseers was too abhorrent for any free labor system, and slavery thrived in the South Carolina low country more luxuriantly than anywhere else in the colonies. Neighboring Georgia remained backward and discontented until the colony legalized slavery in 1750.

During the eighteenth century the supply of slaves tended to exceed the demand, and all thirteen states took early occasion to prohibit the African trade after independence. Georgia and South Carolina later reopened the trade, but after 1808 it was prohibited by national law. Slave buyers thereafter were obliged to rely on the interstate slave trade or on slaves smuggled from Africa. The slave trade was an aspect of the peculiar institution which southerners themselves preferred to overlook. Much was said of the advantages of Christianity and civilization which awaited the Negroes who survived the middle passage, but of the voyage itself as little was said as possible.

With the decay of tobacco production along the Chesapeake and the loss of the protected British market for South Carolina indigo, slavery threatened, at the close of the eighteenth century, to become an intolerable burden to the South. Then cotton revived it. Cotton moved into the western regions of South Carolina and the adajacent areas in north central Georgia, converting the area from subsistence farms to plantations and converting the society from a free yeomanry to a slave plantation order. Cotton production became moderately important to Virginia and North Carolina in the first decade of the nineteenth century, and in the second decade it moved rapidly into central Tennessee, Alabama, Mississippi and Louisiana. In the forties it moved into Texas. In the thirty-five years preceding the Civil War cotton production increased thirty-fold, an expansion made possible by the invention of the cotton gin, the tremendous demand, the vast areas of virgin land, the large supply of slave labor, and the development of large scale farming techniques. In the eleven states that seceded from the Union there were three and one-half million slaves out of a total population of nine million. The value of slaves had been rising for a generation, and the demand was increasingly being made to reopen the African slave trade.

Probably three-fourths of the southern whites owned no slaves at all. Of those who did own slaves, about half were more or less well-to-do yeoman farmers, working side-by-side in the fields with their bondsmen, hopeful for a turn of fortune which would raise them to gentlemanly station, and anxious lest some turn of ill luck drop them to the status of the poor whites and the slaves about them. More than half of all the slaves were owned by 12 per cent of the white population, the owners of twenty or more slaves. And from this select squirearchy there rose the still more select planter aristocracy, the ten thousand families of the South which were supported by a force of fifty or more slaves. These were the groups—the squirearchy and the aristocracy—which absorbed the advantages of slavery; all other major classes in the South suffered from the system. To the great planters slavery remained profitable, economically as well as socially and politically, at the time the South seceded from the Union.

The status of the slave was an ambiguous one, for he was at the same time a human being and a piece of property. As a southern judge explained the matter, a slave was "not in the condition of a horse. . . . He had mental capacities, and an immortal principle in his nature." The law did not "extinguish his high-born nature nor deprive him of many rights which are inherent in man." The southern states all passed slave codes for the double purpose of securing to the slave his natural rights and securing to the owner his property rights. Where the two purposes conflicted, the law naturally tended to be most sensitive to the owner's property rights. One right which all states guaranteed to the slave was the right to life. An owner who killed his slave was a murderer in the eyes of the law, and the law sometimes dealt with him as such. If the death were the accidental consequence of brutal discipline the master might still be sentenced for murder. Otherwise the slave had no clear rights generally recognized in law. He could not hold property, marry, or make any form of contract without his master's permission. And if he made a contract with his master, to work out his freedom for instance, his master was not bound to honor the contract when the terms had been satisfied.

The main intent of the slave codes was to protect the owner in his rights and to protect white society from slave insurrection, violence, dishonesty, or insolence. During the first half of the nineteenth century the slave codes were frequently revised with the view to securing more effective control over the slaves. White men were prohibited from fraternizing with slaves. Masters were prohibited from teaching their slaves to read and write. Slaves were restricted to within a short radius of their place of residence except on pass, and if caught beyond that point they were arrested as runaways. Free Negroes were more feared than slaves as possible insurrectionists, and special codes minutely circumscribed their activities.

While southern society attempted to guard the slave against disciplinary action resulting in murder, it remained all but unanimous in its approval of corporal punishment vigorously and methodically applied. It was the whip, or the fear of the whip, that made the system go. Good business sense might deter the planters from inflicting crippling punishments. Compassion might move him to moderate discipline at the cost of his profits. Skillful handling of slaves might reduce the necessity for corporal punishment to the minimum. The planter might even place the slave on a modified wage basis to give him greater incentive. Nevertheless, the system remained one of involuntary servitude. Fear, most particularly fear of the whip, was the indispensable principle.

II

Anglo-Saxons throughout the world have been notably exclusive as colonizers. On this score the colonial Virginia slaveholder William Byrd chided New Englanders for their foolish delicacy in their relations with the Indians. A more cordial relationship would have worked to their advantage, he wrote, for the "Natives could, by no means, persuade themselves that the English were heartily their friends, so long as they disdained to intermarry with them. . . . Nor would the shade of the skin have been any reproach at this day; for if a Moor may be washt white in 3 generations, surely an Indian might have been blancht in two." The French, he observed, "have not been so squeamish in Canada, who upon trial find abundance of attraction in the Indians. . . . By this piece of

policy we find the French interest very much strengthened. . . ."

> It was certainly an unreasonable nicety, that prevented
> their entering into so good-natur'd an alliance. All nations of
> men have the same natural dignity, and we all know that very
> bright talents may be lodg'd under a very dark skin. The prin-
> ciple difference between one people and another proceeds only
> from the different opportunities of improvement.

This was William Byrd the enlightened and urbane
aristocrat speaking, not William Byrd the slaveholder. Miscegenation in Virginia was a matter for neither levity nor
eighteenth-century reason. The most enlightened southerner
suspended his belief in natural law where it would logically
have sanctioned interracial marriages.

The Anglo-Saxon distaste for such alliances was early
written into law. Interracial marriages with Negroes, although
not with Indians, were outlawed, and heavy penalties were
inflicted upon any white man found to be the parent of a
mulatto, the child inheriting the status of his mother. Nevertheless, the rising mulatto population demonstrated what all
southerners knew to be true, that sanctions of society were
constantly being transgressed. Family resemblances in the
rising mullato population demonstrated one more thing that
people knew already. These transgressions occurred at all
levels of society. The universal consciousness of the habitual
violation of so deep-rooted a taboo could not fail to influence
southern culture, and, once the system of slavery had come
under attack from the North, the abolitionist were quick to
notice southern sensitivity on this point.

Racial purity in the South became a more fiercely ex-
halted ideal for the southern sense of guilt and the southern
rage at northern attacks. This ideal of racial purity was epito-
mized in the idealization of southern womanhood. "On the
one hand, wrote W. J. Cash,

the convention must be set up that the thing simply did not exist; and enforced under penalty of being shot; and on the other, the woman must be compensated, the revolting suspicion in the male that he might be slipping into bestiality got rid of, by glorifying her; the Yankee must be answered by proclaiming from the housetops that Southern Virtue so far from being inferior was superior, not alone to the North's but to any on earth, and adducing Southern Womanhood in proof.

So southern women, enveloped in sentimental protectiveness, lost much of the freedom enjoyed by women outside the slave belt.

Africanization of the South having been averted by the assertion of racial exclusiveness and the maintenance of slavery, the southerner accepted the Negro as an intimate part of southern life and allowed himself to be profoundly influenced by the association. Negro slavery developed in the South a tolerance for outlandish behavior and an attitude of social forebearance which stood in contrast to the northern democratic insistence upon outward conformity. It was expected that the slave would act irresponsibly and often strangely, and tolerance for similar behavior extended itself to the southern white as well. But tolerance toward the slave was limited to his individual actions. All group activity was dangerous. The Negro religious assembly led by a Negro preacher was a potential company of rebels. Negroes, when they acted in groups, were closely supervised, and this became true also of the white community. Labor unions, for instance, were ruthlessly suppressed in the South, at a time when they were gaining recognition and some legal protection in the North. Group action in opposition to the status quo was instinctly suspect, and instinctively it was viewed in its relation to the Negro question.

The time had been, before Nat Turner's insurrection in 1830, before the publication of Garrison's *Liberator* a year later, and before the coming of King Cotton, when southern gentlemen had concerned themselves soberly with the problem

of slavery as an evil to be eradicated. During the Revolutionary era many of these men had faced the fact that arguments concerning the rights of man ought logically to be
applied to Negroes as well as whites. "Sir, it is really matter
of astonishment to me," William Pinkney declared in the Maryland House of Delegates, "that the people of Maryland do
not blush at the very name of Freedom. . . . Is she not at once
the fair temple of freedom, and the abominable nursery of
slaves . . . ?" In South Carolina even Henry Laurens, himself long involved in the slave trade, came, under the impact
of the Revolutionary War, to view the trade as a phase of
English tyranny which should be abolished.

A select company of slaveholding Virginia aristocrats,
including Jefferson, Madison, Washington, John Randolph,
George Mason, and John Taylor of Caroline, were emphatic
in their condemnation of the institution. "Taught to regard
a part of our own species in the most abject & contemptible
degree below us," wrote Mason, "we lose that idea of the
dignity of man, which the hand of nature had planted in us,
for great and useful purposes." The Virginians not infre-
quently willed the freedom of their slaves upon their death,
and the revolutionary agitation brought legal changes in
Virginia and Maryland facilitating manumission of tens of
thousands of slaves.

Enchanted with the idea of the natural rights of man,
the gentlemen of Virginia were yet unable to be thorough-
going in their application of the doctrine. The best known
proponent of natural equality and the best known opponent
of slavery in Virginia was the slaveholder Thomas Jefferson.
Jefferson was appointed, by the first assembly of the state of
Virginia, to the committee in charge of purging the legal
code of "principles inconsistent with Republicanism." The
committee returned with a proposal to emancipate all slaves
born after passage of the act as soon as they had reached
their maturity. Thereafter they were to be colonized wherever

a Negro nation might be established. The suggestion was never brought to a vote. Liberal slaveholders generally preferred, with John Taylor of Caroline, to couple disapproval of the institution with the observation that its continued existence was inescapable.

Jefferson himself never contemplated emancipation unaccompanied by wholesale expulsion. "Deep rooted prejudices of the white," he wrote, "ten thousand recollections of blacks of injuries sustained, new provocations, the real distinction nature has made and many other circumstances will divide us into parties and produce convulsions which will probably never end but in the extermination of one or the other race." He shared the Anglo-Saxon aversion to miscegenation, and he thought all hopes for coexistence on a basis of equality between Negro and white were folly.

Theoretically convinced of the natural equality of man, Jefferson was unable to convince himself empirically of the natural equality of the Negro and the white man. To begin with there was the color difference. Then there were differences in physical structure. The Negro appeared to be different by nature. A careful examination of the subject seemed to Jefferson to demonstrate that the Negro was inferior to the white man intellectually. There had been, it was true, instances of Negroes producing creditable poetry and prose, but Jefferson had been unable to discover any that would have merited attention had it not been created by a Negro. As a scientist he was driven reluctantly to the tentative conclusion that the Negro did not fit his cherished theory of the equality of man, although he never arrived at a final judgment on the matter. Jefferson continued to his death in his hope of a solution to the problem through colonization. He never thought of emancipation in any other terms. His was enlightened anti-slavery opinion at its most radical in the South, and he had nothing but a hopelessly impractical scheme to offer. This scheme was attempted during Jeffer-

son's lifetime in the organization of the American Colonization Society and the establishment of the independent Negro
nation of Liberia, an experiment which absorbed the devoted
attention of American humanitarians in both the North and
the South, but one which failed to have any effect on the
institution of slavery in America.

In the meantime, a new generation had emerged in the
South. New lands were being settled, and a new economy
was establishing itself. Negro slavery seemed indispensable
to this economy, and to the new generation the enlightenment
was an old dream and no more than that. It came to seem
so, even to some of the old friends of emancipation. In his
fight for the admission of Missouri as a slave state, William
Pinkney did not pause to "blush at the very name of Freedom."
Instead he looked upon slavery and found it good. Nor did
it violate true republican principles, for it was in accordance
with those very principles that "rights political and civil, may
be qualified by the fundamental law, upon such inducements
as the freemen of the country deem sufficient."

The debates in 1820 over the admission of Missouri as
a slave state abruptly revealed the new slavocracy to a startled
nation. To northerners, who for more than a generation
had thought of slavery as a dying institution, the debates
came as a shocking surprise. Accustomed to hearing slavery
defended as a necessary evil, they now heard it extolled as
a positive good, and from men who themselves had earlier
condemned it. The venerable Jeffersonian Republican Nathaniel Macon of North Carolina invited Congressmen to visit
his plantation, where a hundred Negro slaves worked his
fields. The plantation, he said, formed a happy, healthy,
isolated community. It provided the kind of life ideally suited
to the needs and capacities of the Negro. Slavery was a positive good for the slave as well as for society in general.

In the next decades the aggressive defense of slavery won
the devoted service of scholars, politicians, planters, and poor

whites. Slavery had become "the greatest of all the great blessings which a kind Providence has bestowed upon our glorious region." The slaves were the happiest creatures in the world. The system was "the most safe and stable basis for free institutions in the world." Nor need peoples outside the South be condemned to forego its advantages. The South's peculiar institution was "not condemned to any lattitude, but . . . is catholic as humanity in its character, and is capable of extension to the utmost limits of the habitable globe." If union with the North prohibited the natural growth of slavery, southerners increasingly argued, then the evils of union outweighed its blessings, and the time had arrived to form a separate southern nation based entirely on southern principles.

The defense of slavery, though it required a thorough-going repudiation of Jeffersonian political theory, was readily and easily accomplished, once the slaveowners found themselves under attack. That the Negro represented a distinct, inferior, separately created race was a belief which was current in the eighteenth century and one which gained new adherents in the nineteenth. So distinguished a northern scientist as Louis Agassiz gave vigorous support to this theory. The *Essay on the Inequality of Human Races* by Count Arthur de Gobineau was published in America, and it naturally received wide acclaim in the South.

Jefferson had supposed that, even if the existence of inferior races could be proved, this did not effect their equality with all others in their possession of natural rights. The first widely influential repudiation of this Jeffersonian thesis was given by Thomas R. Dew, a professor at William and Mary College, in an argument against emancipation, before the Virginia legislature of 1831-32. Throughout history, Dew asserted, slavery has been the means by which civilization was created, giving the superior few the leisure necessary to the advancement of society. The persistence of the institution throughout history gave it abundant human sanction, while divine sanction was incontestably present in the Bible. Under any circumstances some such a system was inevitable, by whatever name it might be identified, the inferior peoples inevitably being forced to do the bidding of the superior ones.

In South Carolina, Chancellor Harper endorsed the Dew argument and proceeded, himself, to demolish the argument of the Declaration of Independence line by line. Man is born, he said, in a state of subjection and remains in that state at least until he is an adult. It is his natural proclivity either to domineer or to be subservient. In the struggle of life, men find their natural places and then society and law confirm them in their proper ranks and privileges. The Negros represented a sordid, servile, laborious race, remarkably indifferent to personal liberty. They had been created to perform sordid, servile and laborious work. They were lacking in morals and they were accordingly well-suited to the task of absorbing such immorality as was inevitable in all society. There was virtually no such thing as white prostitution in the slave states, Chancellor Harper asserted, because of the presence of female slaves. George Fitzhugh, in *Sociology for the South,* argued that society must be organized for positive purposes. The persistence of servile classes was a law of nature, and society should be organized accordingly. The South had the good fortune to possess a distinct, inferior race. The problem was made more difficult in the North by the lack of one, but the northern industrialist should nevertheless own his workers and be responsible for them.

Lending color to these arguments were the neo-feudalistic notions of the romantic movement, most widely popularized in the novels of Sir Walter Scott, with their knights and ladies and faithful servitors. Scott, Mark Twain said, had driven the South wild with his feudal romances. Not content with riding to the hounds after the manner of the English gentry, some southern pinks of chivalry held tournaments where armoured knights unhorsed one another for the honor of their ladies. Dueling, which had elsewhere fallen into disrepute, continued as an important social form in the South down to the Civil War. Young aristocrats spoke of themselves as "the chivalry" and described their culture as "southron." Southern woman was "fair" and women taken together were "southern womanhood." The same style of talk was heard elsewhere in the nation, but in the South, where Negro slavery created a different setting and required a positive justification, popular notions of feudalism were adopted in dead seriousness as a permanent guide for southern life. They became the stuff of southern nationalism.

Cheek by jowl with romantic feudalism, a Greek revival flourished—again nationally, but especially in the South—in sign of which Greek columns were nailed onto the fronts of houses. As a justification for slavery, the new feudalism was probably more congenial to southerners than the new classicism, but the Greek revival provided the more telling argument in a democracy. Southern democracy, it was explained, like Greek democracy, rested securely upon the foundation of slavery, the indispensible foundation for any civilized society. Aristotle was repeatedly cited for his conclusion that slavery was a necessary part of a complete community.

III

The planter class of the South, on the basis of its moderately nationalistic Whig party record, could disclaim responsibility for the rise of a southern slavocracy as a nation within the nation. Yet the planter aristocracy, while working to preserve national union down to the moment of secession, had in concert with its slaves, done much to create the conditions out of which southern nationalism emerged. The planter almost alone, in the South, reaped economic benefits from slavery. In addition, it was the basis for his aristocratic social position, and it was the basis for his political power. The planters' interests were at many points antagonistic to those

of the non-slaveholding yeomanry, and the planter tended
naturally to act in his own behalf.

The excellent southern river system connected the planter
directly with his northern market as well as with his northern
source of supplies and capital. In the forties and fifties this
connection was improved by direct railroad communications.
Such transportation facilities were sufficient to his needs. He
saw no need for a network of good country roads and railroad
spurs connecting the rest of the southern back country to the
outside world or even to the major plantations. It was simpler
to be supplied, even with foodstuffs, from the northern sources
with which he maintained his one vital economic connection.
As a result the yeomanry, isolated from the markets which
internal improvements opened up to northern farmers, were
held back to a permanent near-subsistence economy and to
a narrowly provincial view of the world.

The extent to which the planter relied upon the North
for almost everything but raw cotton is to be seen in the
stunted condition of southern urban development. Five
southern states in 1860 did not have a single town with a
population of ten thousand. New Orleans was the only metropolis in the South. Richmond, Virginia, with its iron works,
was the only important manufacturing center. An urban as
well as rural middle class, such as provided the economic basis
for democracy in the North, failed to develop in the Old
South. For this the planter bore blame. He went beyond a
simple failure to encourage local enterprise to a positively
doctrinaire disapproval of it. The colonial aristocracies of
both Virginia and South Carolina had engaged actively in
commercial enterprises, but following the Revolution such
activities became ungentlemanly.

Planter policy isolated the southern yeomanry intellectually as well as physically from the outside world. As the
chief taxpayers of the South, the planters kept tax rates too
low to provide adequate educational facilities for the majority

of the population. Only in Kentucky and North Carolina, before the war, were advances made in public education comparable to those being made in northern states. The planter, as the owner of the slaves, was faced with the responsibility of keeping them in order. To do so it was perhaps best to keep them illiterate, but under any circumstances it was vital to deny them access to the abolitionist literature which was calculated to incite them to insurrection. So dangerous was such literature that the planters, in common with all classes of southern whites, saw a need for censorship which included rigid policing of the mails. The planter class was not anti-intellectual, and, for itself, it kept in touch with the outside world. But outside the planter class and the supporting lawyers and merchant groups, the South was kept largely in ignorance, even of day-by-day national affairs. When Lincoln ran for President in 1860, many southerners believed that he was an outspoken abolitionist and that his running mate was a mulatto.

If the comparative poverty, isolation, and ignorance of most southerners were only accidentally fostered by planter policy, these qualities supported the anti-democratic purposes of the planter policy. The southern aristocracy was determined to defend itself against the ravages of democracy. Aristocracies in the North had been similarly determined, but their institutions of local government were in most cases less aristocratic to begin with, and they were driven back by the powerful middle and lower middle classes. The South lacked a broad middle class, but the bulk of the southern white population was made up of that self-sufficient yeomanry which, according to Jeffersonian theory, was the one sure basis for a free republican society. The theory was not borne out in practice. Whatever slavery was widespread, the predominant yeoman class generally failed to live up to Jeffersonian expectations in defending its own rights and interests. The yeomanry, in common with the large planters, came to view issues instinctively in relation to the slavery question, and, being less securely placed in society than the great planter, they were generally the more concerned to see that the Negro be kept in his place beneath them. Responsibility for this task naturally rested with the slaveowner, and the planter therefore came to be viewed by the non-slaveholder as performing a vital function for the whole community. Slavery, while it robbed the yeoman of economic opportunity, at the same time disposed him favorably toward the idea that the affairs of society as a whole were the special trust of the slaveowners. The yeomanry demanded and gained political rights, but they were less assured and less successful in gaining political power.

By the eve of the war, property qualifications for voting had been abolished in all southern states, in Virginia and South Carolina under threat of revolt by the western sections of the states. Such reforms, however, were not permitted to unhorse the planter class politically. Virginia did not provide for direct election of governor and county officials until 1850, even then retaining a voting superiority through apportionment by total population rather than by white voting population. Louisiana in like manner coupled manhood suffrage with apportionment by total population, and in practice, politics in Louisiana remained in the hands of the planters. Of all the states, South Carolina remained the most thoroughly aristocratic in its political structure, which rested upon the compromise of 1808 between the tidewater region and the up-country. The compromise provided that half the lower house of the state legislature should represent property—land and slaves—as registered by taxation. In 1860 South Carolina was the only state in the Union where the presidential electors, the governor, and the state officials were chosen by the legislature. The governor of South Carolina was still required by law to be a wealthy man.

In many areas aristocracy was even more securely per-petuated in local government. Justices of the peace were appointed by the governor in Virginia down to 1851. They met four times a year to try cases and transact legislative and administrative duties. They were the chief means by which the local ruling group retained its control. The fight for manhood suffrage triumphed in the older southern states as well as in the older northern states, but slavery offered the planters opportunities, which they seized, to secure political aristocracy behind a democratic facade.

In the West generally, where an entrenched aristocracy had not existed at the time of statehood, political democracy advanced more rapidly than in the East, but the slave West was from the first less democratic than the free West. Missis-sippi, admitted to the Union in 1817, framed a constitution distinctly in the pre-Revolutionary mode. It required land ownership for voting. It imposed a very high property qualifi-cation for the office of governor, and sizeable ones for legis-lators. The electorate was further restricted to persons who were enrolled in the militia and who believed in the existence of God and future state of rewards and punishments. While reforms were later instituted, Mississippi's first constitution was a testament to the aristocratic influence of slavery, even on the frontier.

Slave-state constitutions inevitably were based on quasi-democratic notions, at best. The Mississippi constitution fol-lowed the form by then generally established in southern states when it declared, "That all freemen, when they form a social compact, are equal in rights." As a theoretical basis for democracy this was notably narrower than the statement in the Indiana constitution of the preceding year,

> That the general, great and essential principles of liberty and free Government may be recognized and unalterably estab-lished; we declare, that all men are born equally free and inde-pendent, and have certain natural inherent, and unalienable

rights; among which are the enjoying and defending life and
liberty, and of acquiring, possessing and protecting property
and pursuing and obtaining happiness and safety.

A subsequent Indiana constitution declared that "No negro
or mulatto shall come into, or settle in the State, after the
adoption of this constitution." Most citizens of the Northwest probably took almost as unfriendly a view of Negro
rights as those of the Southwest, but they did not live in a
Negro community where they would feel constantly obliged
to apply an undemocratic principle.

IV

The slavocracy found its intellectual leader in John C.
Calhoun, the Senator from South Carolina. Successively a
staunch nationalist, a states rights nullifier, and an advocate of southern autonomy within the Union, Calhoun was
always first of all the loyal servant of the hundred men, more
or less, who composed the tightly knit aristocracy of Charleston, South Carolina. So long as Charleston might control the
Democratic party, Calhoun was a nationalist. While it was
able to control only the politics of the state, he was a nullifier.
When it was able to dominate southern politics he would become a southern nationalist. Praised as an advocate of minority rights, Calhoun, in his public acts, always had one
specific, tiny, slaveholding minority in mind.

It was not that the Charleston *Beau Monde* composed in
Calhoun's estimation an exceptionally able ruling class. On
the contrary, he was disgusted by the irresponsibility and de-
bauchery of the Charleston set. It was rather that according to his political theory a ruling elite was the basis for a
healthy society, and the Charleston elite was the one at hand.
He therefore took it up, moulded it as well as he could, and
used it as an instrument to impress his will upon the nation.

Calhoun's reputation as a political theorist rests primarily on his brief *Disquisition on Government* and, to a lesser degree, on his *A Discourse on the Constitution and Govern-*

ment of the United States. In the field of political theory the interest in the *Disquisition* rests in its concern for the problem of securing minority rights in a majoritarian democracy. Calhoun's solution is a system of "concurrent majorities," whereby the minority group in the nation—as if there would be only one— would hold veto power against majority dictation. Although argued in theoretical terms, the *Disquisition* is really almost meaningless apart from the American political situation at the time of the Compromise of 1850. It was an argument which, if taken sufficiently seriously outside the South, would have given the southern slaveholding planter that extraordinary control over national policy which the imperious Calhoun thought proper. It is not to be supposed, from a reading of the *Disquisition,* that Calhoun would countenance the extension of his principle to smaller "concurrent majorities" within the South itself. As for his defense of the peculiar institution, Calhoun repeated the arguments which had been developed by Dew, Harper, Fitzhugh and others.

Calhoun's career was remarkably similar to that of Alexander Hamilton. Each rose from obscure and provincial origins to marry into an exclusive, wealthy, cosmopolitan society, and each assumed the role of guardian over his adopted society. Each brought to the task an austere probity such as was highly unusual in American politics. These two men— the two most formidable opponents of the democratic rights of man in the history of American political theory—brought to their tasks a settled belief in the natural inequality and the basic depravity of man. For both, the key to an orderly society was the creation of a ruling elite whose own selfish interest would be served by the maintenance of a stable society. Calhoun's elite happened to dominate a slave society, while Hamilton's dominated a free one; and Calhoun's situation called for policies of free trade and states rights, while Hamilton's called for the tariff and a strong central government. Such differences were comparatively superficial. Calhoun said as much, repeatedly, to the northern business interests. In the broad outlines of northern and southern society the role of the southern slave did not differ materially from the role of the northern worker. In all civilized societies there were such divisions. The leisure of the few, he argued with Fitzhugh and others, always required the labor of the many, and the true interest of northern employer and southern slaveholder lay in uniting to maintain a stable society of masters and servants.

This was good Hamiltonian social theory, but coming from the most radical anti-tariff, states-rights spokesman of South Carolina it was altogether unacceptable to the northern business community. After all, just such an understanding, expressed in a fashion less harshly doctrinaire, already existed between northern and southern Whigs, and it was being seriously embarrassed by the activities of Calhoun and the South Carolina Democrats. The Whig planters resisted Calhoun's leadership as long as they possibly could, but in the end Calhoun, the self-appointed savior of the cotton capitalist and the dour prophet of southern nationalism, became the acknowledged political philosopher of the new slavocracy.

Brought to life by the Missouri Compromise debates, southern nationalism expanded as the South shrank further into its minority position within the nation. Wielding disproportionate control over the Senate, the Presidency, the Supreme Court, and the dominant Democratic party, the South nevertheless placed increasing emphasis upon states rights and the acquisition of new slave territories. There were fire-eaters in the South, especially in South Carolina, who began, a generation before the Civil War, to form their section into an independent nation. They were supported in this by the Garrisonian abolitionists, who wished the North to withdraw immediately from any association with slavery.

Both abolitionists and fire-eaters found their issue after

the Mexican War in the largely academic question of the extension of slavery into the conquered territories. From the first introduction of the Wilmot Proviso in Congress in 1846, prohibiting the extension of slavery into the territories, the sectional dispute revolved around this issue. It dominated the discussion surrounding the Compromise of 1850. It absorbed the attention of the Nashville Convention that year. It was the issue which created the Republican party in 1854. It was the chief theme of the Lincoln-Douglas debates in 1858, and it was the only aspect of the slavery question alluded to in the Republican platform of 1860. In the ordinances of secession drawn up by the southern states, northern opposition to the extension of slavery was given as a primary grievance; yet southerners themselves admitted that the territories would become free states eventually, even if slaves were admitted during the period of settlement. The New Orleans *Bee* wrote during the campaign of 1860:

> The restlessness of the South touching the agitation of the slavery question arises rather from the apprehension of what the aggressive policy of the North may hereafter effect, than from what it has already accomplished. For . . . we may safely affirm that thus far no practical injury has resulted.

As to the failure to capture Kansas as a slave state, "prudent and far-seeing men predicted the utter impracticability of carrying the design into execution. . . . Slavery will go where it will pay."

The election of Lincoln provided the occasion for secession by the deep South, but—to paraphrase John Adams on American independence—the revolution had already taken place in the hearts and minds of the southern people. There was already a southern nation in 1860, a slavocracy supported by its own separate accents, traditions, religious denominations, social ideals, political theories, and expansionists ambitions. The Confederacy gave political form to a self-conscious nation which in its loyalties, oriented to a Negro slave society, already had seceded from democratic America.

Chapter 13

LITERATURE AND DEMOCRACY

IN AMERICAN intellectual history the mid-nineteenth century was the age of literature, as the late eighteenth had been the age of politics and the seventeenth the age of theology. Democracy made its appearance in America without the benefit of any political theory adequate to explain it, and a generation of democratic politics failed to produce one. To the extent that American democracy may be said to have had its philosopher at all, it was no American democrat but instead the French aristocrat, Alexis de Tocqueville. No philosophical justification for democracy emerged in America such as the Philosophical Radicalism which developed in England to support British liberalism. Fundamental changes in academic American political thought awaited the influence of Herbert Spencer and Thomas Huxley, during the intellectual doldrums of the post-Civil War period. Meanwhile, men of genius emerged in America in the field of literature, concerned with American democracy as artists rather than as political theorists.

The wish of the most original observers in America was not to invent a new political system or to contrive a theoretical justification for the existing one; it was to create a new literature out of the new society which had come, unasked, into existence. The half-decade of 1850-55 saw the appearance of *Representative Men* (1850), *The Scarlet Letter* (1850), *The House of Seven Gables* (1851), *Moby-Dick* (1851), *Pierre* (1852), *Walden* (1854) and *Leaves of Grass* (1855). "You might search all the rest of American literature," wrote F. O. Matthiessen, "without being able to collect a group of books equal to these in imaginative vitality." They were produced at the climax of the fresh democratic experiment, and they represented the chief intellectual fruit of the experiment.

From the age of Jackson to the age of Eisenhower, the main theme of American intellectual history has been the struggle to bring the dead level of democracy to terms with the aristocracy of the intellect. There were to be periods of disillusionment, notably in the Gilded Age and the Roaring Twenties, but the age of Jackson was not one of these. Never again did creative American intellectuals wage the struggle with such optimistic enthusiasm as in this, America's great literary age of democratic faith. It is true that in Brahmin Boston and in the slave states of the deep South some literary gentlemen held aloof from the general rush of democratic nationalism. But to American men of genius such a disengaged attitude was intolerable. However critical they might be of one another, these men were united in a mission to create an authentic American culture out of authentic New World materials. The literature they created was by design the literature of democracy, so many contributions to a green age of creative idealism, an age to be destroyed by the Civil War.

I

Ralph Waldo Emerson's Phi Beta Kappa address, *The American Scholar,* delivered at Harvard in 1837, has often been called America's literary declaration of independence from England, but outside the confines of Boston the struggle for literary independence had been the major theme of American letters for two generations. Literary men of the most divergent political views had united in this. Wrote the radical republican Philip Freneau during the revolutionary era:

> Can we never be thought to have learning or grace
> Unless it be brought from that horrible place
> Where tyranny reigns with her impudent face. . . .

And Noah Webster, arch-Federalist and the arch-nation-
alist of the literary world, declared, "America must be as independent in *literature* as she is in *politics,* as famous for
arts as for *arms."* Webster, that stalwart foe of democracy,
devoted his life to this fight for an American system of education and an American system of spelling, writing an American
version of the Bible and compiling *An American Dictionary
of the English Language.* But in this Webster was something
of a sport among his fellow Federalists. Others among them
did also indeed, advert to the need for an American literature,
but the Boston Federalists who wrote for *Port Folio* and *North
American Review* hoped that it could all be kept within the
old bounds. American letters, the *North American Review*
announced at the climax of the War of 1812, "must wait
for all improvements from abroad, acquire a literary tone
from the mother country, . . . and wait for decision on its
merits or demerits, from the higher authorities of London."

For those who wanted to make the clean break, the wish
was not always father to the deed. Freneau lent his talents
as a poet to the cause of independence and Jeffersonian republicanism with reams of contentious doggerel. The verses
upon which his reputation as a poet rests, however, are essentially English lyric poems with American place names.
The career of William Cullen Bryant as the outstanding poet
of republican America is similarly quite separate from his
career as the crusading Jeffersonian editor of the New York
Evening Post. Excelling Freneau as a poet, Bryant, while
calling for an indigenous American literature, Americanized
his own art to the extent of selecting American subjects, but
hardly more than that.

Charles Brockden Brown, an ardent republican, made the
patriotic effort to devote himself entirely to writing, trusting
for his support in the American reading public. "Our manners
and customs are in many respects peculiar to ourselves," he
wrote,

> Every community is distinguished in the same manner. Hence it is, that there exists emphatically *American opinions and customs.* . . . That our national character is not yet established, is true in a limited sense; . . . This difference of manners ought to be strengthened and extended, as an engine to produce the *amor patriae,* and a more ardent attachment to our excellent Constitution.

But Brown was able to achieve little more than gothic romances peopled with frontiersmen and Indians, and, failing to receive the support of the republic, he gave up his attempt.

Among the nation's early writers, Hugh Henry Brackenridge, westerner and democrat, achieved much the greatest success in the common effort to produce a distinctly American literature. A radical patriot, Brackenridge in 1772 co-authored with Freneau *The Rising Glory of America.* In 1776 he composed a verse drama, *The Battle of Bunkers-Hill,* glorifying the fighting ability of Americans. These were but minor efforts on which Brackenridge placed little store. His chief work, *Modern Chivalry,* was a lengthy picaresque novel which he commenced to write in 1792 and completed during the next generation. The heroes of the novel, Captain John Farrago and Teague O'Regen, were modeled upon Don Quixote and Sancho Panza, but they were themselves freshly created out of American life (although Brackenridge chose an Irishman for his comic lead because he felt that the American character had not yet sufficiently developed to support the part). Their adventures took place in the America of Brackenridge's experience, and the style of the tales is simply Brackenridge's own. *Modern Chivalry* is one long lampoon of democracy by a democrat for democrats; "a more thoroughly American book," according to Henry Adams, "than any written before 1833."

Modern Chivalry was American and democratic and at the same time devoid of sober democratic missionary zeal. In this respect its like was not to be seen again in formal

American literature for several generations, hardly until the coming of Mark Twain. In the first quarter of the nineteenth century, Washington Irving, much the best American writer of his day, wrote with the same lack of missionary zeal concerning a wide variety of American subjects, but without the same ability to contribute through his writings to the independence in literature which Noah Webster urged. Much like Robert Louis Stevenson, he was an exceptional literary craftsman, who could write equally well of Captain Bonneville's western explorations or his own touring of Spain, but who was moved in his writing by no burning ideal except the ideal of lucid expression. His reputation, like that of Stevenson's, has suffered as a consequence. Irving's writings won him popular acclaim at home and abroad, but American literary critics apparently have never forgiven him his apparent lack of literary patriotism and grand dedication. They have tended to save their praises rather for Irving's contemporary, James Fenimore Cooper, or even for Charles Brockden Brown, writers who, although inferior to Irving in craftsmanship, assumed earnestly the task of helping to create an authentic American literature.

Until the War of 1812, America's writers found less to complain of from foreign critics than from their own fellow Americans. Irving and Bryant won generous praise abroad, and other writers, Timothy Dwight, John Trumball, and Joel Barlow, for instance, won similar welcome, and it appeared that this foreign praise was necessary to domestic success. "We do not praise a thing," Bryant complained, "until we see the seal of transatlantic approbation upon it." The public continued, in democratic America, to neglect its most ambitious literary men. The American writers, in the meantime, following the War of 1812, faced a rising hostility from the English literary quarterlies, which sharply heightened their sense of mission.

These English attacks, which from 1814 on were so often repeated as to become a distinct literary *genre,* reached a climax of volume and fury in 1820. The classic of the *genre* was composed that year by the Reverend Sydney Smith in the *Edinburgh Review.* Ostensibly reviewing Adam Seybert's *Statistical Annuals of the United States,* Smith first summarized the contents of the book, and then, somewhat irrelevantly, moved on to attack American culture generally. "Such," he said, "is the land of Jonathan, and thus has it been governed. In his honest endeavors to better his condition and in his manly purpose of resisting injury and insult we most cordially sympathize. Thus far we are friends and admirers of Jonathan. But he must not grow vain. . . ."

> In the four quarters of the globe, who reads an American book? or goes to an American play? or looks at an American picture or statue? What does the world yet owe to American physicians or surgeons? What new substances have their chemists discovered, or what old ones have they analyzed? What new constellations have been discovered by the telescopes of Americans? What have they done in mathematics? Who drinks out of American glasses? or eats from American plates? or wears American coats or gowns? or sleeps in American blankets? Finally, under which of the old tyrannical governments of Europe is every sixth man a slave, whom his fellow creatures may buy and sell and torture? When these questions are fairly and favorably answered their lauditory epithets may be allowed.

The American literary reviews were in conservative hands, and the American defense was assumed mainly by conservative literary men. Timothy Dwight, the formidable Pooh-Bah of Connecticut, had already entered the lists in his role as poet, critic, and arbiter of American literary taste. Now, in response to the charges of Dr. Smith, the genteel editor of the *North American Review,* Edward Everett, took up the lance. America, Everett explained, labored under disadvantages, including "the number of low-bred persons who have fled from justice in their native land and crossed the

Atlantic to traverse and vilify ours." He denied the charge that Americans were smarting under adverse English criticism of the American epic poem *Columbiad,* written by that radical republican Joel Barlow. "The multitude of new and worthless words the poet coined," Everett maintained, "were the cause of far more unsparing criticism here than in England." Nor was that all. "The persecution of Americanisms at large has nowhere in Great Britain been pursued with such keenness as in America." Everett credited his nation with having actually preserved some authentic English words which in England had passed out of usage since the seventeenth century.

For the generation of American literary men growing up outside of Boston in the years after the War of 1812, such slavish Anglophilism did not do. "It were the vilest thing you could say of a true American author that he were an American Tompkins," Herman Melville wrote. "Call him an American and have done for you cannot say a nobler thing of him. . . . Let us away with this leaven of literary flunkeyism toward England." A bad American writer, who wrote out of his American experience, was vastly to be preferred to an excellent imitator of English styles. "Let America, then, prize and cherish her writers; yea, let her glorify them. . . . let America first praise mediocrity even, in her children, before she praises . . . the best excellence in the children of any other land." And to be American was to be democratic, to "breathe that unshackled, democratic spirit of Christianity in all things, which now takes the practical lead in this world, though at the same time led by ourselves—us Americans."

II

Democratic America possessed two literary capitols, Boston and New York. Everett spoke for the aristocratic niceness of the former and Melville for the democratic nationalism of the latter. Boston, rising a generation after New York to literary prominence in the national period, displayed virtually its full claim to literary eminence in the membership list of the Saturday Club, established in 1856. Included among the members were Ralph Waldo Emerson, Richard Henry Dana, James Russell Lowell, Henry Wadsworth Longfellow, Oliver Wendell Holmes, John Greenleaf Whittier, Nathaniel Hawthorne, and Edward Everett. In politics all of them were Whigs except Hawthorne, who, Everett complained indignantly, was "on the side of barbarism & vandalism against order, law, & constitutional liberty." Which was to say that Hawthorne belonged to the Democratic party. The historians John Lothrop Motley and William H. Prescott were also members. The two local citizens who, in retrospect, are most conspicuous by their absence were the historian and Jacksonian democrat George Bancroft and the nonconformist poet and essayist Henry David Thoreau.

New York boasted an equally brilliant and more diverse array of talent. Philip Freneau, Charles Brockden Brown, Washington Irving, James Kirke Paulding, Herman Melville, James Fenimore Cooper, and Walt Whitman were all a part of the New York literary scene, while Edgar Allen Poe was more closely associated with New York in his literary activities than with his native Virginia. All of these men were Jeffersonian Republicans or, later, Jacksonian Democrats. They tended to be broadly national in their outlook, whereas the cluster of literary men in the northern capitol tended, with a few exceptions, to be distinctly Bostonian.

Literary New Yorkers of aristocratic position naturally faced difficulties and embarrassments in their attempt to express the American democratic spirit. Irving was so polite about it as to be forgiven by his own class. As time went on, however, he detached himself from any active role in the politics of the Democratic party in deference to the sensibilities of his social class. It was the very aristocratic James Fenimore Cooper of Cooperstown who met the issue head-on. A vigorous man and a copious writer, Cooper drove himself repeatedly into impossible positions and then maintained them against violent opposition.

In politics Cooper became a Jacksonian mainly out of an agrarian distrust of the money power. In art he became a democrat in democratic America by force of patriotic instinct: the wish to identify himself artistically with the national culture. In the same vigorous patriotic spirit, he set himself the task of correcting his countrymen's views upon the subject of democracy. "Some men," he wrote, "fancy that a democrat can only be one who seeks the level, social, mental and moral, of the majority, a rule that would exclude all men of refinement, education, and taste from the class."

> These persons are enemies of democracy, as they at once render it impracticable. They are usually great sticklers for their own associations and habits, too, though unable to comprehend any of a nature that are superior. They are, in truth, aristocrats in principle, though assuming a contrary pretension; the ground work of all their feelings and arguments being self.

Cooper wove this tangled line of argument into an entire book, *The American Democrat,* and, not able to rest content, he did it over again in additional writings. His difficulty was that, sincerely believing himself to be a true democrat, he was driven to the conclusion that the vast majority of Americans were something else. On the one hand, many men of his own class did not disguise from him the fact that they detested democracy. On the other hand, the common people, although ignorantly believing themselves to be democratic, actually were equalitarian and therefore "enemies of democracy." Finding no true democratic heroes among the common men of his time, Cooper retreated into romance and created one of his own in Natty Bumppo, a pathfinder who was not only fearless and resourceful in the wilderness, but who was also properly servile in the presence of his betters. Cooper ended his life generally reviled and widely libeled for his criticism of American democracy.

Melville traveled a similar course with the reading public in democratic America: from early success to a hostile reaction against his later writings. Where Cooper fought back, Melville retired to a job in the New York customs house. When he died, late in the century, he had fallen into such obscurity that only one New York newspaper mentioned his name in its obituary column. Whether he ceased writing because the public had rejected him or because he had nothing more that he cared to say his biographers are unable to declare with assurance. Welcomed at first as a writer of South Sea Island adventure stories and the man who had lived among cannibals, Melville began to lose his reading public as his writings became increasingly allegorical.

He offended evangelical religious leaders in his first writings by his criticism of missionaries in their attempts to make over Polynesian society along western lines. Later, in *Mardi*, he turned to criticize Americans at home for their chauvinistic self-worship, their failure to appreciate the debt American society owed to England, and the blind faith of Americans in the principle of majority rule. The target of his criticism was an American which had threatened war with England over Oregon Territory and had fought a war of conquest with Mexico. "Hark ye, sovereign kings! cheer not on the yelping pack too furiously. Hunters have been torn by their hounds. . . . Neighboring nations may be free, without coming under your banner."

Americans should not take so much credit for their good fortune. From England they had learned liberty, and in America they had increased their liberty because there had been greater room for freedom, "because you overflow your redundancies within your mighty borders; having a wild western waste, which many shepards with their flocks could not overrun in a day. Yet overrun at last it will be, and the recoil must come." The day might eventually arrive, Melville wrote in *Clarel*, when,

> Dead level of rank commonplace:
> An Anglo-Saxon China see,
> May on your vast plains shame the race
> In the dark Ages of Democracy.

But Melville, for all his questionings, did not become a sour critic of American democracy in the manner of Cooper. America, he wrote, was "the best and happiest land under the sun." His skepticism concerning American democracy was but part of his pessimistic general view of human society, joined to his skeptical view of human religions. In *Typee* and *Omoo* his attacks upon the meddling of missionaries placed him in opposition to the popular religions; but the assumptions of liberal Christianity, of Unitarianism and transcendentalism (especially of transcendentalism), were even more alien to him, in their confident identification of human and divine qualities. The grounds for his skepticism he presented in *Pierre,* in an essay on "Chronometricals and Horologicals (Being not so much the Portal, as part of the temporary scaffold to the Portal of this New Philosophy)."

> Now in an artificial world like ours, the soul of man is further removed from its God and the Heavenly Truth, than the chronometer carried to China, is from Greenwich. And as that chronometer, if at all accurate, will pronounce it to be 12 o'clock midnight; so the chronometric soul, if in this world true to its great Greenwich in the other, will always, in its so-called intuitions of right and wrong, be contradicting the mere local standards and watchmaker's brains of this earth. . . .
>
> And thus, though the earthly wisdom of man be heavenly folly to God; so also, conversely, is the heavenly wisdom of God an earthly folly to man. . . .
>
> A virtuous expediency, then, seems the highest desirable or attainable earthly excellence for the mass of men. . . . the only great original moral doctrine of Christianity (i.e., the Chronometrical gratuitous return of good for evil, as distinguished from the horological forgiveness of injuries taught by some of the Pagan philosophers), has been found (horologically) a false

one; because after 1800 years' inculcation from tens of thousands of pulpits, it has proved entirely impracticable.

Melville was the American Goethe, and *Moby Dick* was his *Faust*. "Melville's basic intellectual program," writes Herbert W. Schneider, "was to approach God by means of the 'heart' rather than the 'head,' imagining that though both men and God are eternal mysteries to themselves and each other, they enter together into a tragedy which both can feel and act." Melville's hero Captain Ahab departed from the course of "virtuous expediency" to attack the white whale, the daemonic force of the universe. "To neither love nor reverence," declared Ahab to this opponent, "wilt thou be kind; and e'en for hate thou canst but kill; and all are killed. No fearless fool now fronts thee. I own thy speechless, placeless power, but to the last gasp of my earthquake life will dispute its unconditional, unintegral mastery in me."

The significance of Melville to American democratic thought lies in the entire rejection of his work by Americans for three-quarters of a century. In Germany school boys were obliged to memorize the names of Goethe's mistresses, so reverently did German society do homage to the romatic irrationality of Goethe's genius. In America Goethe was conventionally revered by genteel literary men such as Lowell, because he was revered in Germany. In America he was additionally popular on the purely sentimental level. His *Sorrows of Werther* became a best seller and the model for innumerable American novels of unrequited love. But the romantic, passionate skepticism of Goethe or Melville found no responsive audience in America. American democratic society was founded squarely upon faith in a God who made mankind His special care. He was the Methodist God who declared His purposes through divine revelation. He was the Unitarian God who endowed man with the gift of reason that man might understand His purposes; or He was the transcendental God whose spirit entered man to guide him intuitively. However bitter the sectarian struggles became in democratic America, and however divergent might be the spirit of evangelism from the spirit of transcendentalism, explicit faith in divine justice was a common spiritual requirement for Americans. Even atheists, while rejecting the existence of God, proceeded nevertheless upon the assumption that such a thing as eternal justice existed. Puzzled by Melville's prose and alienated by his mysterious skepticism, the reading public consigned his writings to obscurity with those of the comprehensible but quarrelsome Cooper, while it exalted the genteel Boston school of writers—undemocratic but perfectly clear and morally pure— as the chief claim of American democracy to literary eminence.

III

Oliver Wendell Holmes, Boston's most distinguished toastmaster, may be called upon to speak for the majority of the Saturday Club, although by no means for all its members, on the subject of literature and democracy. There is in New England, Holmes wrote, "an aristocracy, if you choose to call it so. . . . It has grown to be a *caste*,—not in any odious sense,—but, by the repetition of the same influence, generation after generation, it has acquired a distinct organization and physiognomy. . . ." The difference between the typical plebeian New England boy and an aristocratic youth was so apparent as to be recognized at once on sight.

> The first youth is the common country-boy, whose race has been bred to bodily labor. Nature has adapted the family organization to the kind of life it has lived. The hands and feet by constant use have got more than their share of development, —the organs of thought and expression less than their share. The finer instincts are latent and must be developed. A youth of this kind is raw material in its first stage of elaboration. You must not expect too much of any such. Many of them have force of will and character and become distinguished in practical life; but very few of them ever become great

scholars. A scholar is, in a large proportion of cases, the son of
scholars or scholarly persons.

That is exactly what the other young man is. He comes of
the *Brahmin caste of New England.*

The belief in Lamarkian evolution, upon which this thesis
appears to rest, has been discarded by scientists since Holmes's
time. Holmes's own great contribution to the validity of the
thesis, meanwhile, was the raising of a Brahmin son, Oliver
Wendell Holmes, Jr., to become one of America's greatest
jurists. For himself Holmes earned distinction as a physician
and medical scientist, but won more lasting fame, and apparently more personal gratification, as the author of "Old
Ironsides", "The Chambered Nautilus," and other minor but
memorable pieces of poetry. He essayed the novel as well.
He was necessarily a dilletante, however, though an ambitious
one, and the press of his professional duties forced him to leave
the cause of American poetry largely in the hands of such
fellow Brahmins as Lowell and Longfellow.

Lowell, though he gained wide popularity as a poet,
lacked on one hand Holmes's ability to write memorable verse,
and lacked on the other Longfellow's highly developed craftsmanship. Lowell's influence, despite the large volume and
good sales of his poetry, was exerted less as a poet than as a
critic and editor of *The Atlantic Monthly* and later *The North
American Review.* An early champion of the cause of an
American literature, he lacked the understanding of the democratic America necessary to the making of an American literature. Confining himself to the cultural life of Boston and
Europe, he came, in time, to speak disparagingly of the
"babble" that "is kept up about a national literature."

Lowell did make one wholehearted lunge toward an
Americanized form of writing in his *Biglow Papers,* written
at the time of the Mexican War as an attack upon the extension of slavery. He presented his message as the "homely
common-sense" of New England expressed in the "homely

dialect" of an ignorant, but instinctively right-thinking country fellow, Hosea Biglow. Defending his use of dialect against
the fastidious guardians of formal English, Lowell argued
that,

> True vigor of expression does not pass from page to page, but
> from man to man, where the brain is kindled and the lips are
> limbered by downright living interests and by passions in the
> very throe. Language is the soil of thought; and our own es-
> pecially is a rich leaf-mould, the slow growth of ages. . . .

The experiment was a commercial success, but not an
artistic one. Strongly marked throughout the *Biglow Papers*
is the aristocratic condescension of the author, the cream
of the jest for him so plainly being the incongruity of Brahmin
wisdom from the mouth of an untouchable.

Longfellow, technically the most proficient American
poet of his day, was beyond question the popular poet of
American democracy. And that was paradoxical, for Longfellow was alien by training and by temperament to the democracy of his day. A reserved and cultivated gentleman,
Longfellow, in order to equip himself to teach at Bowdoin
College, spent three years in Europe, absorbing the culture
of the European romantic movement. Then, in order to
equip himself to teach at Harvard, he returned to Europe for
fifteen months more of refreshment. The influence of this
European training is marked in the works of this productive
poet, and in the balance it was a baneful influence. Edgar
Allan Poe was willing to concede, if ungraciously, that Longfellow was the most accomplished poet in America, but he
pointed out quite justly that "Much as we admire the genius
of Mr. Longfellow, we are fully sensible of his many errors
of affectation and immitation." These errors were most
marked in Longfellow's tendency to sponge up the wet senti-
mentalism of the German romantic poets. For subject matter
also, Longfellow went to Europe or to a sentimentalized
American past, rather than to the America in which he lived.

Longfellow's appeal to democratic America was based not on his imitations of European writers nor on his translations of European works. It was based partly on his great ability to tell a story calculated to appeal to the American sentiments of patriotism and romance, stories such as *Paul Revere's Ride* and *The Courtship of Miles Standish*. It was based partly on the sound business instinct which he demonstrated in the effective marketing of his verse. But even more it was based upon the inspirational—what the Victorians called 'edifying'—character of Longfellow both as a poet and as a man.

> Tell me not, in mournful numbers,
> Life is but an empty dream!—
> For the soul is dead that slumbers,
> And things are not what they seem.
>
> Life is real! Life is earnest!
> And the grave is not its goal;
> Dust thou art, to dust returnest,
> Was not spoken of the soul.

To a moralistic America, ready to be "up and doing," Longfellow's message appealed. It was an America furthermore, which Longfellow flattered by giving it verse which was at once well written and easy to comprehend, and which left nothing, not even the obvious moral, to the imagination, but explained it fully in the final verse.

There were members of the Saturday Club who were made restless by the Brahmin provincialism which dominated their set. Hawthorne was the most uncompromising of these. Artistically, he lived in a separate world from his Bowdoin classmate Longfellow. Longfellow's interest in his New England ancestry gave the world the decorous romance between Priscilla and John Alden. Hawthorne's interest in his gave the world *The House of Seven Gables*, with Matthew Maule's curse upon the Pyncheon family for the original sin by which the Pyncheons acquired their property. Hawthorne etched a contrast between the historically guilty, exclusive Pyncheon family and the healthy rising democracy; a contrast, as F. O. Matthiessen pointed out, which extended down to the inbred hens in the Pyncheon garden.

Hawthorne's belief in equalitarian democracy at times seemed to extend to the condemnation of all private property as itself a sin against society. Through all his writings runs the theme that exclusiveness—separation from the mass of society and from the general concerns of the world—is a sin against God and man. Hawthorne, himself withdrawn from society, remained personally diffident in the midst of democracy while he denounced the principle of aristocracy. Morbidly absorbed with his own ancestry, he laid down the rule through one of his characters that "once in every half-century, at longest, a family should be merged into the great obscure mass of humanity, and forget all about its ancestors."

A lifelong admirer of Andrew Jackson, Hawthorne remained a staunch supporter of the Democratic party, a perennial officeholder, and the campaign biographer for Franklin Pierce in 1856. In his life and in his writings the irreconcilable struggle continued between the aristocracy of his artistic ideals and the democracy of his political beliefs. But while he cast wistful backward glances upon the cultivated life of aristocratic England, he kept his faith in the equalitarian ideals of America. American democracy repaid him for his support by a fairly early recognition of his genius and even by the purchase in small quantities of his writings. The limits of his American popularity were largely self-imposed. Possessing a potentially wide literary versatility, Hawthorne chose to perfect his style within the narrow range of stern allegory, on the all but unvarying theme of man's moral duty to society. It was not to be supposed that democratic America would have rewarded him more highly than it did, and Hawthorne, despite occasional explosive complaints, appears to have been satisfied with his receipts.

IV

Emerson, less realistic, less original, and less resolutely equalitarian than Hawthorne, was nevertheless made uncomfortable in democratic America by the genteel Federalism of Beacon Street. He could never go so far as to join the Democratic party. (He wrote Carlyle of Jackson that "a most unfit man in the Presidency has been doing the worst things.") Yet Emerson spoke of the democratic spirit in phrases which fired the zeal of democrats. And while never comporting himself in such a manner as to alienate his colleagues in the Saturday Club, he nevertheless remained on cordial terms with such radicals as George Bancroft, Orestes Brownson, and Wendell Phillips. Emerson conveyed the idea of goodness to radicals like Brownson and Phillips and to Brahmin conservatives like Holmes and Everett as well. The chief reason for this was the fact that he actually was a very good man, and one who positively radiated a spirit of sober, responsible kindliness. If he had wild and irresponsible things to say in theory about the virtue of flagrant lawlessness in obedience to some metaphysical higher law, he was himself obedient, not only to the laws, but also always to the proprieties as well. And if he departed from the Unitarian ministry to preach pantheistic notions, he was himself beyond question a devout and respectable gentleman. His "literary declaration of independence" to the Harvard Phi Beta Kappa in 1837, "daring" though it is often said to have been, caused no concern among the Boston worthies. Edward Everett followed with a eulogy of Emerson, and Holmes obliged with a song. Lowell recalled the speech thirty years later for its inspirational character. Emerson's lectures, which often seemed to advocate anarchy, were hardly such as might seriously disturb the most conservative State Street interests. They were, after all, calls, not for social action, but simply for self-improvement.

Emerson's writings took the form of poems and essays, but he was basically an aphorist. His essays were collections

of brilliant sentences bound together by hardly any organization at all. They achieved their unity by the singleness of
Emerson's purpose—whatever subject he might be discussing
—to propagate the message that God lives in each man and
that the duty of society and the individual is to give the fullest
scope and authority to the inward godliness of the individual.
Self-reliance—Emerson repeated the theme in endless varia-
tions—is trust in God. This was the clear, simple message
of transcendentalism, which, clothed in the brilliance of
Emerson's phrases, endured to appeal equally to Woodrow
Wilson and Henry Ford. To most Americans it might not do
at all as a religion, but it was all that democratic America
needed, or at any rate thought it needed, for a philosophy.
It gave the cold, clear, Jeffersonian libertarian ideal the
warmth and mystery which made it congenial to the romantic
age. It glorified the hero in the age of Jackson, while it fortified the individual against the tyranny of the majority. It
glorified the deeds of John Brown in bleeding Kansas, while
in quiet Concord it remained for Emerson the gospel of self-
respect. It argued freedom from social restraint for the businessman, while it became the standard by which business
conduct might be condemned. In whatever way this versatile
philosophy was used, it served as the deification of American
individualism.

Emersonian transcendentalism presupposed the quiet,
settled, civilized, respectable circumstances of Concord, Massachusetts, but Emerson was not content to be a small-town
philosopher. He aspired to mystical experiences which at the
same time he was too modest seriously to expect, and he
aspired to be the philosopher of a democratic nation which
was too vast, vulgar, superstitious, and violent for his comprehension. He glorified heroism as the supreme example of
divinity operating in the individual. John Brown's attack on
the Federal arsenal at Harpers Ferry seemed to him just
such an heroic response to a higher law, and Emerson, faith-

ful to his convictions, publicly declared that Brown, in hanging for the deed, had served to "make the gallows glorious like the cross." But privately Emerson referred to "the sad Harpers Ferry business," and said of Brown, "He is a true hero but lost his head there." Emerson would have felt easier with a hero who endured than with one who acted.

Thomas Carlyle, who possessed a more robust enthusiasm for heroes than his friend Emerson did, urged Emerson to create a mythical American hero of the circumstances of the frontier. "How beautiful," he wrote, "to think of lean tough Yankee settlers, tough as gutta-percha, with almost *occult* unsubduable fire in their belly, steering over the Western mountains, to annihilate the jungle, and bring bacon and corn out of it for the Posterity of Adam. . . ." Perhaps Emerson would have liked to oblige, but it was a task better suited to the talents of Cooper or William Gilmore Simms or Robert Montgomery Bird. It was also better suited to the talents of Davy Crockett, Jack Downing, and Sam Slick, who, to the disgust of the defenders of taste in American literature, were gaining some serious attention in English literary circles. Emerson's magnificent humility always guarded him against venturing out of his own narrow, well-traversed walk. He admired the American West, but among his intimates Thoreau was the nearest approach to Carlyle's hypothetical hero and Walden Pond the closest facsimile of Carlyle's jungle.

Thoreau lacked Emerson's generous soul, perhaps, and also his good breeding, and was not a member of the Saturday Club. Far from being a club member, Thoreau was not, so far as he could arrange it and still have an occasional audience, a member of society at all. As Emerson said of him, "He was bred to no profession; he never married, he lived alone; he never went to church; he never voted; he refused to pay a tax to the State, he ate no flesh, he drank no wine, he never knew the use of tobacco, and, though a naturalist, he used neither trap nor gun." Thoreau, in addition to being a philosophical and poetic observer of nature, served as the personification of Emerson's transcendental, self-reliant, democratic, and—necessarily—anti-social man.

Thoreau would have been the Emersonian myth in the very flesh, except that he moved one step further away from Calvinism by rejecting Christianity altogether. "A healthy man," he wrote, "with steady employment, as wood chopping at fifty cents a cord, and a camp in the woods, will not be a good subject for Christianity." Emerson admired Thoreau greatly, but when Thoreau went to jail for refusing to pay his state tax in a protest against the Mexican War, Emerson found this particular obedience to a higher law "mean and skulking, and in bad taste." When Bronson Alcott had made the same gesture three years earlier, Thoreau, at first approving, had later complained that Alcott acted as though he had started a revolution. The Concord transcendentalists, as they themselves were painfully aware, acted out their parts not upon the stage of the American continent, but upon the stage of one small New England town.

They believed in heroes, they believed in democracy, and they believed in America, and they always had an eye out for men who could meet the qualifications, men who probably would not come from Concord, Massachusetts. In the field of action they found such a man in John Brown, although Emerson appears afterwards to have changed his mind. In the field of art they found such a man, not in Carlyle's jungle, but in the borough of Brooklyn, New York. Walt Whitman, a newspaperman and by temperament and environment a man of the people, wrote a series of verses entitled *Leaves of Grass,* in 1855. Setting the type himself, Whitman sent copies to all of the literary lights of the day. Out of the general silence which followed, there came a letter from Emerson.

> Dear Sir, I am not blind to the worth of the wonderful gift of *Leaves of Grass.* I find it the most extraordinary piece of wit and wisdom that America has yet contributed. . . . It meets

the demand I am always making of what seemed the sterile
and stingy Nature. . . . I give you joy of your free and brave
thought. I have great joy in it. . . . I greet you at the beginning
of a great career.

Whitman subsequently printed, unauthorized, a quotation from this letter upon the cover of his next edition. It
gave Emerson anguish, but Emerson never denied his enthusiasm, even though it was one which displeased the rest of
the Saturday Club. As for Thoreau, he took up Whitman as
one of the great heroes of the age.

Whitman was a proletarian genius who had not been
proposed either by Carlyle or the transcendentalists, although
Emerson had been an early inspiration to him. He was, among
other things, a harbinger of urbanized, industralized America—something that American democracy, and American
literature, were not quite prepared to think seriously about.
With a great lyrical sense, Whitman combined an observing
eye, an acquaintanceship with all sorts of people, a sensual
feeling of identity with all of them, and an indiscriminate
willingness to discuss life in the round, including—and in fact
especially including—sex life. "Walking freely out from the old
traditions," Whitman wrote Emerson, "as our politics has
walked out, American poets and literats recognize nothing
behind the sturdy living forms of the men and women of
These States, the divinity of sex, the perfect eligibility of the
female with the male, all The States, liberty and equality,
real articals. . . ."

To readers a century later, much of Whitman's poetry
simply goes on and on, apostrophizing inordinately; yet his
greatness as a poet is obvious. It was not obvious to his
own generation. Whitman, writing in blank verse and ap-
propriating his vocabulary from the language of the people
about him, sang praises of a continental democratic America.
He did his best to crowd in everything of American life.
Emerson later complained that he expected Whitman to make

the songs of the nation, but that Whitman seemed content to make the inventories. Abandoning the "language of poetry" and the gentleman's rules as to what one said and what one did not say in print, Whitman succeeded in giving voice to the inarticulate democracy of America as no American poet had even attempted to do before him. He saw his poetry as contributing to the national literary mission to transpose the democratic concept "far beyond Politics into the regions of taste." Many who subscribed to this in theory were at the same time altogether unwilling to enter Whitman's regions of taste. The articulate democracy, with a few exceptions such as Emerson and Thoreau, denounced him as an indecent person.

It was a good number of years before Walt Whitman could find a commercial publisher who would print his poems. In the meantime his poetry hung like an albatross around his neck, as he tried to make a living. Most literate Americans denounced the poems as unGodly and unAmerican, and denounced the author as a subverter of good public order. Losing the chance for a government job when Secretary of the Treasury Chase discovered his identity, Whitman worked efficiently and anonymously at another government post until his identity was revealed, upon which he was immediately fired.

No writer, surely, received a worse reception from the American reading public than Whitman. But by best-selling standards, few of the writers in Young America who by academic sanction have been incorporated into American literature did well. Cooper and Irving sold well in their day, while Longfellow and Whittier were quite successful. None matched the popularity of Scott or Dickens, however, while among domestic literature the "women's books" such as *Fern Leaves from Fanny's Portfolio* and *The Lamplighter* were the books receiving popular attention at the time when Melville, Hawthorne, Emerson, Thoreau, and Whitman were producing their greatest works. The best-selling authors of the day were Mary Jane Holmes, Ann Sophia Stephens, Sarah Josepha Hale, Elizabeth Oakes Smith, Caroline Lee Hentz, and Louise Chandler, to name a few. "America," complained Hawthorne, "is now wholly given over to a d—d mob of scribbling women, and I should have no chance of success while the public taste is occupied with their trash. . . ." Thoreau took it more calmly. Viewing unopened packing cases of his books, sent him by his publisher as unsalable, he commented, "Is it not well that the author should behold the fruits of his labor?" The Civil War ravaged this literary age of democratic faith, but the size of the publishers' checks must already have taken its toll. American writers had won their independence from England, but American readers had not, except for the readers of sentimental "women's novels." Universal education and woman's rights were two bright hopes of the age in the struggle for American democratic millennium. Hawthorne viewed such organized reforms with a skeptical eye, and no doubt his colleagues came increasingly to his view.

THE RECONSTRUCTION OF
AMERICAN DEMOCRACY

A MERICAN federal democracy in 1860 faced the challenge of its life—quite apart from the slavery question—in the need to convert its bucolic political institutions to meet the unknown requirements of democracy in the fast approaching monopolistic industrial state. The crisis was the more acute for the fact that no one understood the nature of the problem. The industrial revolution was proceeding at a velocity beyond the comprehension of contemporaries. That it was rapidly reordering the lives of millions of Americans was unavoidably apparent, and yet the notion that government must reorder itself correspondingly was one which did not suggest itself to men in high places. Many still wished to view the industrial revolution as a passing abberation which an intelligent, vigilant citizenry ought not to tolerate, while others, seeing clearly that the old world of their youth had passed away, became all the more resolute in the conviction that the old ways must be preserved. The one prominent political figure to call for bold political reorientation, John C. Calhoun, was a reactionary whose scheme of concurrent majorities took no account of the possibility of present and future change.

Of all those nations of the world which passed through the industrial revolution in the nineteenth century, none was as ill-arranged politically to control the new development as America was. Jeffersonian republicanism and Jacksonian democracy had presupposed a nation of farmers supported by classes of craftsmen and tradespeople whose area of economic enterprise would be local, small scale, and amenable to municipal, county, and state control. The federal and state governments had been devised at a time when, as Henry Adams observed, the machinery of production and the nation's mode of life were not basically different from those of the Saxons of the eighth century.

It was, of course, also true of England, France, Germany, and Japan that governments formed on the basis of a static, agrarian past were obliged to meet the same challenges of industrialism. Each of these nations, however, was administered by a centralized government at the time the industrial revolution centralized its economy. In the United States, on the other hand, decentralization of government was not only a fact of political life; it was a basic article of faith which was not to be given up. Democratic reformers well into the twentieth century continued to argue, rather helplessly, that industry, to be controlled within the federal system, had to be decentralized, rather than that the federal system needed to be strengthened to cope with the centralized economy. This line of argument was a prominent feature of Wilsonian progressivism.

Had it not been for the slavery crisis and the war, the fifties and sixties might well have been a great age of reform, when many of those issues would have been faced which in fact did not receive serious nationwide attention until the twentieth century. Instead, American politics in the fifties narrowed itself to the issue of whether slaves might be taken into the territories, while civil war and reconstruction absorbed its attention in the sixties and left a legacy of hatreds and distractions in the seventies, eighties, and nineties which did much to drive astray practical major reform efforts.

Consequently in the early twentieth century the men of the progressive era could find comparatively little in the previous half century of the nation's history from which to fashion a program of democratic reform applicable to an industrial society. For the support of a strong national reform tradition they were obliged to rely heavily upon the somewhat anachronistic movements of the largely pre-industrial age of Jefferson and Jackson. The New Deal reforms in their turn were made possible, not by the strength of the reform tradition, but by the catastrophic failure of the existing system. In the crisis of the Great Depression, Franklin D. Roosevelt called not for the implementation of a recognized reform program, but for "bold, persistent experimentation." "It is common sense," he said, "to take a method and try it. If it fails, admit it frankly and try another. But above all, try something." The attempt to reconstruct democracy to fit the requirements of an industrial nation still suffered, seventy years after the event, from the ravages of the Civil War. The war preserved the Union, and, in a rather narrowly literal sense, it freed the slaves, but in the history of American democracy it proved to be a disaster of incalculable proportions.

I

It is deceptively easy to minimize the change which industrialism had wrought upon American society by the eve of the Civil War. Statistical comparisons between the decade of the fifties and that of the seventies, for instance, can create the impression of halting, rather small-scale beginnings in the earlier period. The truth is, the changes that marked the decades of the forties and fifties were in some ways more disturbing to society than those of any later period, because they constituted a more radical break with the past and were new to this period, as to no later one. Most of the main problems arising out of the industrial revolution which beset American society in the late nineteenth and early twentieth centuries were faced for the first time during the generation which preceded the Civil War.

The revolution in transportation was the key to the new industrialism. By the eve of the Civil War, half the iron production in the United States was absorbed by the railroads for tracks and other railroad equipment. The thirties and forties saw much more extensive railroad construction in America than in any other nation of the world, and during the fifties this, itself, was increased fourfold, the greatest volume of new construction serving to bring the western areas in commercial contact with the eastern seaboard. That a transcontinental railroad was not already under construction was due only to sectional rivalry in Congress, dominated by the slavery question. Within this decade innumerable farm communities gained railroad outlets and expanded their markets from the immediate neighborhood to the whole world.

With the broadening of markets came the opportunity, and also the necessity, for a commercialization which radically altered the character of that society upon which the political ideals of Jefferson and Jackson had been founded. In 1815 Mount Pleasant, Ohio, a town of five hundred persons, excluding journeymen, laborers, and transients, supported three saddlers, three hatters, four blacksmiths, four weavers, six shoemakers, eight carpenters, three tailors, three cabinet makers, one baker, one apothecary, two wagon-makers, two tanners, one manufacturer of wool-carding machines, one operator of a machine for spinning wool, a manufactory for spinning thread from flax, a nail manufacturer, and the operator of two wool-carding machines. Within a six-mile radius there were nine merchant mills, two grist mills, twelve saw mills, one paper mill, and a woolen factory. All of this was in addition to the household manufacturers, where most of these processes were duplicated and where many additional ones were performed. Mount Pleasant was typical of much of the nation's rural economy until into the 1840's.

Such small, homespun economies as this were transformed almost at once by railroad contact with the manufacturing world. Commercial farming replaced subsistence farming, household manufacture was largely abandoned, and local craftsmen were ruined by the country store. "In proportion as railroads and canals are constructed," the *Voice of Industry* warned in 1847,

> these mamouth establishments in tanning, shoemaking, saddlery, blacksmithing, and every department of work and skill, send their productions and fabrics to distant parts of the country, and reduce smaller capitalists . . . constantly killing out their rivals and monopolizing the business to themselves.

And in the process "The rich grow richer and the poor poorer, and Mammon is usurping sovereignty in all places."

For the farmers, who still remained the dominant element in the nation, the new development resulted in a higher standard of living and also in a diminished independence. Commercial farming brought rich returns during good times and severe hardship during the panic of '57. But even in good times it brought an unwonted reliance upon world market prices and upon other uncontrollable outside economic factors. Naturally unwilling to return to the old simplicities of subsistence agriculture, the farmers were outraged to find that they had been robbed of their birthright of independence. In 1858, farmers attended meetings to demand state and federal regulation of railroads, of grain elevators, and of financial institutions. They called for the organization of cooperatives to drive out the thieving middlemen and restore to those who labored in the earth the just fruits of their toil. This incipient farmers' revolt was nipped in the bud by war, bumper crops, and soaring farm prices, but the later granger and populist movements were clearly foreshadowed in this early reaction.

The cities experienced their greatest relative growth in the history of the nation during the decade before the Civil War. New York doubled in size during that decade to achieve a population of more than one million. Chicago quadrupled, while the lake ports generally experienced unmanageably large growths; and with the bloating of the cities there developed unprecedented lawlessness, violence, sin, and poverty.

Many who had become otherwise reconciled to democracy were convinced that universal manhood suffrage would never be adaptable to metropolitan communities.

Doubts about the practicality of urban democracy were heightened by the fact that this new population was largely acquired from abroad, especially from Ireland. The decade of the fifties experienced—again relatively speaking—the heaviest immigration in the nation's history, and by 1860 the native-foreign, Protestant-Catholic, rural-urban antipathies were far advanced, which were to play so prominent a part in frustrating democratic reform down to the New Deal.

Nativism, which had first shown its promise with the Anti-Masonic party a generation before, in 1854 ballooned forth in the Know Nothing party. It immediately gained a national following, winning notable victories in Massachusetts against the Irish and California against the Chinese. To many practiced politicians it appeared as the party of the future, but it lacked a positive program and an organization, and it passed abruptly from the scene. Dismissed by historians as a racist enthusiasm, the Know Nothing party gained its support not only from simple nativists, but also from many who wished to see the new industrialism, especially the railroads, brought under regulation, to secure the common people from dictation by a plutocracy. Although more blatantly nativistic than later reform movements, it has some claim to be considered the first reform movement of America's industrial age. Nor was its nativism entirely unrepresentative of the later granger, populist, and progressive crusades.

In the new industrial world the skilled mechanic, unlike the unskilled worker, improved his economic position, but his gains were not commensurate with the rapid increase in the value of his production. That employers were waxing fatter than workers under the new system was ground for grievance, but it was not in the economic struggle that the workingmen most acutely suffered the sense of defeat. "The losses of the

industrial worker in the first half of the century," writes
Norman Ware, "were not comfort losses solely, but losses, as
he conceived it, of status and independence." It was not the
machine which the skilled worker reacted against so much
as it was the system, and the new class distinctions, which the
machine introduced. The journeyman who had received his
training in the first decades of the nineteenth century had
been taught to think of himself as a social equal of his boss.
He had also been brought up to believe that a community of
interest bound the journeyman and the boss together in a
joint enterprise. This journeyman might join a union and
take part in a strike; still, he remained alien to the idea that
there was a logical opposition between capital and labor.
This mechanic was not really a wage earner in the modern
sense of the word. He was paid, not for his labor, but for his
"price," that is, for the value of the product he sold to his
employer.

With the rise of the factory system the mechanic in many
cases ceased to make a product, and instead performed one
or more operations in a mass production process. And, at the
same time, he began working for a daily wage, selling himself instead of his product. The mechanic used the phrase
"wage slave" in a literal sense. With the wage system came
also the demand for the speeding up of production and the
consequent tightening of discipline. Responsibility for maintaining this discipline often came to rest with a boss who was
himself a hired man and not the proprietor of the establishment, as had formerly been the case. The factory owner very
likely had no direct contact with his workers and no interest
in anything about them except their rate of production.

Against this new, impersonal, aristocratic factory system
the workingmen made furious complaint. The beginnings of
this system in the twenties contributed to the unusually energetic participation in politics of the workingmen's parties in
the late twenties and early thirties. Criticisms of capitalism

and of wage slavery were increasingly heard in the following decades. Some of the shoe manufacturers, *The Awl* declared in 1844,

> seem to think that the jours [journeymen] are designed for no other purpose than to be their subjects. . . . They seem to think it a disgrace to labor; that the laborer is not as good as other people. These little stuck-up, self-conceited individuals who have a little second-hand credit. . . . You must do as they wish . . . or you are out of their books; they have no more employment for you.

And the National Typographical Society declared in 1850,

> It is useless for us to disguise from ourselves the fact that, under the present arrangement of things, there exists a perpetual antagonism between Labor and Capital . . . one striving to sell their labor for as much, and the other striving to buy it for as little as they can. . . .

During the fifties skilled labor organized, not, as formerly, mainly to promote general programs of reform, but rather as permanent members of a class, joined together to better their working conditions in the inevitable struggle against capital. The panic of '57 wiped these unions out, however, and skilled workers entered the Civil War period bereft of organizational strength.

Meanwhile the rich, as the workingmen charged, were indeed getting richer. For one thing there was more money than there had been before. California gold had helped to create millionaires in the fifties, and the gold and silver strikes in Nevada, Colorado, and elsewhere were on the verge of creating many additional ones. Factory owners were becoming rich, but the merchant capitalist still led the ranks of wealth, his opportunities greatly enhanced by the transportation revolution. Mass-distribution techniques accounted for the wealth of two of the richest men, the drygoods merchant H. B. Claflin and the department store proprietor A. T. Stewart.

Although the number of millionaires in 1860 was remarkable when compared with a generation earlier, the plutocracy was still barely in its infancy. Railroading had yet to produce its multimillionaires. Cornelius Vanderbilt, who had made a fortune in steamboating, did not enter the railroad field until the late fifties. But in the fifties the way was cleared for the railroad kings. In that decade the Pennsylvania Railroad bought out the competing canal system and gained dominion over the state's transportation. The New York Central was formed in 1853 out of a consolidation of seven independent lines, and in the same year the Baltimore & Ohio Railroad extended its rails to Wheeling. By 1861 Congress had granted eighteen million acres of land to the states for railroad construction, and the Illinois Central had become the chief landed interest in Illinois.

Similarly the foundation for plutocracy was being laid in other areas. Oil was first drilled commercially in 1859, and almost at once the rush was on. The iron ore of the Lake Superior region was first mined in the fifties. Cyrus McCormick established his factory in Chicago in 1848, and the forties and fifties saw the development of the sewing machine, the rotary press, the hydraulic turbine, the electric locomotive, the pneumatic tire, and the beginning of packaging in tin cans. Many of the new enterprises were financed and directed from outside the state. The Illinois Central, for instance, was formed by an association of Boston and New York businessmen. Then too, many of the new enterprises developed into interstate operations, where there were no appropriate provisions for regulation. Certainly serious new problems had presented themselves, but the war came, and they were lost from view.

II

Secession and war brought the immediate, accidental, and quite unpremeditated triumph of capitalism in American politics. Although long frustrated by southern agrarian domination of the national government, the majority of the northern business community in 1860 had favored almost any program of appeasement which would keep the South in the Union. Anxious as they were about any changes which might disrupt the flow of trade, fearful of the possible southern repudiation of debts to northern interests, and terrified of losing the rich southern market, businessmen in 1860 joined the new Constitutional Union party to demand that people stop talking about the slavery issue altogether. Then eleven agrarian states withdrew from the Union, and northern business tumbled almost uncontrollably into power. On top of that, war came and opened up prodigious opportunities for profit. Soon northern business interests were battening themselves voraciously on the spoils of war, while in Congress they were wallowing happily in a feast of legislative favors.

These favors most frequently took the form of tariff increases. From 1832 until secession the general tendency had been away from protection and toward free trade. This changed at once. A tariff increase followed immediately upon secession, and during the Civil War every session of Congress made it a part of its business to raise tariffs further. Greater and greater protection for American industry continued to be the rule, despite occasional and generally very minor setbacks, well into the period of the New Deal. In the view of nineteenth-century liberals this new tariff policy, more than any other circumstance, provided the basis for American plutocratic power.

Many bills were passed legislating away the national domain to private interests. Of these the at first widely popular railroad acts were the most momentous. Between 1862 and 1871 more than one hundred and fifty million acres of western land were legislated away by the federal government, about a third of this later being forfeited, however, because of failure to meet the original conditions of the grant. Millions of additional acres were distributed to the railroads by the states. By various other channels, notably the Morrill Land Grant Act, other millions of acres fell, at bargain rates and in units of thousands of acres, into private hands. With the panic of '73 and the revelation of gargantuan corruption, a reaction against these giveaways set in, but the deed was already accomplished. The old American dream of land speculation on the truly grand scale had become a reality, made possible by the coming of the railroad and abetted by secession, civil war, and reconstruction. Meanwhile the old popular demand for free land in modest lots was met with the passage of the Homestead Act, granting 160 acres free to homesteaders. By the time the act was passed, however, the circumstances had changed which had led to its passage. After the Civil War, despite the Homestead law, it was the railroads and not the government that did the real land-office business.

The purpose of the Civil War banking acts was to help finance the war, but the enduring result was the tighter concentration of national credit in the hands of eastern financial institutions. The contract labor law of 1864 permitted the importation of foreign labor under terms of temporary voluntary servitude. After the war the law was repealed, but little effective effort was made to bring a stop to the practice. The war itself did little to stimulate industrial progress; rather it diverted industry into unproductive fields to fill wartime needs. Its benefit to northern capitalism lay almost wholly in the new freedom which resulted from southern secession and wartime necessities.

The reconstruction decade prolonged the condition until, in 1877, the last of the southern states were readmitted on the basis of a broad understanding between northern and southern conservatives. As C. Vann Woodward has demonstrated, complete reunion was accompanied by a "rejuvenation of whiggery." Northern Republicans had been ill at ease with their dirt-poor southern Negro allies. Conservative southerners had been ill at ease in the Democratic party of the common folk, and, having missed out on the division of the national spoils, they wanted their own railroad land grants, river and harbor improvements, and the like. The compromise of 1876-77 did not bring them just what they wanted, but in an informal way it resumed the old conservative alliance of Whig party days. And, until the Populist movement of the nineties, it helped to keep the Democratic party in conservative, business-minded hands, in the South as well as the North, and so to disarm the two-party system as a means of reform. Party politics for the next two decades concerned itself with patronage problems, organization, party loyalty, and the struggle for the compensations to be earned through service to special business interests. As the century drew to a close the system changed to the extent that members of the plutocracy increasingly tended, instead of hiring a senator, to join the Senate themselves. State legislatures were bought in wholesale lots by interested parties, while corruption flourished at its rankest in the cities of the nation.

Politics in the Gilded Age was hardly democratic in the sense of representing the people; yet it entailed no abrupt departure from the political practice of an earlier time. Throughout the national period, politics had been looked upon as a means of gain. Andrew Jackson was willing to use his public influence to promote his personal fortune just as was James G. Blaine. So were Webster, Clay, and Benton, and so were politicians generally. The idea that a public servant might be unfitted for his duties by a conflict of interest between his public and private concerns was one which had not yet entered into the American political tradition. Similarly the robber barons, in their piratical operations, were at worst but selling wooden nutmegs on the grand scale. Shrewd Yankee practice was in the best American tradition. Public opinion might be warm against Rockefeller, but it had no standards by which to condemn Rockefeller's practices.

The small-town ethics of Jacksonian democracy was on the side of plutocracy. A broad change in social standards was evidently required to reorient democratic values to industrial society. The Liberal Republicans attempted to provide it. They bolted against Grant and later against Blaine, calling for honesty in business dealings and an end to corruption and favoritism in government. Liberal Republicanism, however, was too genteel in its leadership and too doctrinaire in its laissez-faire faith to catch the imagination of the people. Populism, with its program of currency reform and government regulation, attracted a broader following and in 1896 captured the Democratic party. Populism, however, remained distinctly a farmers' party, at a time when the farmer had ceased to represent the majority in the nation and had declined, without yet realizing it, to the position of a special interest group. Then too, by the end of the century prosperity returned to the farms of the nation and with it came an end to agrarian reforming zeal. The politics of reform in the Gilded Age failed altogether to formulate a broadly acceptable alternative to plutocratic standards of conduct. It was in the churches of the nation that this task was most effectively carried out.

The social gospel, although it failed to win over American Christianity as a whole, succeeded in capturing the imagination of the upper-middle classes in the last two decades of the nineteenth century, and in doing this it opened the way for a new generation of democratic reform. Christ had come on earth, ministers of the social gospel argued, not alone to bring individuals to salvation, but also to save society as a whole. The duty of the Christian went beyond personal salvation. He must work to make over society along Christian lines, creating an environment suitable to the good Christian life. In all of his public dealings he must be guided by the teachings of Christ, especially by the Golden Rule. The phrase Golden Rule became a key one for ministers, humanitarian reformers, idealistic businessmen, and reforming politicians at the close of the century. The social gospel was broadly interdenominational and undogmatic, concerning itself with the social sciences as much as with theology. It took its text as readily from Henry George's *Progress and Poverty* as from *The Bible*. It won the support of the new generation of academic economists, and, in turn, the American Economic Association gained a significantly large membership from the American ministry.

The origins of the progressive movement are to be traced in the last decade of the nineteenth century to urban good-government drives led often by ministers or by reformers impelled by a strong religious motivation. In their attacks against red-light districts, gambling, and drinking, these reformers won the added support of conservative Protestantism as well. The Anti-Saloon League in some areas brought its great organizational strength to the side of progressivism, where such an alliance worked for the cause of prohibition. Within the Catholic Church the social justice movement similarly worked for the application of Christian principles to the conduct of society. However, Catholic-Protestant antagonism prevented any very effective cooperation, and the progressive movement, while it lacked the explicit anti-Catholicism of earlier reform movements, nevertheless remained distinctly Protestant, as well as middle-class, in its orientation and its following.

This religious orientation of progressivism did much to account both for its success and for its limitations. It provided the movement with a moralistic emotional coherence which to some extent compensated for the lack of any comprehensive program of reform upon which progressives could unite. On the other hand, reforms based on such ambiguous distinctions as the difference between "good" and "bad" trusts were apt to be superficial and ineffective. The progressive movement was a middle-class defense against the consolidated plutocracy above and the burgeoning proletariat beneath. Fear of socialism brought many Americans to the support of economic legislation such as workmen's compensation, industrial safety acts, child labor laws and slum improvement programs. Resentment against the robber barons and fear for democracy in the face of the new economic combinations brought support for legislation to control the great corporations and, if possible, to break up the great monopolies and place the nation on a footing of regulated competition.

The progressive movement occurred during a time of prosperity, however, and few wished to follow any rash course which would endanger the economy. Although Theodore Roosevelt thundered against the great trusts, he did not comport himself in such a way as to lose the financial support of Morgan, Rockefeller, and Harriman in the campaign of 1904, and in the panic of 1907 he proved delicately considerate of corporate interests. Wilson took his stand "where every progressive ought to take his stand, on the proposition that private monopoly is indefensible and intolerable," but when in 1913 the nation began to suffer depression conditions, Wilson was as quick to consult Wall Street as Roosevelt and Taft had been before him. It is significant that the progressive movement was launched nationally at the time when finance capitalism was rapidly completing its consolidations, in the years between 1899 and 1904. Thereafter the masters of capital, secure at last after a generation of danger, accepted moderate regulatory reforms without fury, joined the National Civic Federation to achieve a more harmonious relationship with union labor, and hired experts in public relations, to improve their standing among the people as a whole. The Wall Street broker George Perkins joined Roosevelt's progressive party to assist in the task of regulating the corporations in the interest of the nation as a whole. He was against "social sin" too.

The progressive movement, although it accomplished much in the area of national as well as local reform, failed

to develop a broad program of reform—or a philosophy of reform—to which a majority of the voters would subscribe, and
it failed to turn either major party into a distinctly reform
party. It appeared for a time that Wilson had achieved this
feat in 1916, but Wilsonian progressivism swiftly lost its dominion within the party in the course of Wilson's second administration. As it turned out, it proved to be a war casualty,
but there is good reason to suppose that the Wilsonian coalition would have broken up over progressive issues had America never entered the war. A heterogeneous collection of
farmers, southerners, unionists, intellectuals, humanitarians,
and city bosses, it could hardly have been maintained long as
the party of reform, except where outside pressures were
greater than the great inner stresses and contradictions. In
the event, Wilson ended his second administration amid the
Great Red Scare, at the head of a government more securely
dominated by business interests than any since McKinley's
time. Discredited by the failure of Wilsonian progressivism
and Wilsonian internationalism, the Democratic party fell
to the lowest fortunes of its history in the 1920's, as the nation
kissed democratic reform goodbye.

One main result of the progressive movement, as Arthur
Link has pointed out, was the achievement of the identification of the middle-class American businessman with good government and with those economic reforms which best served
the interests of the nation as a whole. By the close of the
progressive era the businessman had effectively replaced the
farmer as the chief custodian of the national virtues. By then
the businessman, himself, had deserted the progressive cause,
but in the next decade he retained his new prestige and further
enhanced it. At the same time, the managerial revolution
had in the popular imagination replaced the robber baron
with the forward looking business executive, a professional
man trained to administrate industry in the best interest of
the nation, through the uniquely American plan of welfare

capitalism. After a generation of reform the nation had had enough of "politics." Business represented the true national genius, and the nation could safely be entrusted to the businessman. The true measure of liberty, Herbert Hoover explained, was the absence of governmental regimentation. Industrial self-government was the purest form of democracy, and its purest expression was to be found in the America of the twenties. Taking his text from the Declaration of Independence, Hoover preached a machine-age neo-Jeffersonianism, applying the old precepts to the new society with dogmatic finality. This passed for wisdom until late in 1929.

In one respect, the decade of Coolidge Republicanism was undeniably more democratic than any that had preceded it. Strongly supported by the moral forces, the woman suffrage amendment was adopted in 1920, in time for women voters to assist Warren G. Harding to the greatest landslide vote ever accorded a Presidential candidate before or since. Woman suffrage was to prove a disappointment to the moral forces, however, for it has never given national politics quite that high moral spirit which was maintained during the progressive era, comparatively unaided by the women's vote.

It seems to be the consensus of historians that the nineteenth amendment had, in fact, no appreciable impact on politics, but one important piece of circumstantial evidence belies this conclusion. From the election of Jackson to the passage of the nineteenth amendment, no President was elected by a majority of more than the 56.41 per cent which Theodore Roosevelt received in 1904. During the period since the Civil War more than half the contests had been won by a plurality and not a majority of the votes. By contrast, all elections but one, since the adoption of the nineteenth amendment, have been landslide elections, and five of the eleven have been won by a proportionately larger majority than was ever previously accorded a candidate since Monroe's uncontested victory in 1820. So decisive a change in the voting pattern seems to indicate that women voters have changed the character of national elections. The women appear to be largely responsible for that independent vote which has become so important a consideration in the choice of candidates and such a handicap to efficient, uncomplicated party organization.

III

On coming to power in 1933 the New Dealers bothered themselves little, as a practical matter, with progressive precedents or with the whole range of the American reform tradition. They turned rather to America's recent military past for experience and guidance. The immediate aim of the New Deal was not to perfect American democracy, but to mobilize the resources of the nation to meet a desperate emergency. For this purpose the clearly relevant precedents were those which had been established in the course of mobilizing for the first world war. It was upon these that the New Deal chiefly relied in its first two years. The National Recovery Act, the basic recovery program, was a vast scheme for government-directed industrial self-government, developed somewhat along the lines of the War Industries Board. It was directed by General Hugh S. Johnson, whose early training had been with the War Industries Board. Johnson's former colleague on the Board, George Peek, was placed at the head of the Agricultural Adjustment Administration, where he applied his wartime experience in mobilizing agricultural resources. Section 7a of NRA, guaranteeing labor the right to bargain collectively (unsuccessfully as it turned out), had its precedent in the Wilsonian wartime provisions for labor arbitration.

The Tennessee Valley Authority also had its origins during the war, in the dams constructed at Muscle Shoals, Tennessee, to furnish power for nitrate plants. Previous bills authorizing peacetime government operation and extension of these facilities had been passed in Congress, to be vetoed by

Coolidge and Hoover. The war had provided the only precedent to which the New Deal could point for its policy of imposing high income taxes and excess-profits taxes. Reorganization of the railroads similarly benefited from wartime experience. The Public Works Administration, with other relief and pump-priming ventures, represented a departure from past practice for the federal government, but the earlier experience in handling wartime contracts was relevant to the new programs.

For two years the nation continued on this emergency footing ("Fascism, pure fascism," Hoover declared), while general enthusiasm turned to mounting, many-sided opposition. The business community, the chief beneficiary of the system, demanded a return to what it remembered as free enterprise. Organized labor, disappointed in its expectations of strong government support, lashed out in violent, bloody strikes. Millions of impoverished members of the middle and lower-middle classes, who were not included in any politically powerful pressure group, had at the outset welcomed the generous relief handouts and the makework projects. But as they watched the main events from the sidelines for two years, they became increasingly bitter toward the new dispensation. They found their own leaders, and in a loose way they organized. Persuasive demagogues like Father Coughlin gained large and excited followings. The Townsend old-age pension movement enrolled a reputed million members. The Socialist Upton Sinclair seemed for a time likely to win the governorship of California on a wildly radical program. Huey Long, with a following, apparently, of millions, talked of forming a third party on the basis of his "share the wealth" movement.

The year 1934 saw the rise of the common man in America. It was an ugly and frightening sight, as well as a politically disturbing one to the Democratic party, and it was swiftly followed by a series of New Deal reforms which inaugurated a new age of American democracy. In 1935 the

Wagner Act legislated organized labor the support it had been promised under the NRA, and labor at once began to move forward to an unheard-of position of wealth and power. The consequences of the Wagner Act are still working themselves out, and their momentous effects upon American democracy still remain to be determined. At the same time, a new tax bill inaugurated the policy of using the tax power as a social instrument to redistribute the nation's wealth. The NRA having been liquidated by the Supreme Court, the New Deal turned from reliance upon industrial self-government to a bill giving holding companies five years to prove their social usefulness or dissolve. Unorganized labor somewhat later received the Fair Labor Standards Act, with its provisions for minimum wages and maximum hours. The AAA was revised with a view to serving the interests of the nation's poorer farmers as well as those more substantial farmers spoken for by the Farm Bureau Federation.

And, finally, the New Deal departed from the past altogether with the Social Security Act, creating old age and unemployment insurance and providing federal funds for the blind, the crippled, and for dependent children. Formerly it had been true, as Eleanor Roosevelt said that,

> there was no recognition that the government owed an individual certain things as a right. . . . Now it is accepted that the government has an obligation to guard the rights of an individual so carefully that he never reaches a point at which he needs charity.

With its negation of the cherished democratic doctrines of self-help and individualism, so unAmerican a development as the welfare state was one which could hardly be explicitly recognized for what it actually was, and it has not been. Politicians in both parties still defend loudly against encroachments of the welfare state, while continuing to extend the protection of the state to individuals over ever larger areas.

Viewed as a social movement, the New Deal was an

equally radical break with the past. It was the first truly
national, non-middle-class reform movement since the advent of the industrial revolution, and for this, much credit
was due to two major developments of the twenties: prohibition and the immigration restriction laws. Reformers in
America from the Know Nothings to the progressives had
been hobbled by religious and racial conflicts which had fed on
the fears inspired by the ever increasing volume of immigration. Although progressivism had been generally free of
explicit racial and religious antipathies, it had received strong
support from the anti-Catholic, anti-foreign opponents of
the liquor traffic. It had remained basically a Protestant,
middle-class movement, rather than a truly national one,
and a moral crusade rather than a libertarian and equalitarian
struggle.

By the eve of the first world war sophisticated progressives were already tiring of the moralism which had given
the movement its main power, but it was the eighteenth
amendment which broke the stuffy alliance of reformism
and moralism. Prohibition, as Richard Hofstadter has written, was the skeleton at the feast, a grim reminder of the
moral frenzy that so many wished to forget. Before prohibition, leaders of the anti-liquor forces had themselves often
been imbued with the radical idealism of social Christianity,
and under any circumstances they were all on the side of
change. After the victory, the Anti-Saloon League turned
from agitation to the maintenance of the status quo, and
from a degree of democratic idealism to the study of methods
for circumventing various of the first ten amendments to the
Constitution, in the interests of more effective law enforcement. At the same time, Protestantism in the twenties became
notorious at one end of the social scale for its renewed defense of wealth and became notorious at the other for its
renewed attacks upon evolutionary science. The depression
found the Protestant churches at the nadir of their influence,

outside the rural areas of the nation, and the New Deal consequently was a secular movement such as the nation had not
witnessed since the days of Jeffersonian republicanism.

Pressure for immigration restriction, rising irresistibly
throughout the progressive era, resulted in the Immigration
Act of 1921, limiting the annual admission of aliens to three
per cent of the population of each nationality living in the
United States in 1910. Amid the climax of racist fury and the
rapid expansion of the Ku Klux Klan, the law of 1924 was
passed, reducing the annual quota to two per cent and removing the base period to 1890, in order to defend against
continued immigration from southern and eastern Europe.
Further limitations were imposed by the National Origins
Act of 1929, but it was especially the law of 1924 which provided one of the most important watersheds in all of American social history. The rush of racism which preceded the
law abated almost at once following its passage. Numbers
of professional racists found themselves practically without
means of employment. In 1928 a new kind of political leader
appeared on the national scene, when Al Smith won the nomination of the Democratic party. The resulting campaign was
a scandal for its Catholic-baiting, the solid South cracked
under the strain, and Smith was thoroughly defeated, but he
still made a much better showing than his two Democratic
predecessors had made. 1928 was not the year for a Democratic victory under any circumstances, and it has never been
demonstrated that Smith lost more votes by his Catholicism
than he gained by it. In the meantime, he was the harbinger
of the new age when American democracy had ceased to be
American Protestant democracy.

It was not only that immigration restriction quieted the
fears which had divided the reformers from the newer immigrants; it was also that the new laws profoundly altered
the attitudes of the newer immigrants themselves. Until the
1920's they were part of an army of Europeans establishing

themselves in an alien land. With an end to unlimited immigration they became citizens of an exclusive nation. Their interest in the old country was transformed from the xenophobias of the twenties to the artistic folkishness of the thirties and forties. If improvements of conditions in the American ghettoes had seemed hopeless to progressive reformers, it had seemed at least as hopeless to the slum-dwellers themselves. Immigration restriction changed this. The return of prosperity in the forties found the first and second generation immigrants in an unprecedented position to improve their fortunes and in so doing to divest themselves further of the old feeling of separateness. The immigration restriction laws, because of their illiberal origins, have received unsparing denunciation from historians; yet in their consequences they have proved among the most powerful democratic influences in recent American history.

The tremendous impact of the first world war upon American society is even yet not clearly discernible. The second world war, the Korean war, and the cold war, as they have involved the United States so much more deeply and enduringly, have had a vastly more profound impact upon American democracy. They have necessitated governmental operations on a scale never contemplated by the New Dealers. They have entailed a radical departure from the American democratic tradition in the major role accorded to the military in wide areas of American political and economic life. With this has come a measure of secrecy surrounding the conduct of government which obviously limits the authority of the electorate.

On the other hand, America in the cold war feels the vital need to justify itself and its system of government before the world as never before, and this feeling exerts a strong influence upon business and labor, as well as upon the government. The most obvious beneficiaries of this new self-consciousness are the Negroes, who in the past fifteen years have won victories in the struggle for civil rights such as could never have been anticipated on the basis of their history in America from emancipation to the opening of the second world war. The great gains for democracy won during the New Deal in the meantime are securely ensconced in the American democratic tradition. McCarthyism demonstrated once more that in times of stress equalitarianism and majority rule can be dangerous to liberty, but in the end the American Constitutional system got the best of McCarthyism as it has of previous such outbursts. Whether the tremendous changes of the past generation have won or lost for the causes of majority rule, equal rights, individual liberty and justice for all is, under any circumstances, a subject which ought properly be left by the historian to the more daring of the social scientists.

BIBLIOGRAPHY

CHAPTER I

The best study of English society as it relates to American settlement is Wallace Notestein, *The English People on the Eve of Colonization, 1603-1630* (1954). Based upon a wide range of sources, it concentrates on those aspects of English life which are especially relevant to an understanding of colonial society. It supersedes E. P. Cheyney, *European Background of American History 1300-1600* (1904), so far as the English backgrounds are concerned, but Cheyney's work, which discusses the European background of all the colonizing nations, remains a very useful study.

For general reference I have relied on the Oxford histories of England: J. D. Mackie, *The Early Tudors, 1485-1558* (1952); J. B. Black, *The Reign of Elizabeth, 1558-1603* (1936); and Godfrey Davies, *The Early Stuarts, 1603-1660* (1937). Other general surveys I found especially useful were S. T. Bindoff, *Tudor England* (1951), and G. M. Treveleyn, *England under the Stuarts* (1904). For biographical reference, in addition to the Leslie Stephen and Sidney Lee, eds., *Dictionary of National Biography* (63 vols., 1885-1901), the brief biographies in Katharine Garvin, ed., *The Great Tudors* (1935), were helpful.

George Bancroft's *History of the United States from Discovery of the American Continent* (10 vols., 1852-78), remains a stimulating and highly valuable work, despite its fiercely partisan manner. Under any circumstances it cannot be ignored, because it contains much information based upon sources not available to later historians. Of other general works covering the period of settlement, C. M. Andrews, *The Colonial Period of American History* (4 vols., 1934-38), gives the clearest, most detailed and authoritative account, while Edward Channing, *A History of the United States* (6 vols., 1905-25), is as valuable for its historical interpretations and emphases as for its factual presentation. Colonizing ventures are presented from the point of view of the homeland in J. A. Williamson, *A Short History of British Expansion* (2 vols., 1922-1943), and A. D. Innes, *The Maritime and Colonial Expansion of England under the Stuarts* (1932). The standard work on joint stock companies is W. R. Scott, *Constitution and Finance of English, Scottish and Irish Joint Stock Companies to 1720* (3 vols., 1910-12). The charters of Sir Humphrey Gilbert and Sir Walter Raleigh are included in F. N. Thorpe, ed., *Federal and State Constitutions, Colonial Charters, and Other Organic Laws* (7 vols., 1909).

G. P. Gooch, *English Democratic Ideas in the Seventeenth Century with Supplementary Notes and Appendices by Harold Laski* (1927), is directly relevant to the origins of democratic thought in America. W. G. Zeeveld, *Foundations of Tudor Policy* (1948), includes a discussion of equalitarian aspects of Tudor England. For James I see D. H. Willson, *King James VI and I* (1956). James' political views received special attention in J. N. Figgis, *The Theory of the Divine Rights of Kings* (1896); enlarged, 1914. A. O. Lovejoy, *The Great Chain of Being* (1936), discusses the idea of the chain of being in ancient and medieval cosmology. A discussion of the same subject more relevant to English and American history is E. M. W. Tillyard, *The Elizabethan World Picture* (1943).

For a brief, readable, and sensible discussion of the impact of the Black Death upon England see G. G. Coulton, *The Black Death* (1930). For the chief lines of argument in the controversy over the subject, see T. W. Page, *The End of Villeinage in England* (1900), the review of Page's book by P. Vinogradoff in the *English Historical Review*, XV (1900), H. L. Gray "The commutation of Villein Services in England before the Black Death," *English Historical Review*, XXIX (1914), and Ada E. Levett, *The Black Death on The Estates of the See of Winchester* . . . (1916).

For a discussion of Tudor and Stuart society, in addition to Notestein, *The English People,* and Cheyney *European Background,* see L. B. Wright, *Middle-Class Culture in Elizabethan England* (1935), Mildred Campbell, *The English Yeoman under Elizabeth and the Early Stuarts* (1942), R. H. Tawney, *The Agrarian Problem in the Sixteenth Century* (1912), and H. R. Trevor-Roper, *The Gentry, 1540-1640* (1953). On the question of whether the English gentry was on the rise or on the decline in this period there is a lengthy, contentious literature which continues to appear in historical journals.

The standard survey of Parliamentary history is A. F. Pollard, *The Evolution of Parliament* (1926). J R. Tanner, *Tudor Constitutional Documents, A. D. 1485-1603* (1930), contains excellent commentaries. F. W. Maitland, *The Constitutional History of England* (posthumous; edited by H. A. L. Fisher, 1908), remains a remarkably lucid and readable and, of course, authoritative series of lectures. J. E. Neale, *The Elizabethan House of Commons* (1950), is a study of the way Parliament actually was constituted. For English law see W. S. Holdsworth, *The Influence of the Legal Profession on the Growth of the English Constitution* (1926), in addition to his major work, *A History of English Law* (12 vols., 1924-56). J. W. Gough, *Fundamental Law in English Constitutional History* (1955), discusses questions concerning the nature of Parliament which are particularly relevant to American law and constitutional theory. A. B. White presents his argument in *Self-Government at the King's Command; a Study in the Beginnings of English Democracy* (1933).

The quotation from the fifteenth-century work by Sir John Fortescue describing the great chain of being is taken from Tillyard, *Elizabethan World Picture;* the Charles I quotation, from Gooch, *English Democratic Ideas;* the F. M. Powicke statement from his *Medieval England, 1066-1485* (1931); the Webbs' statement from their *English Local Government from the Revolution to the Municipal Corporations Act: The Parish and the County* (1924). The statement of Queen Elizabeth's minister concerning Parliament and that of the historian Henry Hallam concerning the Crown are both quoted in Black, *Reign of Elizabeth.* Lord Acton's comment is from his *Lectures on Modern History* (1921).

CHAPTER II

The authority I have chiefly relied upon is Andrews, *The Colonial Period in America,* which is at its best on political and constitutional matters and on the period of settlement. L. B. Wright, *The Atlantic Frontier; Colonial American Civilization, 1607-1763* (1947), is thoroughly readable and enlightening and is especially good for the colonies south of New England, as is the case with Carl Bridenbaugh, *Myths and Realities; Societies of the Colonial South* (1952), for the colonies south of Pennsylvania. C. E. Merriam, *A History of American Political Theories* (1920), remains a sound, scholarly, readable survey which no later study has entirely supplanted. Generally speaking, the period of settlement is no longer the center of attention for colonial historians, as it was until a generation ago, the formerly neglected first half of the eighteenth century having come into its own in recent years.

Among the many accounts of the settlement of Virginia, that in Channing, *History of the United States,* is notably successful in depicting that episode for the bloody beachhead landing that it was. Among special studies of the founding of Virginia, the standard work, from the political point of view, remains P. A. Bruce, *Institutional History of Virginia in the Seventeenth Century* (2 vols., 1910). For the Virginia Company itself, Scott, *Joint-Stock Companies,* is authoritative. For Virginia society and government as it had developed by the mid-eighteenth century, see Charles Sydnor, *Gentleman Freeholders; Political Practices in Washington's Virginia* (1952), and Carl Bridenbaugh, *Seat of Empire; The Political Role of Eighteenth-Century Williamsburg* (1950). For Maryland I have relied primarily on M. P. Andrews, *Founding of Maryland* (1933).

For the activities of Gorges, see H. M. Fuller, *Sir Fernando Gorges,*

1566-1647 (1952). My account of the settlement of Massachusetts is based primarily on Andrews, *Colonial Period,* S. E. Morison, *Builders of the Bay Colony* (1930), and J. F. Sly, *Town Government in Massachusetts, 1620-1930* (1930). E. S. Morgan, *The Puritan Dilemma: The Story of John Winthrop* (1958), argues that Winthrop was a less authoritarian leader than is generally supposed, and that from the first he favored giving the vote to church members. Max Farrand has edited *The Laws and Liberties of Massachusetts* (1929).

For a brief, lucid introduction to New England theology see Alan Simpson, *Puritanism in Old and New England* (1955), and for an equally readable account of Puritanism in practice, Ola E. Winslow, *Meetinghouse Hill, 1630-1783* (1952). The most exhaustive discussion in New England Puritanism is in the writings of Perry Miller, including *Orthodoxy in Massachusetts, 1630-1650* (1933), *The New England Mind; The Seventeenth Century* (1939), and *The New England Mind; From Colony to Province* (1953). His *New England Mind* is the most thoroughgoing account available of Massachusetts theology, but surely it implies a greater uniformity of belief among the early Puritan clergy than can conceivably have existed. S. E. Morison, *The Puritan Pronaos* (1936), is an excellent brief account of the intellectual life of early Massachusetts and its relation to Puritanism. An ambitious effort to discover the origins of modern American democratic society in New England Puritanism is to be found in R. B. Perry, *Puritanism and Democracy* (1944). See also C. K. Shipton, "Puritanism and Modern Democracy," *New England Historical and Genealogical Register,* CI (1947); Morison, *Builders of the Bay Colony;* B. Katherine Brown, "Freemanship in Puritan Massachusetts," *American Historical Review,* LIX (1954); Morrison Sharp, "Leadership and Democracy in Early New England Defense," *Ibid.,* L (1945); and D. H. Fowler, "Connecticut's Freemen: The First Forty Years," *William and Mary Quarterly,* Ser. 3, XV (1958).

Two controversies have surrounded the settlement of Connecticut in relation to the development of American democracy. One of them, the nature of Connecticut's early legal code, was long since fairly successfully laid to rest by W. F. Prince in his article, "Peter's Blue Laws," *American Historical Association Report* (1898). The other, the extent to which Connecticut was more democratic than Massachusetts, is apparently still open for discussion. An influential article by Perry Miller, "Hooker and the Democracy of Early Connecticut," *New England Quarterly,* IV (1931), argues that the democracy of Hooker and of early Connecticut is perhaps apparent, but certainly not real.

Interest in early Rhode Island history has centered around Roger Williams and the relevance of his ideas to modern democracy. S. H. Brockunier, *The Irrepressible Democrat, Roger Williams* (1940), presents the argument which is implicit in the title. Support for this position is given also in C. L. Rossiter, *Seedtime of the Republic* (1953). Two recent biographies take the view that Williams is properly to be understood only in seventeenth-century theological terms, and that what appears akin to twentieth-century liberalism in his writings was largely incidental to his religious outlook. These biographies are Ola E. Winslow, *Master Roger Williams: A Biography* (1957), and Perry Miller, *Roger Williams: His Contribution to the American Tradition* (1953). This latter view receives support also from Alan Simpson, "How Democratic was Roger Williams?" *William and Mary Quarterly*, Ser. 3, XIII (1956).

For South Carolina I have relied mainly on D. D. Wallace, *The History of South Carolina* (4 vols., 1934), and Bridenbaugh, *Myths and Realities*. On the perhaps unanswerable question of the role played by John Locke in the writing of the *Fundamental Constitutions*, see M. W. Cranston, *John Locke, A Biography* (1957). For New York I have relied upon A. C. Flick, ed., *History of the State of New York . . .* (10 vols., 1933-37), Wright, *Atlantic Frontier* and especially A. E. McKinley, "Transition from Dutch to English Rule," *American Historical Review*, VI (1900). For Pennsylvania, F. B. Tolles, *Meeting House and Counting House; the Quaker Merchants of Colonial Philadelphia, 1682-1763* (1948), was especially useful.

My source for the legislative demands of the House of Burgesses was Andrews, *Colonial History*. The source for the statements of John Winthrop and of Roger Williams was H. R. Warfel, R. H. Gabriel, and S. T. Williams, eds., *American Mind; Selections from The Literature of The United States* (1947). The comment concerning "opulent and lordly planters . . ." was made by Josiah Quincy as quoted in Bridenbaugh, *Myths and Realities*. The statement of the first New Haven constitution concerning the Scriptures is from Thorpe, ed., *Constitutions and Charters*.

CHAPTER III

An excellent introduction to imperial relations in the eighteenth century and to the politics of the colonial assemblies may be found in the text book by E. B. Greene, *Foundations of American Nationality* (1922). The standard work on imperial relations is O. M. Dickerson, *American Colonial Government, 1696-1765* (1912), while for the later period the most detailed account is L. H. Gipson, *The British Empire Before the American Revolution* (9 vols., 1936-56). For the history of the Anglican church see A. L. Cross, *The Anglican Episcopate and the American Colonies* (1902). For statistics concerning colonial population seen Virginia D. Harrington and E. B. Greene, *American Population before the Federal Census of 1790* (1932); for urban expansion see Carl Bridenbaugh, *Cities in the Wilderness; The First Century of Urban Life in America, 1625-1742* (1938), and *Cities in Revolt; Urban Life in America, 1743-1776* (1955). For the conditions facing the newer immigrants see A. E. Smith, *Colonists in Bondage* (1947), and M. W. Jernegan, *Laboring and Dependent Classes in Colonial America, 1607-1783* (1931).

For the western insurrections see J. S. Bassett, "Regulators in North Carolina," American Historical Association *Report* (1894), and Brook Hindle, "March of the Paxton Boys," *William and Mary Quarterly*, Ser. 3, III (1946). With respect to the East-West conflicts which developed on the eve of the Revolution, a difference of opinion has developed among historians over the truth of Carl Becker's famous statement that the question was not home rule, but who should rule at home. See Carl Becker, *The History of Political Parties in the Province of New York, 1760-1776* (1909). R. E. Brown, *Middle Class Democracy and the Revolution in Massachusetts, 1691-1780* (1955), finds no evidence in his study to support such a view where Massachusetts is concerned; while Bridenbaugh, *Myths and Realities*, finds colonial western Virginia to have been well governed and contented with the political system as it existed. And while he finds western animosity prevalent in the Carolinas, he does not find it to be informed by any democratic spirit. For a brief, comprehensive application of the Becker thesis to each individual colony, see Merrill Jensen, *The Articles of Confederation . . . 1774-1781* (1940).

Charles Warren, *A History of the American Bar* (1911), remains the only general account of the subject for the colonial period. No monograph has been written concerning the meteoric rise of the American legal profession during little more than a generation before the Revolution. A significant article bearing on this subject, however, is Milton M. Klein, "The Rise of the New York Bar: The Legal Career of William Livingston," *William and Mary Quarterly*, Ser. 3, XV (1958). See also R. B. Morris, "Massachusetts and the Common Law," *American Historical Review*, XXXI (1926), and *Studies in the History of American Law* (1930). Numerous additional articles may be found in various law reviews.

The best brief introduction to colonial voting regulations is J. B. McMaster, *The Acquisition of Political, Social and Industrial Rights of Man in America* (1903). For a more recent brief survey, see W. Neil

Franklin, "Some Aspects of Representation in the American Colonies," *North Carolina Historical Review*, VI (1929). The standard studies are C. F. Bishop, *History of Elections in the American Colonies* (1893), and A. E. McKinley, *The Suffrage Franchise in the Thirteen English Colonies in America* (1905). Their emphasis upon the narrowness of the colonial franchise is challenged by Brown, *Middle-Class Democracy*, a study which receives support from J. R. Pole, "Suffrage and Representation in Massachusetts: A Statistical Note," *William and Mary Quarterly*, Ser. 3, XIV (1957). R. P. McCormick, *The History of Voting in New Jersey . . . 1664-1911* (1953), concurs as to the breadth of the suffrage but emphasizes other limitations in practice. See also Sister Joan de Lourdes, C. S. J., "Elections in Colonial Pennsylvania," *William and Mary Quarterly*, Ser. 3, XI (1954), and articles bearing on this subject noted in bibliography for chapter II. J. F. Jameson, "Did the Fathers Vote?" *New England Magazine*, I (1890), attempts in a brief article to discover, not only whether colonists had the right to vote, but also whether those who had the franchise used it. His statistics indicate that very few did. This obviously important aspect of the subject has as yet received little attention from historians.

The main general study of American class consciousness is Dixon Wecter, *The Saga of American Society . . . 1606-1937* (1937). E. H. Cady, *The Gentleman in America* (1949), examines the subject from the point of view of American literary history. For Virginia see L. B. Wright, *First Gentlemen of Virginia; Intellectual Qualities of the Early Colonial Ruling Class* (1940), Sydnor, *Gentlemen Freeholders*, and Bridenbaugh, *Seat of Empire*. For New England see S. E. Morison, "Precedence at Harvard College in the Seventeenth Century," American Antiquarian Society, *Proceedings*, XLII (1932), and N. H. Dawes, "Titles as Symbols of Prestige," *William and Mary Quarterly*, Ser. 3, VI (1949).

W. W. Sweet, *The Story of Religion in America* (1939), remains the best introduction to the history of colonial religion, while Sweet's collections of materials on the individual major denominations gives excellent insights into the day to day activities of the churches. For the Great Awakenings see C. H. Maxson, *The Great Awakening in Middle Colonies* (1920), W. M. Gewehr, *The Great Awakening in Virginia, 1740-90* (1930), and E. E. White, "Decline of the Great Awakening in New England," *New England Quarterly*, Ser. 3, XXIV (1951). L. J. Trinterud, *The Forming of an American Tradition, A Reexamination of Colonial Presbyterianism* (1949), is an important work which sheds new light on the Great Awakenings as a whole.

The quotation of Governor Spotswood is from F. J. Turner, *The Frontier in American History* (1920). Jefferson on Blackstone's *Commentaries* is from Warren, *American Bar*, as is John Adams' observations. The General Court ruling of 1651 is from Morison, "Precedence at Harvard." Governor Gooch's statement was taken from Wecter, *Saga of Society*.

CHAPTER IV

E. S. Morgan, *The Birth of the Republic, 1763-89* (1956), is brief, clear, scholarly, and witty and provides an excellent introduction to the subject. Among more detailed studies J. C. Miller, *Origins of the American Revolution* (1943), is recent, authoritative, and readable. For the Sons of Liberty the most useful studies are Helen M. and E. S. Morgan, *The Stamp Act Crisis* (1953), and Miller, *Origins of the Revolution*. The quotations in this chapter dealing with either the Stamp Act or the Sons of Liberty are to be found in one or the other book. Much of the material for the activities of the New York Sons was taken from H. M. Morais, "The Sons of Liberty in New York," R. B. Morris, ed., *The Era of the American Revolution* (1938). See also Becker, *Political Parties in New York;* Carl Bridenbaugh, *The Colonial Craftsman* (1950); P. G. Davidson, "Sons of Liberty and Stamp Men," *North Carolina Historical Review*, IX (1932); and A. M. Schlesinger, "Political Mobs and the American Revolution, 1765-1776," American Philosophical Society, *Proceedings*, XCIX (1955). For the role of the merchants see Schlesinger, *The Colonial Merchants and the American Revolution, 1763-1776* (1918).

For the role played by the newspapers see A. M. Schlesinger, *Prelude to Independence; The Newspaper War on Britain, 1764-1776* (1957), and his "Colonial Newspapers and the Stamp Act" *New England Quarterly*, VIII (1935), as well as P. G. Davidson, *Propaganda and the American Revolution, 1763-1783* (1941). See also Sidney Kobre, *The Development of the Colonial Newspaper* (1944), and L. C. Wroth, *The Colonial Printer* (1938). Vincent Buranelli, ed., *The Trial of Peter Zenger* (1957), contains the transcript of the trial.

Merriam, *American Political Theory*, provides a good introduction to the political theory of the revolution, while the subject receives more thorough attention in C. F. Mullett, *Fundamental Law and the American Revolution, 1760-1776* (1933). Rossiter, *Seedtime of the Republic*, discusses colonial American political thought from a primarily biographical approach. C. H. McIlwain, *The American Revolution: A Constitutional Interpretation* (1923), argues that Parliament had never possessed lawful authority outside the realm of England, a view with which R. L. Schuyler, *Parliament and the British Empire* (1929), takes issue. C. F. Mullett, "Tory Imperialism on the Eve of the Declaration of Independence," *Canadian Historical Review*, XII (1931), is an excellent discussion of the loyalist argument, which also receives extended treatment in Davidson, *Propaganda and the Revolution,* and in M. C. Tyler, *The Literary History of the American Revolution, 1763-1783* (2 vols., 1897). See also Cross, *American Episcopate.*

Mullett, *Fundamental Law,* and Rossiter, *Seedtime of the Republic,* both argue that Locke's importance to the Revolution has been overemphasized. Still, Locke's *Second Treatise on Civil Government* remains the classic statement of the natural rights philosophy upon which the revolutionists finally rested their case. The best biography is Cranston, *John Locke.* Willmoore Kendall, *John Locke and the Doctrine of Majority Rule* (1941), is an interesting discussion of a central ambiguity in Locke's political theory. See also Peter Laslett, "The English Revolution and Locke's *Two Treatises of Government,*" *Cambridge Historical Journal,* XII, no. I (1956); Carl Becker, *The Declaration of Independence* (1922); and B. F. Wright, *American Interpretations of Natural Law* (1931). H. M. Jones, *The Pursuit of Happiness* (1953), is an entertaining account of the legal difficulties which the phrase has presented where it has been incorporated into state constitutions.

The statement by Archibald Kennedy is quoted in Rossiter, *Seedtime of the Republic.* Jefferson's appraisal of Locke's *Treatises* is quoted in Merriam, *American Political Theory.*

CHAPTER V

E. P. Douglass, *Rebels and Democrats; The Struggle for Equal Political Rights and Majority Rule During the American Revolution* (1955), surveys in a sensible and scholarly manner the democratic political developments of the Revolutionary era, giving detailed attention to the politics of individual states. J. F. Jameson, *The American Revolution considered as a Social Movement* (1926), summarizes the anti-aristocratic influences of the Revolution. Together the two books provide a well rounded history of the course of American democracy in these years.

The standard political history remains A. C. McLaughlin, *The Confederation and The Constitution, 1783-1789* (1905), an interesting and generally reliable survey, but one which is limited by an inability to take the Anti-Federalists seriously. A much less scholarly work written from a more severely doctrinaire Federalist point of view is John Fiske,

The Critical Period in American History, 1783-1789 (1888), a work of considerable importance for its influence, both on historians and on the general reading public, in dramatizing the stereotype of an age of chaos from which the framers of the Constitution rescued the nation. Allan Nevins, *The American States During and After the Revolution, 1775-1789* (1924), is an extremely useful state by state compendium of events presented from the Federalist point of view. Thorpe, *Constitutions and Charters,* is, of course, basic to the study of state-making.

On the other hand, the Confederation regimes receive staunch support from Merrill Jensen, *The New Nation; A History of the United States During The Confederation, 1781-1789* (1950). Jensen argues here, and in his *Articles of Confederation* (1940), that in the agrarian age of the late eighteenth century, democracy was better secured by local than by national control, and that the main theme of the period was the struggle between states-rights democrats and nationalistic, anti-democratic conservatives. Politically he finds this to have been not a critical period, but an age of democratic achievement, except in those states where irreconcilable conservatives defeated reasonable schemes. In his defense of the states' financial arrangements he receives support from E. J. Ferguson, "State Assumption of the Federal Debt During the Confederation," *Mississippi Valley Historical Review,* XXXVIII (1951). More broadly conceived than the previously mentioned studies, *The New Nation* is most valuable for its treatment of the social and economic history of the period. For a good commentary on these various interpretations see R. B. Morris, "The Confederation Period and the American Historian," *William and Mary Quarterly,* Ser. 3, XIII (1956). Morris notes, concerning Jensen's thesis, that the main issue "does not seem to have been one between radicals and conservatives but between extreme particularists of the Clinton stripe and continental nationalists of varying shades and degrees."

The statement concerning leveling sentiment in the Pennsylvania convention is quoted in Nevins, *American States,* as is that from the report of the North Carolina drafting committee. The Loyalist Declaration of Independence is quoted in C. H. Van Tyne, *The Loyalists in the American Revolution* (1929). John Adams' plan of government is contained in a rather brief letter to R. H. Lee in 1776 and published in John Adams *Works,* C. F. Adams, ed. (10 vols., 1850-56). Gouverneur Morris and Rufus King are quoted in McLaughlin, *Confederation and Constitution,* as is the statement from the Newburg Addresses. Mercy Warren is quoted in Mary and C. A. Beard, *A Basic History of the United States* (1944).

CHAPTER VI

Max Farrand, *Framing of the Constitution of the United States* (1913), is a readable and authoritative survey by the editor of *The Records of the Federal Convention of 1787* (4 vols., 1911-37). C. A. Beard, *An Economic Interpretation of the Constitution of the United States* (1913), remains the chief focal point of controversy, with its carefully—not to say cagily—presented thesis that the Convention was dominated by holders of personal property, and that the Constitution was an economic document, drawn up to defend their special interests and to defend also against the encroachments of democracy. The study has recently come under comprehensive attacks in two monographs, R. E. Brown, *Charles Beard and the Constitution* (1956), and Forrest McDonald, *We the People: the Economic Origins of the Constitution* (1958). Both studies charge Beard with use of faulty statistics and with false reasoning from the statistics he does use. Both argue that the Convention was much more representative of the people as a whole than Beard contends and that the division was neither between the creditor-debtor classes nor between the seaboard and western areas. See also Jensen, *New Nation*, which is in the Beard tradition.

A good introduction to the political thought of the founding fathers is in H. W. Schneider, *A History of American Philosophy* (1946), and Richard Hofstadter, *The American Political Tradition and the Men who Made It* (1948). *The Federalist Papers*, brief, clear, and readable, are the classic contemporary defense of the Constitution.

For the two-party system W. E. Binkley, *American Political Parties, Their Natural History*, rev. ed. (1958), provides an excellent introduction. Edward Stanwood, *History of the Presidency* (1904), is a very useful reference work, as is E. H. Roseboom, *A History of Presidential Elections* (1957). For the beginnings of party politics see S. G. Brown, *The First Republicans; Political Philosophy and Public Policy in the Party of Jefferson and Madison* (1954), N. E. Cunningham, *The Jeffersonian Republicans; The Formation of Party Organization, 1789-1801* (1957), and Joseph Charles, "Hamilton and Washington: The Origins of the American Party System," *William and Mary Quarterly*, Ser. 3, XIV (1955), as well as C. G. Bowers, *Jefferson and Hamilton* (1925). These studies all tend to neglect the history of actual party organization from the precinct level up, however, and in this important respect, much the best work remains G. D. Luetscher, *Early Political Machinery* (1903). See also M. I. Ostrogorski, *Democracy and the Organization of Political Parties* (2 vols., 1908).

Columbia University is currently paying honor to its most illustrious alumnus with a series of studies of Alexander Hamilton, all tending to rescue him from the invidious position to which he was relegated by more than a generation of historians. See Broadus Mitchell, *Alexander Hamilton, Youth to Maturity, 1755-1788* (1957), L. M. Hacker, *Alexander Hamilton in the American Tradition* (1957), and R. B. Morris, ed., *Alexander Hamilton and the Founding of the Nation* (1957), an extremely useful compilation of Hamilton's writings. Two recent studies shed new light on John Adams' administration, and both are highly successful in the trying task of defending Adams' reputation. They are M. J. Dauer, *The Adams Federalists* (1953), and S. G. Kurtz, *The Presidency of John Adams* (1957). See also Adrienne Koch and William Peden, eds., *The Selected Writings of John Adams and John Quincy Adams* (1946).

For the American reaction to the French Revolution see E. P. Link, *Democratic-Republican Societies, 1790-1800* (1942); G. A. Koch, *Republican Religion; The American Revolution and The Cult of Reason* (1933); H. M. Morais, *Deism in Eighteenth Century America* (1934); and C. D. Hazen, *Contemporary American Opinion of the French Revolution* (1897). The definitive work on the alien and sedition acts is J. M. Smith, *Freedom's Fetters; The Alien and Sedition Laws* . . . (1956).

The best biography of Burr is the highly partisan S. H. Wandell and Meade Minnegerode, *Aaron Burr* (2 vols., 1925). No special study has been made of Burr's political career in New York, but Channing, *U. S. History*, contains a good account of his role in the election of 1800. See also D. S. Alexander, *A Political History of the State of New York* (3 vols., 1906-09), and Gustavus Myers, *The History of Tammany Hall* (1901).

Two books together provide an excellent introduction to the thought of Thomas Jefferson: Adrienne Koch, *Jefferson and Madison; The Great Collaboration* (1950), and Lester Cappon, ed., *The Adams-Jefferson Letters* (2 vols., 1959). In these works Jefferson is allowed to speak for himself on politics and political theory as well as on many other subjects. For Jefferson's views at an earlier period see his classic, *Notes on Virginia*, edited by William Peden (1954). Despite the volume of writings on Jefferson, no full length biography has been completed since H. S. Randall, *The Life of Thomas Jefferson* (3 vols., 1858). Two such biographies are in preparation: Marie Kimball, *Jefferson* (3 vols., 1943-50), and Dumas Malone, *Jefferson and His Time* (2 vols., 1948-51). Among the shorter works, a good biography is Gilbert Chinard, *Thomas Jefferson, The Apostle of Americanism* (1929), while A. J.

Nock, *Thomas Jefferson* (1926), is a brilliant interpretive biography. C. A. Beard, *Economic Origins of Jeffersonian Democracy* (1915), is an influential and—except for the first third of the book—basically sound study.

The statement by McMaster is from his *Rights of Man in America*. John Dickinson is quoted in Farrand, *Framing of the Constitution;* the J. F. Jameson statement is from *American Revolution as Social Movement;* Madison's statements are all from the *Federalist;* John Adams on political parties, from Binkley, *American Political Parties;* William Maclay from Nock, *Jefferson;* Beard from his *Economic Origins;* Henry Adams from his *John Randolph* (1882); Washington from J. C. Fitzpatrick, ed., *The Writings of George Washington . . . 1745-1799* (39 vols., 1931-44), and John Adams on Shays's Rebellion from Cappon, ed., *Adams-Jefferson Letters.*

<h2 style="text-align:center">CHAPTER VII</h2>

The classic general work, one of the great works in American historiography, is Henry Adams, *History of the United States of America During The Administrations of Thomas Jefferson and James Madison* (9 vols., 1889-91). Federalist in outlook, Adams tends always to give Jefferson the disadvantage of the doubt, while habitually employing the subtly defacing weapon of irony against the Jeffersonian Republicans. The work has been enormously influential in fixing historical opinion concerning the period. Edward Channing, *The Jeffersonian System, 1801-1811* (1906), remains the standard survey. For the period from the close of the War of 1812 to the close of Monroe's second term George Dangerfield, *The Era of Good Feelings* (1952), is a substantial, stimulating, eminently readable general work. J. B. McMaster, *A History of the People of The United States from the Revolution to the Civil War* (8 vols., 1883-1913), is crammed with interesting, significant information for the period. For Madison see the staunchly partisan biography still in preparation, Irving Brant, *James Madison . . .* (4 vols., 1941-53). For Gallatin see Raymond Walters, Jr., *Albert Gallatin* (1957). For Jefferson see the bibliography for chapter VI, D. J. Boorstin, *The Lost World of Thomas Jefferson* (1948), and C. M. Wiltse, *The Jeffersonian Tradition in American Democracy* (1935).

The best possible introduction to American society at the turn of the century is the opening chapters of Henry Adams' *History,* printed separately as *United States in 1800* (1955). For the early history of the West the colorful, scholarly *The Winning of the West* (4 vols., 1889-96) by Theodore Roosevelt has yet to be superceded. Among the survey histories of the West, the most extensive and detailed is Ray

Billington, *Westward Expansion* (1949). For the period following the War of 1812, F. J. Turner, *Rise of the New West, 1819-1829* (1906), dominated throughout by the Turner thesis, is full of interesting and significant information. See also R. H. Brown, *Historical Geography of the United States* (1948). Margaret and A. G. Bogue, " 'Profits' and the Frontier Land Speculator," *Journal of Economic History,* XVII (1957), gives a good survey of the findings of other scholars on that subject, as well as the results of the authors' own researches.

T. P. Abernethy, *Three Virginia Frontiers* (1940), is a brilliant, brief, interpretive introduction to the subject of frontier democracy—surely the truest thing that has been written on the matter—while his *From Frontier to Plantation in Tennessee, A Study in Frontier Democracy* (1932) is the standard work on the subject. See also T. D. Clark, *A History of Kentucky* (1937), and E. H. Roseboom and F. P. Weisenburger, *A History of Ohio,* rev. ed. (1954). For the constitutions of these states, of course, the basic source is Thorpe, *Constitutions and Charters.*

For a social as well as economic history of industrial and urban development the best survey is G. R. Taylor, *The Transportation Revolution, 1815-1860* (1951). The standard and abundantly usable work is V. S. Clark, *History of Manufacturers in the United States, 1607-1860* (3 vol., 1929). The standard work in labor history is J. R. Commons *et. al.,* eds., *History of Labor in the United States* (4 vols., 1918-1935), and Commons *et. al., Documentary History of American Industrial Society* (10 vols., 1958). For the early period of the century see W. A. Sullivan, *The Industrial Worker in Pennsylvania, 1800-1840* (1955).

For immigration see M. L. Hansen, *The Atlantic Migration, 1607-1860* (1940). For a study of the servant class see Lucy M. Salmon, *Domestic Service* (1897), and any of the published travelers' reports for the period written by women. The history of the free servant classes in America is a highly significant subject, and one which Harriet Martineau found to be "a continual amusement;" yet it has so far been mainly ignored by historians.

Jefferson's statements are taken from his *Writings,* P. L. Ford, ed., (10 vols., 1892-99), the current, exhaustive Jefferson *Papers* J. P. Boyd *et. al.,* eds. (14 vols., 1950-58), extending as yet only to the year 1789. Calhoun and Madison are both quoted in Julius Pratt, "James Madison," in Allen Johnson and Dumas Malone, eds., *Dictionary of American Biography* (22 vols., 1928-44). The Hezekiah Miles statements are quoted in Taylor, *Transportation Revolution,* as is the observation of

Tench Coxe. Timothy Flint makes his observation in his *Recollections of the Last Ten Years* (1826). The Duc De Liancourt and Albert Gallatin are quoted in Adams, *United States;* the Abernethy statement is from his *Three Frontiers.*

CHAPTER VIII

The best introduction to the constitutional histories of the states in the first quarter of the nineteenth century remains McMaster, *Rights of Man in America.* For a recent, good, brief, comprehensive account, see Leland Baldwin's text book, *The Stream of American History* (2 vols., 1952). Bayard Still, "Statehood Process, 1800-1850," *Mississippi Valley Historical Review,* XXIII (1936), is a general essay on the subject, emphasizing the importance placed in the constitutions of this period on annual elections and on powerful legislatures, as opposed to powerful governors. A standard work is J. Q. Dealey, *Growth of American State Constitutions* (1915), while the standard work for history of the franchise is K. H. Porter, *A History of Suffrage in the United States* (1918). F. M. Green, *Constitutional Development in the South Atlantic States, 1776-1860* (1930), gives a good account for that area. For the states where the major changes took place see D. R. Fox, *The Decline of Aristocracy in the Politics of New York* (1919), A. B. Darling, *Political Changes in Massachusetts* (1925), and J. M. Morse, *A Neglected Period of Connecticut's History, 1818-1850* (1933). See also W. R. Fell, *Transition from Aristocracy to Democracy* (1933), and W. R. Fee, *The Transition from Aristocracy to Democracy in New Jersey, 1789-1829* (1933).

For the Panic of 1819 see Taylor, *Transportation Revolution;* McMaster, *History of American People;* Bray Hammond, *Banks and Politics in America, from the Revolution to the Civil War* (1957); Thomas H. Greer, "Economic and Social Effects of the Depression of 1819 in the Old Northwest," *Indiana Magazine of History,* XLIV (1948)); and Samuel Rezneck, "The Depression of 1819-1822: A Social History," *American Historical Review,* XXXIX (1933). C. S. Sydnor, "The One-Party Period of American History," *American Historical Review,* LI (1946), is an excellent account of the collapse both of party politics and of public interest in the presidential election of 1820.

Since the Richmond Junto was a secret organization, little exact information is available concerning its activities and influence. A good brief account is Rex Beach, "Spencer Roane and the Richmond Junto," *William and Mary Quarterly,* Ser. 2, XXII (1942). See also C. H. Ambler, *Sectionalism in Virginia* (1910), and Ambler, *Thomas Ritchie* (1913). For New York politics and the rise of the Albany Regency see

Ostrogorski, *Democracy and Political Parties,* and Fox, *Decline of Aristocracy.* Considering Van Buren's great importance to American political history, remarkably little of a scholarly nature has been written about him, although he has a number of biographies. Van Buren's own *Inquiry Into the Origin of Political Parties* (1867), however, is both a shrewd and a revealing study.

For the election of 1824 see Roseboom, *History of Presidential Elections,* and Dangerfield, *Era of Good Feelings.* The fullest and most recent study of John Quincy Adams' administration is S. F. Bemis, *John Quincy Adams and the Union* (1956). Koch and Peden, eds., *Selected Writings of John Adams and John Quincy Adams* is worth reading throughout. For the Pennsylvania convention of 1824 see P. S. Klein's excellent *Pennsylvania Politics, 1817-1832* (1940). E. M. Carroll, *Origins of the Whig Party* (1925), sheds light on the political developments of the period generally.

C. G. Sellers, "Andrew Jackson versus the Historians," *Mississippi Valley Historical Review,* XLIV (1958) is a useful summary of historical writings on Jackson. James Parton, *A Life of Andrew Jackson,* (3 vols., 1859-60), remains the fullest, and in many ways most authoritative, study. While highly critical of Jackson as President, Parton nevertheless gives his subject sympathetic and admiring treatment. J. S. Bassett, *The Life of Andrew Jackson* (2 vols., 1911), presents Jackson more favorably as a great leader of the democratic movement, a thesis which receives unqualified support from C. G. Bowers, *The Party Battles of the Jackson Period* (1922), and A. M. Schlesinger, Jr., *Age of Jackson* (1945). Schlesinger presents Jackson as the leader of a class struggle in which the urban workers as well as farmers played a vital role. Abernethy in *Frontier to Plantation* and in his "Andrew Jackson and the Rise of Southwestern Democracy," *American Historical Review,* XXXIII (1927), sees Jackson as an opportunist, belatedly leading a movement which he had consistently opposed in Tennessee politics until the movement itself swept him into national power. The view of Jackson as the symbol of the democratic movement in the minds of the people is explored in John Ward, *Andrew Jackson, Symbol for an Age* (1955). Marvin Meyers, *The Jacksonian Persuasion* (1957) discusses various significant figures and various aspects of the Jacksonian movement.

Chancellor Kent, Webster and Van Buren on the suffrage are quoted in McMaster, *Rights of Man in America.* Benton's statement is from his *Thirty Years View* . . . (2 vols., 1854-56). The John Quincy Adams comments are from Koch and Peden, eds., *Selected Writings.* Thurlow Weed and Henry Clay are quoted in Carroll, *Whig Party.*

Van Buren's account of the joining of the anti-Adams forces is quoted in Ostrogorski, *Democracy and Political Parties.* The Congressman's praise of Jackson is quoted in Ward, *Andrew Jackson;* George M. Dallas is quoted in Klein, *Pennsylvania Politics.*

CHAPTER IX

For the Jackson administration see the bibliography for chapter VIII. The standard work for the period is G. G. Van Deusen, *The Jacksonian Era, 1828-1848* (1959). H. C. Syrett, *Andrew Jackson* (1953), is a useful selection of Jackson's writings with a brief, valuable introduction. J. L. Blau, ed., *Social Theories of Jacksonian Democracy . . . 1825-1850* (1947), is a collection of writings by Jacksonian democrats, with an emphasis upon the radical spokesmen for the movement. F. J. Turner, *The United States, 1830-1850* (1935), gives a detailed examination of the major sections of the nation. Hofstadter, *American Political Tradition,* contains an influential chapter which describes Jacksonian democracy as a struggle for liberal capitalism.

Some of the best history of this period is contained in biographies. C. M. Wiltse, *John C. Calhoun* (3 vols., 1944-51), a highly appreciative biography, is also one of the most complete recently written histories of the period. Two recent biographies of Thomas Hart Benton, both of them good, attempt to raise Benton in stature and place him at the head of the democratic movement. They are W. N. Chambers, *Old Bullion Benton . . . 1782-1858* (1956), and E. B. Smith, *Magnificent Missourian; The Life of Thomas Hart Benton* (1957). C. G. Sellers, *James K. Polk, Jacksonian, 1795-1843* (1957), is an intimate study of Jacksonian politics in Tennessee. G. G. Van Deusen, *Thurlow Weed, Wizard of the Lobby* (1947), is the best examination of the methods by which Weed gained his great political power.

For the bank fight see Hammond, *Banks and Politics;* R. C. H. Catteral, *Second Bank of the United States* (1903); and G. R. Taylor, ed., *Jackson Versus Biddle* (1949), a collection of writings on both sides of the controversy. See also M. G. Madeleine, *Monetary and Banking Theories of Jacksonian Democracy* (1943), and R. C. McGrane, *Panic of 1837* (1924). C. R. Fish, *The Civil Service and the Patronage* (1904), is the standard work for that subject.

For the relationship of the state governments to economic enterprise see Mary F. and Oscar Handlin, *Commonwealth; . . . Massachusetts, 1744-1861* (1947); Louis Hartz, *Economic Policy and Democratic Thought; Pennsylvania, 1776-1860* (1948); J. N. Primm, *Economic Policy in the Development of a Western State; Missouri, 1820-1860* (1954); and M. S. Heath, *Constructive Liberalism . . . Georgia to 1860*

(1954). All these studies attest abundantly to the absence of laissez faire in American economic life before the Civil War. See also Joseph Dorfman, *The Economic Mind in American Civilization* (5 vols., 1946-59), especially for the academic thought of the time. For a significant as well as enjoyable account of the campaign of 1840 see R. G. Gunderson, *The Log Cabin Campaign* (1957).

Alexis de Tocqueville, *Democracy in America*, Phillips Bradley, ed., (2 vols., 1945), is a great classic, much the most penetrating, perceptive, sensible and complete examination of Jacksonian democracy in existence. If it may be said to have a basic theme, it is the problem of reconciling equality with liberty and with those civilized values which in France were inextricably associated with aristocracy. The introduction to the Bradley edition gives an interesting and significant account of the history of the reception of the work both abroad and in America. See also G. W. Pierson, *Tocqueville and Beaumont in America* (1938).

The story of Joseph Palmer is told in Clara E. Sears, *Bronson Alcotts' Fruitlands* . . . (1915). Jackson's "The bank is trying to kill me . . . " is quoted in Hofstadter, *American Political Tradition;* Benton's complaint against local banks is quoted in Schlesinger, Jr., *Age of Jackson;* Thurlow Weed, in Carroll, *Whig Party;* John Quincy Adams, in Koch and Peden, eds., *Selected Writings;* Horace Greeley, in Gunderson, *Log Cabin Campaign,* and the log cabin and hard cider quotation, in McMaster, *History of American People.*

CHAPTER X

The pioneer historian of American religions from an historical rather than a denominational point of view is W. W. Sweet, and his *Story of Religion in America* (1939) is the standard survey of the subject, although recent research has modified some of his conclusions. His source books on the Methodist, Baptist, Presbyterian, and Congregational churches reveal the day to day workings of these denominations. For Deism see Morias, *Deism in Eighteenth Century America.* Conrad Wright, *The Beginnings of Unitarianism in America* (1955), is a clear, authoritative account. See also N. H. Sonne, *Liberal Kentucky, 1780-1828* (1939). An excellent account of revived Calvinism in Connecticut is C. R. Keller, *The Second Great Awakening in Connecticut* (1942). Catherine C. Cleveland, *The Great Revival in the West, 1797-1805* (1916), is an account of the first years of the movement at the turn of the century. W. R. Cross, *The Burnt-Over District; The Social and Intellectual History of Enthusiastic Religion in Western New York, 1800-1850* (1950), is a good account of religious activity in upstate New York, where Mormonism, Millerism, and Spiritualism originated and where a remarkably large number of leaders of the revivals began their careers. C. A. Johnson, *The Frontier Camp Meeting* (1955), is a readable and scholarly account of that institution.

For the role of religion in American reform movements see Alice F. Tyler, *Freedom's Ferment; Phases of American Social History to 1860* (1944). Three recent studies attempt to link the evangelical churches with humanitarian reform movements. They are C. C. Cole, Jr., *The Social Ideas of the Northern Evangelists, 1826-1860* (1954), J. R. Bodo, *The Protestant Clergy and Public Issues, 1812-1848* (1954), and T. L. Smith, *Revivalism and Social Reform in Mid-Nineteenth Century America* (1957). Except for the demonstration of a widespread support for the temperance and anti-slavery movements and a very frugal support of charitable institutions, these studies are not notably successful in establishing a clear connection. The first chapter of Smith's work is an excellent introduction to each of the major Protestant denominations in this period. R. S. Fletcher, *A History of Oberlin College from Its Foundation Through the Civil War* (2 vols., 1943), is a history of the institution which played a key role in the training of a militant evangelical ministry for the West. See also C. S. Griffin, "Religious Benevolence as Social Control, 1815-1860," *Mississippi Valley Historical Review*, LXIV (1957).

No satisfactory full history has yet been written of the doctrine of separation of church and state in America. The crucial period of the mid-nineteenth century, when the nation argued out the relevance of the doctrine to public education, has, in particular, received remarkably little attention. One of the best discussions of the subject remains Toqueville, *Democracy in America*. J. L. Blau, *Cornerstones of Religious Freedom in America* (1949), is a good brief collection of documents relating to the question, as the question is understood from a twentieth-century liberal point of view. S. H. Cobb, *The Rise of Religious Liberty in America* (1902), covers the subject throughout the colonial period. R. F. Butts, *The American Tradition in Religion and Education* (1950), is a brief survey of that aspect of the subject, but one which pays little attention to this period. W. G. Torpey, *Judicial Doctrines of Religious Rights in America* (1948), is an informative, scholarly account which does not, however, treat the subject from an historical point of view. Reinhold Niebuhr has written a number of books and essays bearing on the subject of the relationship of religion and society in America, works which display brilliant insights but not very extensive historical knowledge.

Jefferson on the need for religion is quoted in Boorstin, *Lost World of Thomas Jefferson;* Adams to Jefferson in Cappon, ed., *Adams-Jefferson Letters;* the Baptist minister on the decline in religious fervor in Sweet, *Story of Religion.* The comment of the "Connecticut gentleman," the comment by Thomas Robbins, and the quotation from the preamble to the Connecticut Home Missionary Society are quoted in Keller, *Second Awakening.* D. R. Fox is quoted from his *Ideas in Motion* (1935); the reports of the Society for the Prevention of Pauperism, from Mc-Master, *History of American People;* the comments on the War of 1812, from Ward, *Symbol for an Age,* and Robert Owen from Bertrand Russell, *Freedom Versus Organization, 1814-1914* (1934).

CHAPTER XI

Probably the best general survey of the material covered in this chapter is C. R. Fish, *Rise of the Common Man* (1927), in the History of American Life series. There is no study which examines the American missionary spirit in this period as it manifested itself simultaneously in domestic reform and in territorial expansion. The nearest approach is R. H. Gabriel, *The Course of American Democratic Thought,* rev. ed., (1956). For the study of domestic reform the one major comprehensive work is Tyler, *Freedom's Ferment,* while the standard work on the expansionist spirit is A. K. Weinberg, *Manifest Destiny; A Study of Nationalist Expansionism in American History* (1935).

An interesting and enjoyable sample of European travelers' impressions of America is to be found in Oscar Handlin, ed., *This Was America* (1949). See also Allan Nevins, ed., *America Through British Eyes* (1948). For the Greek Revolution see M. A. Cline, *American Attitude Toward the Greek War of Independence* (1930). Dexter Perkins, *Hands Off; A History of the Monroe Doctrine* (1941), is the standard authority, while S. F. Bemis, *John Quincy Adams and the Foundations of American Foreign Policy* (1949), is the latest word on the origins of the Monroe Doctrine. For the ideology of westward expansion, see, in addition to Weinberg, *Manifest Destiny,* H. N. Smith, *Virgin Land; The American West as Symbol and Myth* (1950). Merle Curti, *The American Peace Crusade . . . 1815-1860* (1929), is the standard study.

G. V. Seldes, *Stammering Century* (1928), is a delightful account of mid-nineteenth century reform movements, with an emphasis upon the lunatic fringe. For this element in the reform movement see also J. D. Davies, *Phrenology . . . a 19th Century American Crusade* (1955). R. H. Shryock, "Sylvester Graham and the Health Reform Movement," *Mississippi Valley Historical Review,* XVIII (1931), is excellent. The most balanced account of the women's rights movement is in Tyler, *Freedom's Ferment.* See also E. A. Hecker, *A Short History of Women's*

Rights (1910). For the utopian movements the major work is *History of American Socialisms* (1870), by one of the most successful leaders in the movement, J. H. Noyes. See also A. E. Bestor, Jr., *Backwoods Utopias; The Sectarian and Owenite Phases of Communitarian Socialism in America, 1663-1829* (1950), and Lindsay Swift, *Brook Farm* (1900).

For the history of treatment of the poor see R. H. Bremner, *From the Depths; the Discovery of Poverty in the United States* (1956), a highly readable, scholarly study of a somewhat neglected subject. See also D. T. McColgan, *Joseph Tuckerman* (1940). For prison reform the standard work is Blake McKelvey, *American Prisons* (1936). For treatment of the insane see Albert Deutch, *Mentally Ill in America,* rev. ed., (1949), and H. E. Marshall, *Dorothea Dix: Forgotten Samaritan* (1937). For educational reform see E. D. Grizzell, *Origin of the High School in New England before 1865* (1923); B. A. Hinsdale, *Horace Mann* (1898); and a valuable article, H. M. Jones, "Horace Mann's Crusade," in Daniel Aaron, ed., *America in Crisis* (1952).

J. A. Krout, *The Origins of Prohibition* (1925), is a good account of the temperance movement down to the Civil War and the only scholarly account on the subject available. A. F. Fehlandt, *A Century of Drink Reform in the United States* (1904), is also useful, as is Deet Pickett, ed., *Cyclopedia of Temperance and Prohibition and Public Morals* (1817). For the abolitionist movement the most authoritative studies are G. H. Barnes, *Anti-Slavery Impulse, 1830-1844* (1933), and D. L. Dumond, *Antislavery Origins of the Civil War in the United States* (1939). Of especial relevance to the history of American democracy is R. B. Nye, *Fettered Freedom: Civil Liberties and the Slavery Controversy, 1830-1840* (1949). See also Fletcher, *Oberlin,* for an account of the college which was the center of the most effective antislavery activity, and Constance M. Rourke, *Trumpets of Jubilee* (1927), an extremely well-written series of biographies, including an excellent one of Lyman Beecher.

Andrew Jackson is quoted in Syrett, ed., *Andrew Jackson;* Jefferson and Edward Everett, in Weinberg, *Manifest Destiny;* Emerson to Carlyle in R. L. Rusk, ed., *The Letters of Ralph Waldo Emerson* (6 vols., 1939); and Emerson on the Friends of Universal Reform, in Mary and C. A. Beard, *The Rise of American Civilization,* rev. ed. (2 vols., 1949). Sylvester Graham is quoted in Shryock, "Health Reform Movement." David Dudley Field is quoted in Tyler, *Freedom's Ferment,* as is the statement by Tocqueville and Beaumont. Horace Mann is quoted in Jones, "Horace Mann's Crusade;" the secretary of the American Temperance Union, in Fehlandt, *Century of Drink Reform;* the comment on

Beecher, in Rourke, *Trumpets of Jubilee;* and the Lane rebels Charles Stuart and Theodore Weld in Dumond, *Antislavery Origins.*

CHAPTER XII

A. O. Craven, *The Growth of Southern Nationalism, 1848-1861* (1953), is a recent, scholarly, sensible, and detailed study of the subject. The two major works on American slavery are U. B. Phillips, *American Negro Slavery* (1918), and Kenneth Stampp, *The Peculiar Institution* (1956). Phillips approaches the subject from a point of view sympathetic to the planter. He treats slavery as a system for which the Negroes were not ill-suited and one from which they benefited in many ways. Stampp, proceeding from the assumption that Negroes were no more suited to slavery by nature than any other people, views the system as a grossly evil one, which—however benign it might have been in operation—robbed the slave of the freedom which he desired as much as anyone else did. Both studies are scholarly and well written.

J. H. Franklin, *From Slavery to Freedom: A History of American Negroes,* rev. ed. (1956), is a good brief survey of the subject. For Virginia the standard work is J. C. Ballagh, *History of Slavery in Virginia . . .* (1902). See also Mary and Oscar Handlin, "Origins of the Southern Labor System," *William and Mary Quarterly,* Ser. 3, VII (1950), and Elizabeth Donnan, ed., *Documents Illustrative of the History of the Slave Trade to America* (4 vols., 1930-35). W. E. Dodd, *The Cotton Kingdom* (1919), is a good brief introduction to that subject, while a more detailed account of cotton production itself may be found in L. C. Gray, *History of Agriculture in Southern United States to 1860* (2 vols., 1933).

W. J. Cash, *The Mind of the South* (1941), is a brilliant, compellingly written historical examination of southern culture. Clement Eaton, *A History of the Old South* (1949), is a good brief survey, while Eaton, *Freedom of Thought in the Old South* (1940), is a detailed account of the impact of slavery and the slavery controversy upon southern thought. W. S. Jenkins, *Pro-Slavery Thought in the Old South* (1935), is a thorough examination of southern attitudes against as well as for the institution. See also A. M. Lloyd, *The Slavery Controversy, 1831-1860* (1939), J. T. Carpenter, *The South as a Conscious Minority, 1789-1861* (1930), and Kenneth Stampp, "The Fate of Southern Anti-Slavery Sentiment," *Journal of Negro History,* XXVIII (1943). Dangerfield, *Era of Good Feelings,* contains a good account of the Missouri Compromise debates. F. M. Green, "Democracy in the Old South," *Journal of Southern History,* XII (1946), stresses the extent of democracy in southern states.

A good introduction to the southern defense of the peculiar institution is W. E. Dodd, "The Social Philosophy of the Old South," *American Journal of Sociology*, XXIII (1918), while essays on the subject by Dew, Harper, and others are to be found in *The Pro-Slavery Argument* (1852). See also Edward Lurie, "Louis Agassiz and the Races of Man," *Isis*, VL (1954), and J. C. Greene, "American Debate on the Negro's Place in Nature, 1780-1815," *Journal of the History of Ideas*, XV (1954). R. G. Osterweis, *Romanticism and Nationalism in the Old South* (1949), contains interesting information concerning neo-feudalism in southern life. For a study of the southern yeomanry see Frank Owsley, *Plain Folk of the Old South* (1949). See also R. B. Morris, "The Measure of Bondage in the Slave States," *Mississippi Valley Historical Review*, LXII (1954), for varying degrees of white as well as Negro servitude.

There are a number of good biographies of Calhoun, of which the most detailed are Wiltse, *John C. Calhoun*, and W. M. Meigs, *The Life of John Caldwell Calhoun* (2 vols., 1917). There is, in addition, a good deal of literature concerning Calhoun's political theory, of which the most recent study is A. O. Spain, *The Political Theory of John C. Calhoun* (1951). J. M. Anderson, ed., *Calhoun: Basic Documents* (1952), contains the *Disquisition on Government* as well as eleven of Calhoun's most important speeches. For a broad examination of American society immediately preceding the Civil War see Kenneth Stampp, *And the War Came; The North and the Secession Crisis, 1860-1861* (1950). See also U. B. Phillips, *The Course of the South to Secession* (1939).

The statement concerning the slave's natural rights is quoted in Ballagh, *Slavery in Virginia*. William Byrd is quoted from his *Histories of the Dividing Line Betwixt Virginia and North Carolina*, W. K. Boyd, ed., (1929). Pinkney and Mason in opposition to slavery are quoted in Jenkins, *Pro-Slavery Thought*, as are the unidentified miscellaneous praises of slavery. Jefferson's statement is from his *Notes on Virginia*. Pinkney's defense of slavery at the time of the Missouri Compromise is quoted in Dangerfield, *Era of Good Feelings*. The New Orleans *Bee* is quoted in Phillips, *Course of South to Secession*.

CHAPTER XIII

B. T. Spencer, *The Quest for Nationality; An American Literary Campaign* (1957), is a thorough study of literary nationalism in America in this period, giving attention to lesser literary figures as well as to the major ones. See also R. W. B. Lewis, *The American Adam; Innocence, Tragedy and Tradition in the Nineteenth Century* (1955), and F. I. Carpenter, *American Literature and the Dream* (1955), for more interpretive studies of the American literary mission. The most enjoyable and meaningful introduction to the history of American literature in the nineteenth century is Edmund Wilson, ed., *The Shock of Recognition; The Development of Literature in the United States Recorded by the Men Who Made It* (1943), a compilation of criticism of American writers by other writers. V. W. Brooks, *Makers and Finders; A History of the Writer in America, 1800-1915* (5 vols., 1936-52), is a readable series, which gives a remarkably broad coverage of the subject. The standard reference work is R. E. Spiller, et. al., *Literary History of the United States* (3 vols., 1948), containing, in addition to articles on literary movements and individual writers, detailed bibliographies. V. L. Parrington, *Main Currents in American Thought* (3 vols., 1927-30), is an extremely influential intellectual history which relates American literature of the time to Jeffersonian agrarian thought.

For individual writers of the early national period see L. G. Leary, *That Rascal Freneau* (1941); H. R. Warfel, *Noah Webster: Schoolmaster to America* (1936); Parke Godwin, *A Biography of William Cullen Bryant* . . . (2 vols., 1883); C. M. Newlin, *The Life and Writings of Hugh Henry Brackenridge* (1932); S. T. Williams, *The Life of Washington Irving* (2 vols., 1935); and Leon Howard, *Connecticut Wits* (1943). McMaster, *History of the People of the United States,* contains an extensive account of the attack upon American writers by the English literary quarterlies. See also J. C. McCloskey, "The Campaign of Periodicals after the War of 1812 for National American Literature," *Publications of the Modern Language Association,* L (1935).

For an important study of the major writers of the mid-nineteenth century see F. O. Matthiessen, *American Renaissance* (1941). For a general account of the New York literary scene, see Perry Miller, *The Raven and the Whale; The War of Words and Wits in the Era of Poe and Melville* (1956). For the Saturday Club see E. W. Emerson, *The Early Years of the Saturday Club, 1855-1870* (1918). R. E. Spiller, *Fenimore Cooper, A Critic of His Times* (1931), is the standard biography, while, among the voluminous writings on Melville, Leon Howard, *Herman Melville, A Biography* (1951), is a recent, scholarly account, and Jay Leyda, *The Melville Log* (1951), is revealing. Schneider, *American Philosophy* contains an especially penetrating essay on Melville, from which I have borrowed a great deal. See also the essay in Gabriel, *The Course of American Democratic Thought.* For other New England writers see M. A. DeW. Howe, *Holmes of the Breakfast Table* (1939); H. E. Scudder, *James Russell Lowell: A Biography* (2 vols., 1901); Samuel Longfellow, *Life of Henry Wadsworth*

Longfellow . . . (3 vols., 1891) ; and Newton Arvin, *Hawthorne* (1929).

G. E. Woodberry, *Ralph Waldo Emerson* (1907), is a brilliant, brief study, while the best larger work is R. L. Rusk, *The Life of Ralph Waldo Emerson* (1949). H. S. Canby, *Thoreau* (1939), and Canby, *Walt Whitman* (1943), are scholarly, readable biographies. For the writers of popular women's books see F. L. Pattee, *The Feminine Fifties* (1940), and J. D. Hart, *The Popular Book; A History of America's Literary Taste* (1950).

Freneau is quoted in Warfel, Gabriel, and Williams, *American Mind,* as is Oliver Wendell Holmes. Charles Brockden Brown is quoted in Wilson, ed., *Shock of Recognition,* as are Noah Webster, William Cullen Bryant, Edgar Allen Poe, James Russell Lowell, Thoreau, Whitman, and Herman Melville. Sidney Smith is quoted in McMaster, *History of American People,* as is the reply of Edward Everett. Everett's comment on Hawthorne's Democratic party membership is quoted in Schlesinger, Jr., *Age of Jackson.* Emerson is quoted from his *Miscellanies* (1895), and from Rusk, ed., *Letters.* Carlyle is quoted in Matthiessen, *American Renaissance.* Emerson on Thoreau's disobedience is quoted in Canby, *Thoreau.*

CHAPTER XIV

For an excellent study of the impact of the industrial revolution upon society see Norman Ware, *The Industrial Worker, 1840-1860* (1924). See also Taylor, *Transportation Revolution* and Commons, *et. al., History of Labor in United States.* For developments in the industrial revolution, see Clark, *History of Manufacturers;* W. B. Kaempffert, ed., *A Popular History of American Invention* (2 vols., 1924) ; L. E. Atherton, *The Pioneer Merchant in Mid-America* (1939) ; and Atherton, *The Southern Country Store, 1800-1860* (1949). R. A. Billington, *The Protestant Crusade, 1800-1860: A Study of the Origins of American Nativism* (1938), is the standard study of nativism for the period.

For northern business on the eve of the Civil War see G. W. Van Vleck, *The Panic of 1857* (1943) ; P. S. Foner, *Business and Slavery; The New York Merchants and the Irrepressible Conflict* (1941) ; and Stampp, *And the War Came.* For the home front during the Civil War see E. D. Fite, *Social and Industrial Conditions in the North during the Civil War* (1910) ; V. S. Clark, "Manufacturing Development during the Civil War," *Military Historian and Economist,* III (1918) ; Gustavus Myers, *History of the Great American Fortunes* (3 vols., 1909) ; T. C. Cochran and William Miller, *The Age of Enterprise; A Social History of Industrial America* (1942) ; and the famous chapter in Mary and C. A. Beard, *Rise of American Civilization,* treating the Civil War as the second American revolution, one by which business freed itself from agrarian political domination.

For the economic issues of the Reconstruction period see H. K. Beale, *The Critical Year; A Study of Andrew Johnson and Reconstruction* (1930), a detailed account of the Congressional election of 1866, and C. V. Woodward, *Reunion and Reaction; The Compromise of 1877 and the End of Reconstruction* (1951), pointing up the key role played by economic factors in the political reconciliation. See also W. M. Persons, *et. al.,* "Business and Financial Conditions Following the Civil War," *Review of Economic Statistics,* II (1920), Supplement 2. See L. M. Hacker, *The Triumph of American Capitalism* (1940); C. F. and Henry Adams, *Chapters of Erie* (1956); F. A. Shannon, *The Farmer's Last Frontier; Agriculture, 1860-1897* (1945); P. H. Buck, *Road to Reunion* (1927); and Allan Nevins, *Emergence of Modern America, 1865-1878* (1927). For a thorough account of politics in the Gilded Age see Matthew Josephson, *The Politicos, 1865-1896* (1938). A good summary account of this subject, and one which takes very much Josephson's point of view, is the chapter on the spoilsmen in Hofstadter, *The American Political Tradition.*

For brief, readable, recent, scholarly surveys of the periods from the Gilded Age to the present, see the following volumes from the Chicago History of American Civilization series: S. P. Hays, *The Response to Industrialism, 1885-1914* (1957); W. E. Leuchtenburg, *The Perils of Prosperity, 1914-32* (1958); Dexter Perkins, *The New Age of Franklin Roosevelt, 1932-45* (1957); and Herbert Agar, *The Price of Power; America Since 1945* (1957). Two readable and influential studies of American democratic reform since the Civil War have recently been published. They are E. F. Goldman, *Rendezvous with Destiny; A History of Modern American Reform* (1952), an account which places extremely heavy emphasis upon the role of the intellectuals in the reform movements, and Richard Hofstadter, *The Age of Reform from Bryan to F. D. R.* (1955), an account which stresses the provincial, self-interested character of populism and the middle-class desire for status as a central motive in the progressive movement. Irvin Wyllie, *The Self-Made Man in America; The Myth of Rags to Riches* (1954), is a good, brief study of that subject. The standard study of populism is J. D. Hicks, *The Populist Revolt* (1931). The best studies of the social gospel are H. F. May, *Protestant Churches and Industrial America* (1949), and Aaron Abell, *The Urban Impact on American Protestantism, 1865-1900* (1943). R. D. Cross, *The Emergence of*

Liberal Catholicism in America (1958), is an excellent study in an area where until recently little work had been done.

Good, recent, readable studies of the progressive movement include George Mowry, *The Era of Theodore Roosevelt, 1900-1912* (1958); J. M. Blum, *The Republican Roosevelt* (1954); Blum, *Woodrow Wilson and the Politics of Morality* (1956); A. S. Link, *Woodrow Wilson and the Progressive Era, 1910-1917* (1954); and R. B. Nye, *Midwestern Progressive Politics . . . 1870-1958* (1958). See Arthur Link, "What Happened to the Progressive Movement in the 1920's," *American Historical Review,* XLIV (1959), for an original and subtle account of that problem.

For industrial mobilization during the first world war see Bernard Baruch, *American Industry in War . . .* (1941), and G. B. Clarkson, *Industrial America in the World War* (1923). George Mowry, "The First World War and American Democracy," Jesse Clarkson and T. S. Cochran, eds., *War as a Social Institution . . .* (1941), discusses the anti-democratic influences of the war, and Max Lerner adds a shrewd criticism of Mowry's article, noting the fact of later applications of war-born administrative techniques to depression problems. For a detailed, scholarly biography of a man who was an important connecting link between wartime mobilization and mobilization for recovery under the New Deal see Margaret L. Coit, *Mr. Baruch* (1957). Basil Rauch, *The History of the New Deal, 1933-1938* (1944), is a standard account, which first developed the idea of the separate first and second New Deals. The best single-volume study of Franklin D. Roosevelt is J. M. Burns, *Roosevelt: The Lion and the Fox* (1956). For the impact of the depression upon American society see Dixon Wecter, *The Age of the Great Depression, 1929-1941* (1948), and F. L. Allen, *Since Yesterday; The Nineteen-Thirties in America* (1940). John Higham, *Strangers in the Land; Patterns of American Nativism, 1860-1925* (1955), is an excellent study of nativism, which, unfortunately, stops short of the depression period. For the Catholic issue in the election of 1928 see E. A. Moore, *A Catholic Runs for President* (1956) and Oscar Handlin, *Al Smith and His America* (1958).

Two opposing studies of the present state of American democracy, each of them most misleadingly selective in the material presented, are well worth reading together. F. L. Allen, *The Big Change . . . 1900-1950* (1952), presents an impressive fund of evidence to show that American society was incomparably more democratic at mid-century than it was fifty years earlier, or, presumably, at any previous time. C. W. Mills, *The Power Elite* (1956), presents equally abundant evidence to show that American democracy has become an empty form, that society is obsessed with class distinctions, and that control of the nation is in the hands of an elite, which is, itself, beyond the control of the electorate. Both books are extremely well written. Samuel Lubell, in *The Future of American Politics* (1952), and *Revolt of the Moderates* (1956), makes stimulating forecasts of American democracy on the basis of years spent interviewing citizens personally throughout the nation. E. F. Goldman, *The Crucial Decade: America, 1945-1955* (1956), is a readable survey of the immediate American past.

FDR on "persistent experimentation" is quoted in Hofstadter, *American Political Tradition;* the description of Mount Pleasant, Ohio, is from *Niles Register* as quoted in Taylor, *Transportation Revolution,* and the quotations from the *Voice of Industry, The Awl* and the National Typographical Society are from Ware, *Industrial Worker.* Hoover on the New Deal as Fascism is quoted in Goldman, *Rendezvous with Destiny,* as is Mrs. Roosevelt on social security. Hofstadter is quoted from his *Age of Reform.*

INDEX

Date Due

OCT 1 6 '6⁹			
DEC 7 '64			
SEP 29 '65			
OCT 6 '65			
MAY 10 '66			
NOV 1 3 '70			
AP 22 '82			
	PRINTED IN U. S. A.		